$14.95 BT
123
38
009

D0224290

LIVING IN THE SPIRIT:

THE WAY OF SALVATION

LIVING IN THE SPIRIT:
THE WAY OF SALVATION

REVISED AND EXPANDED EDITION

R. HOLLIS GAUSE

CCU Library
8787 W. Alameda Ave,
Lakewood, CO 80226

CPT Press
Cleveland, Tennessee USA

Published by CPT Press
900 Walker ST NE
Cleveland, TN 37311
email: cptpress@pentecostaltheology.org
website: www.pentecostaltheology.org

First edition published by Pathway Press, 1980

Revised and Expanded Edition
Copyright © 2009 CPT Press
All rights reserved. No part of this book may be reproduced or translated in any form, by print, photoprint, microfilm, microfiche, electronic database, internet database, or any other means without written permission from the publisher.

ISBN-10: 0981965105
ISBN-13: 9780981965109

DEDICATION

'The king's daughter is all glorious within' (Ps. 45.13). With thanks to God for the beauty of a godly woman, for her love, loyalty, and encouragement, I dedicate this volume to my wife, Beulah Hunt Gause.

Addendum: This revision comes more than twenty years after the original publication. In this time my wife became afflicted with memory loss and became physically invalid. In all of her illness she was very much aware of her relationship with the Lord Jesus Christ. During a part of this time she was confined to a long term health care facility; there she became known for her singing, praying and recollection of Scripture. In God's care she was able to spend the last eight months of her earthly life in our own home.

On December 15, 2002, she went home to be with the Lord. Though I have a deep sense of loss, I am even more aware of the appropriateness of my original dedication printed above. With gratitude to God for keeping us for each other for almost fifty-five years, I renew my dedication of this book to her.

CONTENTS

ACKNOWLEDGEMENTS

The work that is presented here is the product of study and presentation under many circumstances: the classroom, the pulpit, presentation to research groups, and so forth. All of these circumstances and the people involved have been provocative and have contributed to the work. I am grateful for the opportunities to minister under these circumstances and to the people who have thus contributed to this material.

A number of individuals have been particularly helpful. The personnel at Pathway Press—O.C. McCane, O.W. Polen, James D. Jenkins, Homer Rhea, Hoyt Stone, and Van Henderson have been encouraging and have contributed to the progress of the work and its publication. Robert E. Fisher, General Director of Education for the Church of God, has contributed a great deal to this material by suggestions for clarification and by emphasizing the need for application.

I am particularly grateful to Mrs. Arnold McQueen for her secretarial assistance in preparing most of this manuscript. Mrs. Douglas Stuman also assisted me in this area.

The extent to which the wife of a writer contributes to a work is seldom fully understood and appreciated. I wish to thank my wife for her encouragement, critical judgments, and excitement which she shares with me in this endeavor.

A note of clarification should be made concerning the Scripture citations in this work. Most of the quotations are the result of translations (in some cases paraphrases) of the original text by the author. Other quotations are from the King James Version.

ACKNOWLEDGEMENTS:
REVISED AND EXPANDED EDITION

The faculty members at the Church of God Theological Seminary have been very helpful in responding to a great deal of the material in the book, especially the chapters that have been added in this edition. They have responded to the material in formal and informal settings. Their criticisms and suggestions for refinement have been very helpful. I am grateful to them, and to God for allowing me to minister in such a community of faith and scholarship.

Two people among my colleagues deserve special mention. Dr. Kimberly Ervin Alexander has been my frequent colleague in team teaching; I have shared much of this material with her in manuscript and lecture form. She is a valued and able critic. Dr. Steven Jack Land, President of the seminary, has been most encouraging. I am grateful to him for recommending and arranging a sabbatical from my teaching duties at the Seminary.

The final drafts of this material were prepared during my sabbatical in 2004. During this time, Dr. Gary Moncher, President of Patten University (Oakland, CA) has provided living quarters for me at the University. He has also invited me to deliver a series of lectures on Pentecostal Wesleyan Theology. The privilege of delivering these lectures has been helpful in refining the material.

For all of these I am grateful, but especially to God His grace in my life and ministry.

'The lines are fallen unto me in pleasant places; yea, I have a goodly heritage' (Ps. 16.6).

R. Hollis Gause
Cleveland, TN 2009

INTRODUCTION

The title *Living in the Spirit: The Way of Salvation* expresses the involvement of the Spirit of God in every experience of redemption. This is the consistent testimony of Scripture. Much of the rhetoric of Pentecostal preaching reflects this. The Holy Spirit convicts of sin; He[1] calls to repentance. Believers are born of the Spirit and sanctified by Him. Believers are to walk in the Spirit. They are promised baptism with the Holy Spirit[2] and are to be filled with the Spirit.

This title is designed to go a step beyond these considerations and to show that the believer is living in the Spirit from the first moment of faith in Christ. To be saved and to live a godly life is to live in and by the power of the Holy Spirit. The way of salvation is life in the Holy Spirit.

The major thrust of this book is the Holy Spirit filled life. Two emphases prevail here. The first is that receiving baptism with the Holy Spirit is a distinctive experience. It is not to be confused with the experiences of initial salvation: repentance, justification, adop-

---

[1] The author has chosen to capitalize nouns and pronouns that have reference to God, Jesus and the Holy Spirit.

[2] As distinct from references to Spirit baptism in the first edition, the author is attempting in this edition to use with consistency the term 'baptize with the Spirit' or varying adaptations to the context. The expression 'baptize with the Holy Spirit' is preferred because of the analogy of water baptism which is sometimes described as 'baptism with water'. This expresses the idea that the element of baptism is water. In the same way, I wish to represent Spirit baptism as the spiritual baptism that Christ administers by pouring out the Holy Spirit on believers. The Minister of this baptism is the divine Person of the Son of God. The element of baptism is the divine Person of the Holy Spirit. Such an interpretation of the Spirit baptism is consistent (though not the only grammatical possibility) with the Greek phrases in Mt. 3.11; Mk 1.8; Lk. 3.16; Jn 1.33; Acts 1.5; 11.16. F. Blass and A. deBrunner suggest the meaning of this phrase (ἐν πνεύματι) in Lk. 3.16 and Acts 1.5 as examples of the instrumental use: hence 'with the Spirit'. *A Greek Grammar of the New Testament* (University of Chicago Press, 1961, section 195).

tion and regeneration. Neither is it to be confused with the subsequent crisis experience of sanctification. The second is to show that being filled with the Spirit is a quality of being and a manner of life. It is the manner of life expected of and provided for all those who have been born again. All of the prior experiences in redemption anticipate and are culminated in baptism with the Holy Spirit.

Repentance is turning from sin to the pursuit of holiness. Justification anticipates and requires holiness of life. Adoption anticipates the life of a child of God in the Spirit of adoption who is witness of adoption, guide to the children of God and intercessor for the saints. Regeneration by the Spirit anticipates living in the Spirit who is the Begetter of the new life in Christ. We use the metaphor of the mountain:

As the pinnacle of the mountain is distinct from the path leading to it, baptism with the Holy Spirit is distinct from those experiences which anticipate it. On the other hand, as the pinnacle and the mountain are integral to each other, all the prior experiences are bound up in the life in the Holy Spirit. Though the base of the mountain is distinct from the peak, it is one mountain. Progression along the slope of the mountain provides different experiences and vantage points. It is still one mountain.

A brief description of the experiences which are specifically identifiable in the order of salvation will be helpful. These definitions will put the experiences of redemption in logical and experiential order.

Repentance

Repentance is a gift of divine grace; it cannot originate out of the depraved heart. It is wrought by the word and Spirit of God upon the mind, emotions and will of the individual. There is a renewal of the mind so that the individual is convinced of guilt, corruption, and offensiveness to God. There is a renewal of the individual's emotions so that he/she comes to be sorry for and to despise the sinful condition and manner of life. The individual is renewed in will so that she/he turns from sin and seeks a life of obedience to the law of the Lord. Since this is an experience in grace, it is an experience of faith.

Repentance is a way of live for the believer in Christ. It is lived out in a continuing heart search, assessment of the manner of living and likeness to Jesus Christ.

Justification

Justification is a judicial act of God; that is, it occurs in an act of divine judgment. It is an act of God's grace in which God remits the sins of the believer and declares him/her to be righteous before God. The sole basis for this declaration of forgiveness and transmission of righteousness is the obedience of Christ—the active obedience in which He fulfilled all righteousness and the passive righteousness in which He was crucified for us, shedding His blood for a covering (i.e. an atonement) for us. This righteousness is transferred to the believer, giving her/him a standing before God clothed in righteousness. This declaration frees the believer from judgment and gives the benefits of Christ's full merit.

This act, on God's part, is judicial in nature. By justification God pardons the believer even though the past life is one of sinfulness. God further transforms the believer so that he/she becomes a partaker of the divine nature (2 Pet. 1.4), and the love of God is shed abroad in the heart by the Holy Spirit (Rom. 5.5).

The only instrument for receiving this gift of divine grace is faith in Jesus Christ. Its Agents are the word and Spirit of God.

Adoption

Adoption, like justification, is a judicial act of God's grace. It is a personal act of God whereby those who were the children of wrath by nature are received into the family of God. They are declared to be children of God and are numbered among His children with all the rights and privileges as heirs of God and joint heirs with Jesus Christ, the only begotten Son of God. This benefit is received by faith alone, and its agents are the Word and Spirit of God.

Some have attempted to deny adoption a distinctive place in the order of salvation. In the absence of adoption, they place the Father-child relationship in the new birth. Adoption as an experience in the order of salvation is called for because we are dealing with individuals whose personal identity, origin and history are alien to God and His household. It is the problem of this alien origin and personal history that adoption addresses. Regeneration creates a new inner nature, but it does not bring into being a new person. In the believer's personal history, she/he was a child of wrath. Nothing can undo or deny this fact of personal history. It can be superseded by the legal act of adoption. Legally, the believer can be withdrawn from the old family with its loyalties and placed in a new family and under its loyalties.

Regeneration

Regeneration (or the new birth) is a creative act of God's grace. God brings into being a new origin of existence. The biblical analogy for this act is the new birth, a birth from above. This creative act implants the seed of the life of Christ and brings forth a new creation in Christ, created anew in mind, emotions and will. The agents of this act of God are His Word and Spirit. The sole instrument of its reception is faith. The evidences that this new creation has occurred are the shedding abroad of the love of God in the heart, the presence of the renewed image of God (manifested in the fruit of the Spirit) and the cessation of the life of sin.

Sanctification

Sanctification is an act of divine grace, the agents of which are the Word and Spirit of God. The basis for this provision and experience is the blood of Christ's atonement whereby the body of sin is crucified and all unrighteousness is purged from the heart of the regenerate, making her/him free from the law of sin and death. By this ex-perience the graces which are implanted in the prior experience of regeneration are released to more fruitful growth in and by the Holy Spirit.

Such a definition of the experience of sanctification is incomplete unless it also addresses itself to the pursuit of holiness. The pursuit of holiness is the normal manner of life for the believer; that is, this life is characterized by freedom from sinning, by the denial of lust of the flesh, lust of the eye and pride of life and by a cultivation of the fruit of the Spirit.

Initial experience and subsequent experience in salvation

In making the distinctions described above a further distinction needs to be recognized. It is the distinction between initial experiences in salvation and subsequent experiences in salvation. The experiences which are to be identified as initial are repentance, justification, adoption and regeneration. The changes of position (viz., legal standing) and nature (viz., transformation of character) occur in union with each other when one first trusts in Christ as Savior.

The experiences which occur later in the course of one's redemptive life are subsequent to initial salvation. These subsequent experiences we identify as sanctification and baptism with the Holy Spirit. By subsequence we mean both the temporal and logical order of experience.

Traditional Wesleyan theology has maintained these distinctions which are also consistent with the theology of John Wesley. The point at which Pentecostal Wesleyan theology is distinct from traditional Wesleyan theology is on the definition of Spirit baptism. Traditional Wesleyan theology has maintained that Spirit baptism occurs with and is indistinguishable from sanctification. Pentecostal Wesleyanism distinguishes the two, making Spirit baptism distinct from and subsequent to sanctification.

Holy Spirit Baptism

Baptism with the Holy Spirit is an anointing and commissioning of the believer. It is the Father's act of providing the anointing and commission which He placed on His Son (Isa. 61.1, 2; Lk. 4.18, 19). It is the Son's act of sharing His commission and anointing with His disciples (Jn 20.19-23). It is the Spirit's act of endowing believers with the power to be witnesses and to occupy themselves in witnessing of God's mission in the world (Acts 1.5-8; 2.1-4, 32; 13.47).

This experience is the climax of all preceding experiences in salvation, and is provided in the atoning work of our Lord Jesus Christ. There is a strong emphasis on vocational/missional purposes of this baptism, but its purpose is not vocational alone.

This experience has a place in redemptive order and experience because of its relationship to and dependence on the Cross, resurrection and ascension of Jesus. As a redemptive experience, it is transformational in the cultivation of righteousness and its anointing for the pursuit of holiness.

All the experiences of initial salvation are preparatory for this experience, as is the experience of sanctification. It is important to keep in mind that this experience is promised only to believers; it is not promised to the world because the world neither knows nor can it receive the Holy Spirit (Jn 14.16, 17). These considerations demonstrate both a logical and a temporal sequence in the order receiving this blessing.

The Unity of Redemptive Experience

All of these experiences are united by four common bases: (1) the unity of redemptive experience, (2) the unity of faith through all redemptive experience, (3) the centrality of the Word of God to redemptive experience and (4) the centrality of the Holy Spirit to the provision and application of redemptive experience.

All redemptive experience is the provision of our Lord Jesus Christ; He is Redeemer. His reconciliation of God to fallen humanity, the justification of the ungodly, and the crucifixion of 'the old man' are accomplished in the atoning death of Jesus, our Lord and Son of God. He provides for the believer's regeneration experience, the pursuit of holiness and bodily resurrection by His own resurrection. As victorious Lord who has ascended to the Father and has received gifts of redemption for us, He pours out the Holy Spirit on His disciples.

All the benefits of divine grace are received by faith. This is true to the character of promise from God, because promise by nature is a claim of faith. This is the unifying thread through all the experiences of grace. Living in grace is the life of faith: 'The manner in which the just live is by believing' (Hab. 2.4).[3] Life in the Holy Spirit is a life of faith, for it is in faith that believers seek and cultivate the Spirit's indwelling and filling.

The Word of God is the announcement of the law of God in the conviction of sin and the announcement of the grace of God in the forgiveness of and healing from sin; as divine Word, it fulfills its own commands and promises. When the law of God speaks, judgment of sin is thereby accomplished. When the gospel of God speaks, salvation is fulfilled. These things are true because the Word of God has in it the power to fulfill its own decree.

The other personal Agent for the realization and application of the benefits of grace is the Holy Spirit, divine Person and member of the Holy Trinity. He is the convicting Agent in the call to repentance, confession and salvation. He is the Executor of God's will in the application of redemptive provision. He is the cultivating Agent who leads the believer through all the experiences of grace. His operations are represented in the various titles and functions which are ascribed to Him. He is the Spirit of grace, the Spirit of life, the

---

[3] Author's own translation.

Spirit of adoption, the Spirit of holiness, the Spirit of truth, the Spirit of glory and many others.

Pentecostal theology must unify its doctrines of salvation and baptism with the Holy Spirit. The definitions cited above and to be discussed in this volume represent an essential step in that direction. There is logical and chronological order in the experiences of redemption; however, this should not lead to a fragmentation in definition. Especially, it should not lead to fragmentation in our experience of life in the Holy Spirit.

I am fully committed theologically and experientially to the Wesleyan distinction between regeneration (and all aspects of initial salvation) and sanctification. I am also fully committed theologically and experientially to the Pentecostal distinction between sanctification and baptism with the Holy Spirit. The intention of this work is to maintain those distinctions without forfeiting the unity of redemptive provision and experience [4]

---

[4] The Pentecostal movement is not uniformly Wesleyan. So the statements above are not intended to encapsulate the views of all Pentecostal denominations or individuals. The position embraced here is representative of a significant segment of the so-called classical Pentecostals. Historically, it seems clear that Wesleyan holiness prevailed as the matrix out of which the modern Pentecostal movement began. Division would occur later with the rise of the 'finished work' doctrine of salvation. This interpretation rejected the experiential order of 'saved, sanctified and filled with the Holy Spirit' and substituted the doctrine of positional sanctification which occurred at the time of conversion.

1

REPENTANCE UNTO LIFE

Introduction

By definition, repentance is a work/gift of divine grace imparted to the individual by the agency of the Word of God and the Spirit of God. It is a reversal of the sinner's attitude and behavior in which he/she turns from disobedience to obedience, from unbelief to faith, from rebellion to submission to God, and from loyalty to satan to loyalty to God. It is a change of masters: from bondage to the devil to willing servitude to God.

These changes involve the entire nature of human personality: mind, emotions and will. Intellectually, the penitent is convinced of guilt, corruption and offensiveness in the sight of God. Emotionally, he/she comes to despise the sinful condition and manner of life, and to fear the wrath of God. Volitionally, the will is prompted and enabled to turn from sin and sinning and to pursue a life of obedience to the law of the Lord.

This experience is essential to salvation. This is the consistent position of religious movements that have emphasized crisis conversion. As a general rule such movements have discussed repentance only in relationship to one's conversion, or initial salvation. Though this has been true of the holiness Pentecostal movement, it is not true to the heritage of Wesleyan theology. Repentance is an essential of the Wesleyan doctrine of conversion. It occurs initially when the sinner is convicted of his/her sins, and turns from the life of sin to a life of godliness and faith in Jesus Christ and the grace which He offers.

In addition to initial repentance, repentance is a grace which is to be practiced throughout one's life in Christ. This is necessitated by two conditions. The first is the growing enlightenment of the believer. As the believer becomes more and more mature, he/she real-

izes patterns of thought and conduct that are not conducive to
growing in grace and Christian perfection. As the believer becomes
aware of these shortcomings, it is necessary for him/her to repent,
turning from these practices and seeking perfection in love. The
second is the occasion of known sin in the life of the believer—for
instance Peter's denial of Christ on the night of His betrayal. Such
an occasion requires the confession of sin. The promise of 1 Jn 1.9
is both awesome and comforting: 'If we confess our sins, He [God]
is faithful and righteous to forgive our sins and to cleanse us from
all unrighteousness'. Proverbs 28.13 sounds the warning and the
promise: 'He that covereth his sins shall not prosper, but whoso
confesseth and forsaketh them shall have mercy'.

The subject of discussion in this chapter is initial repentance.
The continuing practice of repentance in the believer's life will be
the subject of the chapter to follow.

Repentance under all circumstances has to do with sin, and the
Scriptures are clear: 'For all have sinned and come short of the glory
of God' (Rom. 3.23). This text announces the universality of sin,
and requires repentance for salvation. Repentance is a necessity of
the spiritual life, whether in initial salvation or in continuing in
Christ as a believer.

In order to develop this subject it will be necessary to deal with
the following subjects: the glory/holiness of God, the sinfulness of
humankind and the nature and necessity of repentance.

The Glory of God

There are two aspects of the glory of God: His majesty (majestic
holiness) and His purity (ethical holiness). The majesty of God is
represented in Scripture by the appearance of God, especially in
such appearances as the Burning Bush (Exodus 3), the pillar of
cloud and fire that stood between Israel and the Egyptians (Exod.
14.19-22; also called here the 'angel of the Lord'), the fire upon
Mount Sinai (Exod. 19.11-25), the Shekinah that stood over and
within the tabernacle, and especially the holy place (Exodus 33) and
later the temple on the occasion of its dedication (2 Chron. 5.13,
14). This glory was seen and described by the prophets, but especially Isaiah (Isaiah 6) and Ezekiel (Ezekiel 1). This glory of God
covered the countenance of Moses and the people could not look

on this servant of the Lord (Exod. 34.30; 2 Cor. 3.7-18) and they were afraid to look on or touch the holy mountain (Heb. 12.18-29).

This is the glory of God's essential nature which no one has seen nor can see (1 Tim. 6.14-16). This is the majesty that worshipers feared to see lest they die (Heb. 12.20, 21).

The most prominent representation of that glory is in the divine Name(s). It is the Name of the Lord that is to be feared because that Name is the divine presence. It is to be feared as the Person of God is to be feared: '… That thou mightiest fear this glorious and fearful name, the Lord thy God' (Deut. 28.58). When Ezra called the exiles to a renewal of covenant with the Lord by the reading and interpretation of the Law, the Levites exhorted the people to 'stand up and bless the Lord your God forever and ever…' (Neh. 9.5). The exhortation climaxes in a doxology: 'And blessed be thy glorious name, which is exalted above all blessing and praise' (Neh. 9.5). The glory of God and His Name is further represented in this doxology by mentioning God's works of creation, redemption and care (Neh. 9.6-38). These works of glory are as much associated with the Name of God as with His Person; they are inseparable in glory.

The Psalms abound in doxologies that extol the wonder of the divine Name. 'O Lord our Lord, how excellent is thy name in all the earth! Who hast set thy glory above the heavens' (Ps. 8.1). 'The Lord reigneth, He is clothed with majesty. The Lord is clothed with strength, wherewith He hath girded himself: The world also is established that it cannot be moved. Thy throne is established of old: Thou art everlasting' (Ps. 93.1, 2). 'Bless the Lord, O my soul. O Lord my God, thou art very great; thou art clothed with honour and majesty. Who coverest thyself with light as with a garment: Who stretchest out the heaven like a curtain' (Ps. 104.1, 2).

Isaiah's vision of the Lord impresses the glory of the Lord upon the seraphim and the prophet. 'In the year that king Uzziah died I saw the Lord sitting upon a throne, high and lifted up, and his train filled the temple' (Isa. 6.1). The wonder of that glory is shown in the worship response of the seraphim: 'Above it stood the seraphim: each one had six wings; with twain he covered his face, and with twain he covered his feet, and with twain he did fly. And one cried to another, and said, "Holy, holy, holy, is the Lord of hosts: the whole earth is full of his glory" ' (Isa. 6.2, 3). Even the temple itself responded to this glory and the doxology of the seraphim:

'And the posts of the door moved at the voice of him that cried, and the house was filled with smoke' (Isa. 6.4).

The prophet was smitten with this glory and purity: 'Then said I, Woe is me! For I am undone; because I am a man of unclean lips, and I dwell in the midst of a people of unclean lips: for mine eyes have seen the King, the Lord of hosts' (Isa. 6.5).

Such manifestations of glory continue into the New Testament records. Stephen, 'being full of the Holy Ghost, looked up steadfastly into heaven, and saw the glory of God, and Jesus standing on the right hand of God. And said, "Behold, I see the heavens opened, and the Son of man standing on the right hand of God" ' (Acts 7.55, 56).

The light of divine glory appeared to Saul of Tarsus; he fell to the earth and inquired, 'Who art thou, Lord? And the Lord said to him, I am Jesus whom thou persecutest' (Acts 9.3-5). The terror of that glory marked Paul's recollection of that scene as he recalled his conversion and told his story before Agrippa: 'At midday, O King, I saw in the way a light from heaven, above the brightness of the sun, shining round about me and them that journeyed with me' (Acts 26.13; cf. also, Acts 22.6-11). This appearance of the Lord to Saul marked him and his ministry from that point on changing him from persecutor to apostle and from a hater of the people of 'the way' to one of the people of 'the way'.

The appearance of the glory of the Lord reaches its climax in the book of Revelation in which both angels and humankind, and saint and sinner cast themselves before the Lord in His exaltation.

This review of only a few of the instances of the appearance of God shows that God is higher than the heavens and the 'heaven and the heaven of the heavens' cannot contain Him (1 Kgs 8.27). Paul describes Him to the people at the Areopagus: 'God that made the world and all things therein, seeing that he is Lord of heaven and earth, dwelleth not in temples made with hands' (Acts 17.24).

The sum of this glory is that God is infinite, above all things, before all things and by Him all things consist. He is the Creator and all other beings are creature. He is eternal; they are temporal. He is infinitely perfect in power; their power is weak, dependent and corrupted. He governs all things; they are the governed. He is the glory before which godly worshipers fall and cry for mercy. The entire assembly of the Lord trembles before Sinai. Moses radiates His glory after he descended from the presence of the Lord and the people could not look on his face (Exod. 34.29-35; 2 Cor. 3.7, 13).

God's glory lies in the fact that He alone is God. The call for Israel (the Shema) is, 'Hear, O Israel: the Lord our God is One' (Deut. 6.4). Our Lord cites this in His answer to the inquiry concerning the great commandment: 'Hear, O Israel, the Lord our God is one Lord' (Mk 12.29). The point of this text is that, though there are many who are called lords and gods, there is only one who is indeed divine (1 Cor. 8.5). He is not simply the highest in a multitude of gods; He alone is God and all others are non-existent. He is not simply the God of greatest glory; He is the only God and He is infinite in His splendor. All other claimants to deity are corruptions and defilements of the word 'god'.

Exodus 15.11 spells out this contrast between God and all false gods: 'Who is like unto thee, O Lord, among the gods? Who is like unto thee, glorious in holiness, fearful in praises, doing wonders?' This uniqueness of God lies in the fact that He is eternal, having no beginning, changes in age or nature and no end of His being. The writings of Isaiah elaborate on this fact as an explanation of the divine Name YHWH: 'Remember the former things of old: for I am God, and there is none else; I am God and there is none like me' (Isa. 46.9). Earlier, Isaiah recalled the words of God: 'Ye are my witnesses, saith the Lord, and my servant whom I have chosen; that ye may know and believe me, and understand that I am: before me there was no god formed, neither shall there be after me. I, even I, am the Lord; and beside me there is no Savior... Yea, before the day, I am... I am YHWH, your Holy One, the Creator of Israel your King' (Isa. 43.10-15; cf. also Isa. 41.4; 44.6; 48.12; Deut. 32.39, 40; Jn 8.58; Rev. 1.8). Note especially Isa. 44.6, 'Thus says, YHWH, the King of Israel and his Redeemer YHWH of hosts, I am first and I am last; besides me there is no God'.

Any representation of deity besides that which is revealed in Scripture is a lie; the Apostle Paul calls it 'the lie' (Rom. 1.25. 'Who changed the truth of God into the lie who worshipped and served the creature instead of the Creator, who is blessed forever, Amen'). It is the misrepresentation of the I am with a corruption from satan himself. Idolatry is devil worship.

The consequence of the truth of the infinite glory of God is that God must be honored as the only God. Any substitution for this

God is idolatry. Any reduction of His glory is sacrilege. Any dese-cration of His Name, Word or Presence is profanity.

We turn now to the moral excellence of God, which we have called the ethical holiness of God. This understanding of holiness relates to the fact that God is the Fountainhead and Measure of all virtue, and He is entirely free from fault or impurity.

As in the discussion of the majesty of God, we must also em-phasize here the infinity of God. In Him all virtue originates and these virtues are without limit. In Him all virtues stand in perfect harmony with each other so that one does not intrude on, contra-dict or limit the other.[5]

We must emphasize that God is without defilement, and any-thing short of fulfillment is defiling. God is devoid of any impurity; there is no error or sin in Him. We must go beyond this, however.

God is the presence of all virtue, and that virtue is primarily de-fined in the love of God: 'And we have known and believed the love that God hath to us. God is love; and he that dwelleth in love dwelleth in God, and God in him' (I Jn 4.16). The love of God means that all goodness in God is first fulfilled in Holy Trinity, and then directed toward His creatures, especially toward humankind because we were created in His image and redemption aims to re-store that image fully in Christ.

This love is the union of perfection between all the moral attrib-utes of God, in the words of Paul the 'bond of perfectness' (Col. 3.14). His righteous judgments are perfected in His good will, and His justice is the fulfillment of His love. His mercy is the fulfillment of the love of God in harmony with justice. His power is not the ability to do anything, but to do all things perfectly in love. To lie,

---

[5] A common mistake in the explanation of the graces of God is to explain them separately. The result is often that one attribute seems to conflict/compete with another. This is most commonly seen in explanations of mercy and justice as if justice sought retribution and mercy intervened and would not let justice be fulfilled. If this is the case, there is conflict in God and He does not represent the infinite fulfillment of goodness. This perceived conflict is beautifully harmonized by the psalmists. 'Justice and judgment are the habitation of thy throne: mercy and truth shall go before thy face' (Ps. 89.14). In this text 'justice and judgment' and 'mercy and truth' are in parallel. These terms define each other. Justice de-fines mercy and judgment defines truth. Psalm 85.10 states it in this way, 'Mercy and truth are met together; righteousness and peace have kissed each other'. The point of union between these two perfections is the infinite love of God in which all divine qualities are fulfilled. This is true holiness: pure religion and undefiled before God (Jas 1.27).

to be merciless, to be evil, to be unforgiving, to excuse sin (as distinct from forgiving sin), to be viciously destructive, etc., are not possibilities with God because He is love.

These perfections exist in God eternally and unchangeably; they will never fail, are never diminished and do not cease. They exist in Him in His being the eternal 'I AM'. So all the qualities of divine Being are from everlasting to everlasting as He is from everlasting to everlasting.

When we understand the holiness of God in this way, we know that God is entirely pure and that He defines all that is good and He is the Source from whom all good comes and is measured.

It is important to see love and perfection as they are fulfilled in other moral perfections of God. We note the justice of God. All law is derived from divine nature.[6] In His justice God is the Source and Measure of all righteousness because justice is His nature exactly as love and holiness are.

This means that God can by no means clear the guilty except in Christ. He will punish evil in accordance with His nature of righteousness, holiness and love. He will reward righteousness, again in accordance with His nature of righteousness, holiness and love.

In the goodness of God He is the Benefactor of all creatures. Scriptures apply this goodness to the whole realm of nature. Psalm 147 in particular celebrates this goodness in relation to the clouds, the rain, the mountains, the beasts, the nations, the snow and the running water (Ps. 147.7-20). Our Lord applies this to the flight and fall of the sparrows and to lilies of the field as they are beautified by God (Mt. 6.26-30). The point of Christ's emphasis on the goodness of God is that God cares even more for those whom God has made in His own image; 'Your heavenly Father feeds the fowls of the air;

---

[6] A common misunderstanding of the law is that law and legalism are synonymous or coextensive with each other; they are not. The law of the Lord is Word of God just as much as the promises of God are Word of God. It is common for the psalmists to speak of loving the law of the Lord, and to use other terms of affection for divine law. The Scriptures intermix the terms of the law and the terms of the promise because law is predictive of promise, and promise is the end of the law. Loving the law is the same as loving God, and one cannot be a legalist if he/she is in love with the Lawgiver. Legalism is a human construct in which persons and traditions have created regulations which are unrelated to love, faith and the commitment of the heart to obedience. These regulations reduce personal relationship with God to a contract between equals, ignoring our dependent covenant relationship with God.

'Are ye not much better than they?' (Mt. 6.26). He makes the same application to the care of God for the lilies and grass of the field (Mt. 6.30-32).

The pinnacle of God's goodness is stated in Jn 3.16, 'For God so loved the world, that He gave His only begotten Son, that whosoever believeth in Him should not perish, but have everlasting life'. The point of this text is that it is the world (the world of unbelieving and hate filled men and women) that God loves, and He loves them while they are still sinners and are still involved in sinning (Rom. 5.6-10). It would have been possible to discuss the goodness of God in an abstract ('theological') manner, but God's love in Christ puts a face on divine love—the face of Jesus. This Face of love and goodness also places a moral imperative on all human beings. God requires love and goodness of all men and women, not simply the absence of hatred.

The manner in which God created man and woman becomes the divine mandate of their moral obligation. God began the human race by creating man and woman in His image (Gen. 1.26, 27). This means that the splendor of the love and holiness of God was imprinted on both Adam and Eve; they reflected back to God His own nature. True, they were creatures and could only reflect these virtues and could not originate them of themselves. That was the limitation of their creaturehood, but being a creature is not sinful. God saw in them the beauty of holiness.

They were also limited by the fact that they had just begun their stewardship under God. It was a twofold stewardship. First, it was a stewardship over the rest of the earth to transport to the world the order and beauty of the garden of Eden (Gen. 1.28-31; 2.7-9). Second, it was a stewardship of moral perfection. This required of them a perpetuation of their holiness by obedience and trust in God the Creator (Gen. 2.8, 9; 3.2-3). It also required of them growth in the knowledge of God and fulfillment of divine virtues in growing and new relationships with God and the rest of creation. They had not yet reached the end for which God had formed them. Theirs was a worshiping and growing relationship with God their Creator. It was a growing stewardship with their environment including plants, animals and the earth.

This order of creation requires of men and women that they reflect the goodness of God their Creator in their being and behavior. These must be reflected in the manner in which they relate to God, to one another and to their environment. This cannot be satisfied simply by the absence of violence, disobedience or impurity. It can be satisfied only in the fulfillment of harmony, peace, love, obedience and purity.

God fulfills His holiness by truth. The first meaning of truth is integrity: integrity of being, integrity of word and integrity of action.

By integrity of being we mean that God fulfills in His nature all that the name and names of God require. The Name of God indicates sovereignty. The Name Adonai (usually translated Lord) calls on the Bearer of the name to be Master. The name Jehovah (יהוה) means that the One who claims that Name is eternal and unchangeable. The Name Jesus Christ requires that He be Savior the anointed of God. Many other applications would be appropriate in other contexts, but these are sufficient to establish our claims. The being of God requires of Him that infinity, holiness, righteousness, eternity, omnipotence, omnipresence be perfectly realized in Him. His Word and His actions must be consistent with these perfections.

The word of God consists of both law and promise. The law of the Lord is the revelation and explication of His holiness. When God requires of humankind that we must love Him supremely, He is telling us that He alone is God, and that there can be no relationship of love and worship that is not first directed to our relationship with Him. When God tells us that we must love our neighbors as ourselves, He is saying to us that love is the primary and defining relationship that we can have with one another. These qualities define holiness, and that is the reason that these two relationships in love define the whole law of God (Deut. 6.5; Josh. 22.5; Mt. 22.34-40; Mk 12.28-34; Lk. 10.25-28; Rom. 13.8-10). The law of the Lord is true to His nature.

The promise(s) of God have the same relationship to the truth/integrity of God. His promises originate in His nature; therefore they complement the law; they fulfill the law. So law and promise are harmonious with each other because they are both founded in the nature of God. Both law and promise are divine Word— inspired by the Holy Spirit.

These conditions in God define the truth which God requires of the creature. God calls on humankind to fulfill truth in nature, word and behavior. The integrity that defines God's nature must also define the nature of humankind made in the image of God. As in God, there must be integrity of human nature, profession, speech and actions. The psalmist defines this aspect of holiness in the creature in these terms: truth in the inward parts (Ps. 51.6), a clean heart and a right spirit (Ps. 51.7, 10).

The Sinfulness of Humanity

There are three aspects of human sin: sins against God's majesty, sins against His purity/holiness and the general depravity of humankind. First, however, we must define sin.

According to Scripture sin is both a condition and an act. The sinful condition describes the sin cursed nature in which the descendants of Adam are born (Rom. 5.12-21; Ps. 51.5). The sinful act is a knowing and willful transgression of the law of the Lord or omission of righteousness.[7] In relation to transgression, willfulness is an essential consideration.

As a condition of sin-cursed human existence, the transgression and corruption of Adam passed to all his descendants, Christ only excepted: 'Wherefore as by one man sin entered into the world, and death by sin; and so death passed upon all men, for that all have sinned' (Rom. 5.12). This sinful condition in and of itself is not damning; Paul declares, 'For I was alive without the law once: but when the commandment came sin revived and I died' (Rom. 7.9). Sin was present in Paul, but he was not condemned by God because the law had not come to his moral conscience. When that happened spiritual death occurred. Paul continues his explanation of this condition in vv. 10, 11: 'And the commandment, which was ordained to life, I found to be unto death. For sin, taking occasion by the commandment, deceived me and by it slew me.' This is the pattern in which all humankind comes to the awareness and activation of sin.

This condition of sin is usually referred to under terms of depravity, the carnal nature or inbred sin: 'Behold, I was shapen in

---

[7] Thomas C. Oden, *John Wesley's Scriptural Christianity* (Grand Rapids, MI: Zondervan, 1994), p. 248: 'Since natural finitude and physical infirmities are not as such sin, *which is willful negation of a known moral requirement*, [emphasis ours] sanctifying grace does not have as its purpose the ending of either finitude or physical diseases and infirmities, which may become a means of increasing faith, hope and love'.

iniquity; and in sin did my mother conceive me' (Ps. 51.5). This condition is not damning until the latent sin is awakened by the knowledge of the law and the individual chooses sinful actions and embraces his/her depravity.

This choice occurs universally as Paul declares, 'For all have sinned and are coming short of the glory of God' (Rom. 3.23). Sin in its awakening and in its continuing is defined by the law of the Lord. To his own question, 'Is the law sin?' Paul answers, 'God forbid. Nay, I had not known sin, but by the law' (Rom. 7.7; cf., Rom. 3.20). In this sense the law of the Lord defines sin. The law was added because of transgressions in order to bring about the fulfillment of divine promise (Gal. 3.19). Transgression preceded the giving of the law, and the law answers the complaints of the condemned rendering their guilt unquestionable and unassailable (Rom. 3.19).

Even though the law is essential for the definition of sin and the rendering of judgment, sin is not primarily the violation of a code of law. It is violation of divine nature and the disruption of relationship with God. It is violation of trust, and it is a denial of the truth of God's law and judgment. It is a repudiation of God's trustworthiness. This violation (and disruption) occurs in the things we do and say, but most importantly in what we are—sinful and corrupt. Sin is overt; it erupts in such outward manifestations as cursing, lying, stealing, violence, murder, adultery, etc.

These sins begin in the heart and are committed there before they come to the surface in words and actions. In fact, they may exist in the heart (with all damnable consequences) and never be acted on. Even so sin—even covert sin—is damning (Mt. 5.21-28). Christ's analysis of the origin of sinful actions is very clear: 'That which cometh out of a man, that defileth the man. For from within, out of the heart of men, proceed evil thoughts, adulteries, fornications, murders, thefts, covetousness, wickedness, deceit, lasciviousness, an evil eye, blasphemy, pride, foolishness: All these evil things come from within, and defile the man' (Mk 7.20-23).

Sin is not a component of human nature; it is a foreign element in human nature, and is a corruption of its purity. It is a false and Gnostic error to attribute sin (whether of nature or actions) to being human or finite. The first man and woman were fully human in their original condition, which was a sinless condition. Our Lord was fully human, yet He was without sin (Heb. 4.15; 2 Cor. 5.21).

No one sins by accident, nor can sin be excused by one's circumstances, proclivities, weaknesses or predispositions. Certainly these things affect the sinner and create special circumstances of temptation, but they neither predetermine a particular action nor excuse the sin. Gnosticism has a history of offering these excuses. Many modern views of human nature continue to offer these ancient 'fig leaves' as palliatives of the conscience, and religion is often the cohort of such things.

Sin is a transgression of God's nature, described in both law and promise. In transgression the creature violates the relationship with God, because he/she interrupts harmony with God. Sin also consists in failure to fulfill the righteousness and holiness revealed in God and required of the creature. In this light the Scriptures declare the universal character of sin: 'For all have sinned and are coming short of the glory of God' (Rom. 3.23).

We have described the nature of God in terms of His infinite glory/majesty—the majestic holiness of God. We have also described the nature of God in terms of His ethical/moral perfection—the ethical holiness of God. We must describe sin in the same categories.

Sin against the glory of God involves the violation of His Name(s), Being and uniqueness. The creature is not required to possess the glory of God expressed in these terms because they are exclusive to God. In fact this is prohibited. The most heinous violation of God's glory is idolatry. In this sin we change the 'glory of the uncorruptible God into an image made like to corruptible man, and to birds, and four footed beasts, and creeping things' (Rom. 1.23). The most egregious form of that sin is the attempt of the creature to make himself divine claiming for himself powers, glory and infinity which belong only to God (Isaiah 13).

Yet there are many ways more subtle than these by which people sin against the glory of God. We fail to recognize the honor and glory of God appropriately. We profane His Name and His Word by an irreverent attitude toward His presence, and by an empty use of the divine Name and Word. We call the name of God without expecting anything to happen. We cite the word of God without expecting its fulfillment. This sin manifests itself in egotism, self indulgence, elevation of family above the worship of God, selfishness, dependence on and affection for material things and many other attitudes and acts. We love these things more than we love God.

Whatever are its forms, this sin (as all sin) is completely intolerable to God: 'I am the Lord: that is my name: and my glory will I not give to another, neither my praise to graven images' (Isa. 42.8).

The sins against the moral excellence of God exist in act and in condition. Once the sinful nature is embraced, it is sinful to be in the depraved condition. It is to be in a pale of sin; it is the absence of holiness, justice, goodness and truth. In this depravity it is impossible for the individual to lift himself/herself out of it by good deeds, right thinking or correct speech. It is sinful to commit acts that are contrary to the divine nature, to think thoughts unworthy of holiness or to speak contrary to the truth of God. These sins are shown in human history and nature. God is holy; humankind is defiled. God is just; humankind is partial in judgment. God is good; humankind is filled with hate rather than love. In the absence of hatred, humankind simply fails to love. God is long-suffering; humankind is impatient and demanding. God is merciful; humankind vindictive (and not just) in retribution. God is kind; humankind is self-seeking. God is true; humankind is deceitful, a liar to him/herself, to other people and to God.

These forms of actual transgressions proceed from the depraved condition of humankind which is described in Rom. 3.9-18. Among all humankind—Jews and gentiles—there is none righteous. Human philosophies did no better than give finesse to human corruption and idolatry. The Jews in legalism had done no better than make their religion a curiosity which is neither redemptive nor attractive. In mental capacity humankind is corrupt because it has no understanding of God. In volition men and women are corrupt because they have chosen their own way and not the way of the Lord. Emotionally and psychologically—in heart and word—humankind is corrupt because he/she is deceitful, a liar and destructive. Socially humankind is destructive and murderous. He/she has corrupted his/her religions because he/she has no fear of God; he/she does not respect God, and he/she lives as if there were no God to whom he/she must give account. Is Paul describing here only the dregs of human society? No, he is describing all humankind devoid of the saving grace of God. Rom. 3.23 covers these conditions and is applicable to Jews and gentiles, plicable to Jews and gentiles, the 'good moral' persons, and the debauched of society.

These conditions drive us to our next subject: the nature and necessity of repentance.

The Nature and Necessity of Repentance

Repentance, the call to repentance and the response of the sinner to the call do not reside in the unbeliever as a 'spark of the divine' needing only an awakening of human potential. Every aspect of repentance is a provision of the grace of God. This follows from the following considerations. First, repentance is a good thing—spiritually good. So, it can come only from God who alone is the origin of good and the Giver of every good and perfect gift (Jas 1.17). Romans 2.24 indicates that it is the goodness of God that leads people to repentance: 'Or despisest thou the riches of his goodness and forbearance and longsuffering; not knowing that the goodness of God leadeth thee to repentance?'

Second, humankind is dead in trespasses and sins (Eph. 2.1), and cannot produce in itself an attitude of godly sorrow that leads to repentance (2 Cor. 7.10). Repentance is declared to be the gift of God: 'When they [i.e., the spiritual leaders of the church in Jerusalem] heard these things, they held their peace and glorified God, saying, "Then hath God also to the Gentiles granted repentance unto life" ' (Acts 11.18). The unbelieving deserves no right to have the opportunity to repent. The very call to repentance is undeserved; therefore, it is of the grace of God. Fallen human nature has in it no spiritual or moral ground of repentance. It is the divine Word that calls to repentance and not any goodness on the part of those in sin. Neither is it out of his/her wisdom, for in the unbeliever dwelleth no good thing (Rom. 7.18). It is the Holy Spirit who convicts of sin, righteousness and judgment (Jn 16.7-11). It is in the mercy of God that the sinner is not hardened beyond any appeal from the goodness and grace of God.

Third, those who are in sin oppose themselves steeping themselves in sin more and more, keeping themselves away from God and rebelling against His goodness, mercy and grace. Paul tells Timothy, 'In meekness [to instruct] those that oppose themselves; if God peradventure will give them repentance to the acknowledging of the truth' (2 Tim. 2.25). They are so bound by their sinful condition that they stand in the way of their own spiritual good. The word of God and the Spirit of God intervene against this condition to bless sinners with repentance.

Repentance is a work of God's grace in the whole person: mind, emotions and will. These are the exact areas defined in Scripture in the description of human depravity. Since the human being is a sinner in a commitment of his/her entire self to sin, the route of repentance must involve the entire self.

In terms of the mind, it is necessary for the sinner to hear and learn the law of the Lord for conviction. This forces on the unbeliever specific awareness. The individual comes to know the condemnation of God's law and God's present wrath against sin. He/she awakens to the offensiveness of his/her sins and the repulsiveness of his/her person before God. The individual becomes conscious that he/she has no ability in personal strength to cease from sin: 'Can the Ethiopian change his skin, or the leopard his spots? Then may ye also do good, that are accustomed to do evil?' (Jer. 13.23). These are rhetorical questions, and the answer is clearly, 'No'.

In addition to knowing the law of the Lord, the individual must become aware of the promise in the gospel of Christ. He/she must know the mercy of God in Christ, and the promise and power of God to renew the depraved will to cease from sinning.

Repentance is a radical emotional experience. It involves the hatred of one's sins and sinful condition. Repentance reduces the sinner to grief and sorrow for the sinful life and the fact of depravity. This is not the remorse of Esau who wept over the consequences of his selling the birthright but still had no remorse for the act of selling his spiritual heritage (Heb. 12.15-17). It is a godly sorrow— sorrow the gift of God—that works repentance (2 Cor. 7.10). This emotional upheaval shows itself in many ways, but Paul describes it well in his correspondence with the Corinthians: 'What carefulness it wrought in you, yea, what clearing of yourselves, yea, what indignation, yea, what fear, yea, what vehement desire, yea, what zeal, yea, what revenge' (2 Cor. 7.11).

The will of the sinner is essential to repentance. Sin is a willful act; therefore, repentance must also be a willful act. In sin humanity's will is totally enslaved to sin: 'Know ye not, that to whom ye yield yourselves servants to obey, his servants ye are to whom you

obey; whether of sin unto death or of obedience unto righteousness?' (Rom. 6.16). The unbeliever does not have the spiritual re-
sources necessary to make this commitment; so the agency of Word
and Spirit of God are essential to repentance. The will must be
strengthened and renewed by the power of the Holy Spirit.

An important consideration here is the Wesleyan doctrine of
prevenient grace which means the grace that goes before. It is preparatory grace in which God enables the sinner to have a conscience of right and wrong, to remain aware of the goodness of
God that leads to repentance and to be able to respond in the will
to the call to repentance.

> In other words, the doctrine of prevenient grace reveals that
> God takes the first step in the process of salvation and heals
> some of the most damaging effects of original sin. The result of
> this divine action is that humanity now has sufficient grace to be
> able to respond to God's offer of salvation in Jesus Christ. Thus,
> God has not forsaken humanity in its most abject state, but has
> already acted through His Son Jesus Christ by that 'true light that
> enlightens every man' (John 1.9)[8]

The will to repent is expressed in the words of the psalmist: 'I
thought on my ways, and turned my feet unto thy testimonies; I
made haste, and delayed not to keep thy commandments' (Ps.
119.59).

Repentance is a complete reversal of life. As the mind, heart and
will had been committed to disobedience, they are now committed
to obedience. This is a purposing of heart, mind and will to forsake
sin in every aspect and to follow God as we once followed satan.

Such a commitment requires evidence; that evidence is to 'bring
forth fruits meet for repentance' (Mt. 3.7-10; Mk 1.2-7; Lk. 3.7-14).
John the Baptist clearly meant forsaking the past life, restitution,
confession of the sinfulness of the past life, and filling in the future
with following after new obedience. He told those who had two
coats to give one to the person who had none, and to share food in
the same manner. He told publicans (those who had bought their
office of tax collecting for extortion) to exact tax of no one beyond
the legitimate tax. He told soldiers not to use their office for terror,

---

[8] Kenneth J. Collins, *Wesley on Salvation* (Grand Rapids, MI: Francis Asbury
Press, 1989), pp. 23, 24

to bring no false accusation (a common practice for extortion and terror), and be content with their wages (Lk. 3.10-14). These are radical changes in life—a complete reversal of attitude and behavior.

There are specific applications which are incumbent upon all who profess repentance. Repentance calls on the believer to forsake the past, separating from its patterns of fellowship and the manner of life. Restitution for wrongs committed where possible is certainly called for. This involves the restoration of stolen property and stolen reputations. Mending of broken relationships, especially if we caused the break by wrong and hurtful actions, must be a part of our repentance. We are in no position to offer a gift of worship on the altar of God if we have not righted the wrongs that we have committed against our brothers and sisters (Mt. 5.23, 24).

Fundamental to repentance is the confession of sins; this is audible repentance. Confession cannot be fully satisfied in 'secret'. The Scriptures call for confession within the body of Christ; in fact, if we do not confess within the body, our prayers will be hindered (Jas 5.13-16).

The Apostle Paul commended the Corinthian believers because their actions of reversal gave evidence of their repentance: 'For behold this selfsame thing, that ye sorrowed after a godly sort, what carefulness it wrought in you, yea, what clearing of yourselves, yea what indignation, yea, what vehement desire, yea, what zeal, yea, what revenge! In all things ye have approved yourselves to be clear in this matter' (2 Cor. 7.11).

Though we must not codify particular visceral reactions to repentance, we must understand that repentance is a radical emotional upheaval. The description of Peter's repentance following his denial of the Lord shows us a man who wept uncontrollably when he recalled Jesus' warnings, his own arrogance in self confidence and his denials of the Lord ('And when he went out, he kept on weeping', Mk 14.65).

The committing of sin involves the will to sin; likewise, repentance involves the will to repent. In sin the human will is enslaved to sin, but God has preserved in that depraved condition a ground upon which the gospel and the Holy Spirit can work. Depravity does not mean inability to be responsive to the goodness of God; it means inability to save oneself by any good deeds or good resolves.

God's gift of grace addresses the sinner under these circumstances and gives the grace of repentance. The person so moved is enabled to forsake sin and to follow righteousness.

The full meaning of repentance, then, requires a change of direction in heart, mind and will. With purpose of heart, with change of mind and with renewal of the will the penitent forsakes sin and follows God as he/she once followed sin: 'I speak after the manner of men because of the infirmity of your flesh for as ye have yielded your members servants to sin to uncleanness and to iniquity unto iniquity; even so now yield your members servants to righteousness unto holiness' (Rom. 6.19).

Repentance is a recurring theme in both the Old Testament and the New Testament. It is the message that is common to all those who preached the imminence of the kingdom of God: John the Baptist (Mt. 3.2; Mk 1.15), Jesus (Mt. 4.17), those whom Jesus commissioned to preach (Mk 6.12) and the apostles and other ministers after the ascension of Jesus (Acts 2.38; 3.19).

The necessity of repentance is borne out by reason and Scripture. A person must know that he/she is a sinner before he/she will seek to forsake the way of sin. One must know that he/she is lost before there is any desire to be guided to the right path. One must know that he/she is condemned before he/she will seek forgiveness. He/she cannot be forgiven until he/she wants forgiveness. He/she cannot be helped until he/she wants to be helped.

The Scriptures that demand repentance are abundant. There follows here only a partial list.

'Let the wicked forsake his way, and the unrighteous man his thoughts: and let him return unto the Lord, and he will have mercy upon him; and to our God, for he will abundantly pardon' (Isa. 55.7).

'In those days came John the Baptist, preaching in the wilderness of Judaea, and saying, Repent ye: for the kingdom of heaven is at hand' (Mt. 3.1, 2).

'From that time Jesus began to preach, and to say, "Repent ye: for the kingdom of heaven is at hand" ' (Mt. 4.17).

'And they [the Twelve] went out and preached that men should repent' (Mk 6.12).

'I tell you, Nay: but except ye repent, ye shall all likewise perish' (Lk. 13.3, 5).

'And Peter said unto them, "Repent ye, and be baptized every one of you in the name of Jesus Christ unto the remission of sins; and ye shall receive the gift of the Holy Ghost" ' (Acts 2.38).

'And the times of this ignorance God winked at; but now commandeth all men everywhere to repent' (Acts 17.30).

'The Lord is not slack concerning his promise, as some men count slackness; but is longsuffering to us ward, not willing that any should perish, but that all should come to repentance' (2 Pet. 3.9)

Repentance is fundamental to the whole question of morality. The act and practice of repentance are essential to salvation.

2

LIVING A PENITENTIAL LIFE

Introduction

In the preceding chapter we discussed repentance in initial salvation. A study of Scripture shows that repentance is one of the processes of spiritual living that is perpetuated in the cultivation of holiness and the Holy Spirit filled life (Heb. 12.14; Eph. 5.18-21). The encounter with God and the conviction of our sins when we first came to know the Lord set the pattern in which we are always to live in Christ. All the processes of life are like this. We see it in the origin and perpetuation of life in plants and animals. The neglect of these processes is an invitation to ill health. The most serious consequence of this neglect is death. This pattern prevails in spiritual life as well.

We have emphasized initial repentance; by that term we mean the turning around of our lives when we were first convicted of sin, and turned to Jesus Christ. Now we emphasize continual repentance that must be characteristic of life continually lived in fulfilling the divine call to holiness. This is living penitentially. The commitments made upon our first turning to the Lord must be followed through and become the manner in which one lives in covenant with God and the rest of the body of Christ.

The message of repentance must be very clear. First, there is only one kind of repentance—repentance from sin. Second, repentance always takes place in the light of divine judgment. Third, the intention of God for this judgment is redemption not destruction: 'Zion shall be redeemed with judgment, and her converts with righteousness' (Isa. 1.27).

The agency of the Word and the Spirit must remain central to repentance and restoration in its perpetuation. The divine Word is central to all spiritual life; 'Man shall not live by bread alone, but by every word that proceedeth out of the mouth of God' (Mt. 4.4; Deut. 8.3). There may be waves of emotion and crusades to 'get back to basics', but these may be nothing more than exercises in nostalgia and not redemptive experiences in judgment and renewal. Only by living in and by the Word (as Jesus himself did) can spiritual life remain vibrant.

It is by the Holy Spirit that the Lord 'washes away the filth of the daughters of Zion' and purges the 'blood of Jerusalem from the midst thereof'. He is the 'Spirit of judgment and the Spirit of burning' (Isa. 4.4). The redemptive quality of this judgment is clear when the prophet confesses that 'when thy judgments are in the earth, the inhabitants of the world will learn righteousness' (Isa. 26.9).

The Nature of Repentance

The hatred of sin which was awakened when we were first convicted of sin by the Holy Spirit must be perpetuated in life. Paul describes this spiritual grace in 2 Cor. 7.8-13. Upon conviction by the Holy Spirit the Corinthian believers became sorrowful as God intended; this is 'godly sorrow' (v. 9). Godly sorrow leads to repentance (v. 10). This is not the sorrow of the world. It is not a 'guilt trip' or hand-wringing over the consequences of sin (as Esau, Heb. 12.15-17). It is the deep sorrow of knowing that we have offended God, grieved the Holy Spirit, defiled the temple of the Holy Spirit and our own hands and heart. It is sorrow that prevails even when we did not 'get caught'. The product of such sorrow is repentance, and the product of repentance is salvation.

This text describes this sorrow and its manifestations among the Corinthians (v. 11). The first characteristic is earnestness. The second is that the penitent clears himself/herself in confession and redirection of behavior. Paul shouts, 'What eagerness to clear yourselves!' The third characteristic is indignation. Repentance involves a true hatred of sin, especially our own sins. We are playing a game—a damnable game—when we hate the sin in others and do not despise our own sins (Rom. 2.1). The fourth characteristic is fear or alarm. It is the kind of fear that the Hebrews writer described: 'It is a fearful thing to fall into the hands of the living God' (Heb. 10.31). The fifth characteristic is longing—longing for restoration of right relationship with God and His people. The sixth characteristic is zeal—a determination to set things right. It is the desire to see that right (justice) is done.

There are substitutes for repentance which are quite subtle and deceiving.. To habituate oneself to an external pattern of life that is behaviorally acceptable to our society is not repentance. To do by habit the things that are right requires no spiritual decision or commitment. Such a way of life requires no essential moral sensitivity, and no moral choices on our part. The likelihood is that this kind of living will degenerate to a social religion and the mechanical practice of 'good living'. In behavioral manifestations it may be indistinguishable from holy living, but the heart knows and God knows.

Every day of life is a day of encounter with evil. In a penitent life, evil must be deliberately rejected, and holiness must be consciously pursued. In the grace of God encounter with evil is encounter with salvation. To reject the temptation and defeat evil is a reaffirmation and renewal of our repentance. God responds in a reaffirmation of His grace to us in victory. In this reaffirmation, God is the Victor because the battle is His and not ours (1 Sam. 17.47; 2 Chron. 20.15; 1 Cor. 10.13).

Prayers of Repentance

There are many prayers of repentance recorded in Scripture. Four stand out with special prominence: the prayer of Solomon in his dedication of the temple, the prayer of Josiah when the scroll of the law was found in the ruble, the prayer of Ezra when he learned of the compromises among the exiles and the prayer of David recorded in Psalm 51. It is not our purpose to give full expositions of all of these. We will lift up the most prominent aspects of these prayers as they illustrate repentance for us.

The prayer of Solomon (2 Chronicles 6): In this prayer the king established a pattern of repentance for Israel. He imagined four specific circumstances that would show the people their need for repentance (6.24-31). The first circumstance is defeat in battle. He prayed, 'If thy people be put to the worse before the enemy...because they have sinned against thee...' Continuing this prayer Solomon described the essential components of repentance:

'and shall return and confess thy name and pray and make supplication before thee in this house...'

Then the king makes his specific petition: 'then hear thou from heaven and forgive the sin of thy people Israel, and bring them again unto the land which thou gavest to them and to their fathers' (vv. 24, 25).

The second circumstance that Solomon envisions is drought: 'When the heaven is shut up and there is no rain... because they have sinned against thee...' Solomon repeats the pattern of repentance: 'if they pray toward this place, and confess thy name and turn from their sin, when thou dost afflict them...' His petition is the same: 'then hear thou from heaven and forgive the sin of thy servants, thy people Israel... and send rain upon the land...' His specific request beyond forgiveness is, 'send rain upon thy people... (vv. 26, 27).

The third circumstance of chastening is famine and pestilence: 'If there be dearth [famine] in the land... pestilence... blasting or mildew, locusts or caterpillars, if their enemies besiege them...' Solomon asks YHWH, 'Hear thou from heaven thy dwelling place, and forgive, and render unto every man according unto all his ways, whose heart thou knowest; (for thou knowest the hearts of the children of men)' (vv. 28-30).

The fourth eventuality that Solomon anticipates is captivity: 'If they sin and be delivered to their enemies...' He describes repentance again: 'If they bethink themselves... and turn and pray unto thee in the land of their captivity, saying we have sinned, if they turn unto thee with all their heart...' Solomon comes again to forgiveness and restoration: 'Then hear thou from heaven thy dwelling place, and forgive, and render unto every man according to all his ways... that they may fear thee to walk in thy ways... (vv. 28-31).

These petitions are important for this study because of the consistency in which judgment, repentance and restoration are described. As to judgment, every petition makes it clear that these circumstances come on the people of God because they are under divine judgment. Defeat, drought, famine, pestilence and captivity are not merely coincidental. They are divine interventions in which God uses tragedy for His judgments: 'I form the light, and create darkness: I make peace and create evil: I the Lord do all these things' (Isa. 45.7; cf. Exod. 4.11; 1 Sam. 2.6-8; Amos 3.6).

Repentance is described in basically the same terms in all circumstances anticipated. They return from evil; they do not simply turn from one form of sinning to another form of sinning (as in reformation), and in the turning they confess the name of YHWH. They make supplication before YHWH, envisioning His presence in the temple where He manifested His glory in the Shekinah. They acknowledge that they are completely exposed to God, because He knows the hearts of the children of men. Their repentance is agonizing because of the punishments and because of the offensiveness of their deeds: 'Then what prayer or what supplication soever shall be made of any man, or of all thy people Israel, when every man shall know his own sore and his own grief, and shall spread forth his hands in this house, then hear thou from heaven thy dwelling place, and forgive...' (vv. 29, 30). In these petitions sin is understood to be the sins of individuals and their judgment and the sin of the nation and its judgment.

This prayer shows that repentance is a redemptive grace. The assurances offered in this prayer demonstrate this. Israel and we are assured that God will hear. This is witness to His faithfulness, and the knowledge of that faithfulness among God's people. God will hear from the uttermost point of the chastisement of His people. He will hear from the deepest level of despair. He will hear when His people call on him from the lowest point in life: when life is almost gone, with little or no hope of restoration and when life does not seem to be worth living.

The prayer of Josiah (2 Chron. 34.8-33): Josiah had come to the throne of Judah following the reigns of Manasseh (55 years) and Amon (two years, his reign being cut short by assassination). Most of Manasseh's reign was corrupt, and even when he recognized YHWH, he did not fully restore faithful worship in Judah and Jerusalem. Amon for his short reign 'trespassed more and more' (2 Chron. 33.23). With Josiah's reign restoration began and would bring about cleansing and repair of the temple in Jerusalem that had become filled with the corruption of Josiah's predecessors. In the course of the repair and cleansing of the temple, the priests discovered 'the book of the law in the house of the Lord' and it was delivered to the king (2 Chron. 34.15, 16).

The discovery of the scroll of the law in the house of the Lord is a tragic irony. It is ironic that the law should be lost in the temple, of all places. This is the place where God dwelt between the cherubim (2 Kgs 19.15; 1 Chron. 13.6), and the place that Israel was to turn to when they found themselves under judgment. It is ironic that there was not a scroll of the law in the palace because Moses (under God's order) had required that the king of Israel would have a copy of the law of the Lord beside him on his throne: 'And it shall be, when he sitteth upon the throne of his kingdom, that he shall write him a copy of this law in a book out of that which is before the priests the Levites: and it shall be with him, and he shall read therein all the days of his life: that he may learn to fear the Lord his God, to keep all the words of this law and these statutes to do them' (Deut. 17.18, 19).

When the law was brought to Josiah and was read to him he rent his clothes (2 Chron. 34.18, 19). He sent messengers to inquire of God concerning the wrath pronounced in the law. In his inquiry the king confessed, 'For great is the wrath of the Lord that is poured out upon us, because our fathers have not kept the word of the Lord, to do after all that is written this book' (2 Chron. 34.21). He did not rationalize the guilt away by attributing it to another generation. He did not imagine that the judgments which had come upon Judah were natural disasters, the way things are in a sin cursed world, bad political or military decisions, etc. These are the kinds of spiritual mind games that people use (individuals, nations and churches) when they wish to excuse their sins and avoid the real issue of confession: saying about their sins what God says about them.

The prayer of Ezra (Ezra 9.5-15): Of all the prayers that we look at in this study the prayer of Ezra is probably the most emotional. With great personal integrity Ezra had led the people in the restoration of the law and the services of worship in the restored temple: 'For Ezra had prepared his heart to seek the law of the Lord, and to do it, and to teach in Israel statutes and judgments' (Ezra 7.10).

Ezra leaned that many of the leaders of the people, even priests and Levites had not purified themselves in any sense of the word. They had used the restoration of the temple and its worship hypocritically to cover their own sins. Ezra described his own reaction to this news: 'And when I heard this thing, I rent my garment and my mantle, and plucked off he hair of my head and of my beard, and sat down astonied' (Ezra 9.3). There were others among the returned exiles that were equally affected by the knowledge of this sinfulness in Israel. They are described as those who 'trembled at the words of the God of Israel, because of the transgression of those that had been carried away' (Ezra 9.4). They gathered with Ezra as he sat in his consternation until the time of the evening sacrifice (Ezra 9.4).

Ezra's devastation at the knowledge of these sins is dramatically recalled in his great confession: 'O my God, I am ashamed and blush to lift up my face to thee, my God: for our iniquities are increased over our head, and our trespass is grown up unto the heavens' (Ezra 9.6. For similar confessions see Ps. 38.4-10; Isa. 6.5; Dan. 9.13-19). Ezra confessed that these sins had a long tradition in the nation of Israel: 'Since the days of our fathers have we been in great trespass unto this day...' (Ezra 9.7a). Ezra also acknowledged that the misfortunes of the nation had come upon them as the judgments of God for their sins: 'and for our iniquities have we, our kings and our priests, been delivered into the hands of the kings of the lands, to the sword, to captivity, and to a spoil, and to confusion of face as it is this day' (Ezra 9.7b). These conditions are strikingly close to the conditions that Solomon had described in his prayer at the dedication of the temple.

The pattern of repentance: These three prayers show a pattern of penitence. Though they are all from the Old Testament, the spirituality shown is common to both the Old Testament and the New Testament.

The first element common to these prayers is that there is a sense of union with God. There is broken fellowship, but the overall awareness is that God is faithful to His covenant and to His people. In each of the prayers God is still called 'our God', or 'my God'. This is the confession of a child to a loving, understanding and caring Father. This does not mean that He overlooks the sin, and treats it as anything other than a violation of His holiness and covenant. On the other hand it is not confession to an adversary or to a prosecutor. Such a confession ought not carry the fears and terror usually associated with admission of guilt. This is the confession of comfort and reconciliation not of terror. In the New Testament, John puts it in these words: 'I write unto you, my little children, that you sin not. But if anyone sins, he/she has an Advocate (παράκλητον) with the Father; He is Jesus Christ the righteous One. He is not only our atonement, but the atonement for the sins

of the whole world' (1 Jn 2.1, 2). All these prayers reach their fulfillment in Jesus.

The second pattern in these prayers is a sense of personal shame
for having violated the holiness and love of God and having de-
faulted on the redemptive covenant. So, Ezra can describe the sins
of the people as having heaped up over his head and rising to
heaven, and he can say, 'I am ashamed and blush to lift up my face
to thee'. Though Ezra was personally uncompromised, he associated himself with the corporate body to which he was joined in
covenant with God.

The third element in this pattern is the acknowledgment of the
heinousness of the sins and that these sins account for the afflictions on the people. The captivity, the drought, the pestilence are
acknowledged as the just chastisements of the Lord. They are not
accidents of life or the miscalculations of men. These are God's af-
fliction of His own people.

Confession in the biblical sense confesses sin as sin. In Ezek.
6.9, 10 God says:

> And they that escape of you shall remember me among the na-
> tions whither they shall be carried captives, because I am broken
> with their whorish heart, which hath departed from me, and with
> their eyes, which go a whoring after their idols, and they shall
> lothe themselves for the evils which they have committed in all
> their abominations. And they shall know that I am the Lord, and
> that I have not said in vain that I would do this evil unto them.

The final element in this pattern is the matter of righting the
wrongs—restitution. Sins cannot be undone, but the offender can
and must return to a renewal of obedience; if he/she does not,
there is no real evidence that repentance has occurred. The renewal
of vows and obedience is essential to the pursuit of holiness. The
penitent must return to the point of compromise and make a new
beginning with God.

In all of these prayers, there is a somber tone. It would remain
so if it were not for two facts: the faithfulness of God and the
promises of God. God is faithful to Himself and to His people even
in the face of their failures, and even in the midst of captivity under
divine judgment. In fact, His judgments are essential to His faithfulness. God is faithful even in the face of Israel's captivity, whether
in the period of the Judges or in the Babylonian captivity. Israel

learned this in the literal sense of political and military conquest. It is a lesson no less applicable to believers today.

The promises of God are based on and guaranteed by His faithfulness. He responded to the prayer of Solomon by making specific promises. He promised to answer every petition that Solomon had asked: 'If I shut up heaven that there be no rain, or if I command locusts to devour the land, or if I send pestilence among my people…. If my people which are called by my name, shall humble themselves, and pray, and seek my face, and turn from their wicked ways, then I will hear from heaven, and will forgive their sins, and heal their land' (2 Chron. 7.12-14).

The people of God must hear the call of God on the lips of the prophet Hosea: 'Sow to yourselves in righteousness, reap in mercy; break up your fallow ground: for it is time to seek the Lord, till he come and rain righteousness upon you' (Hos. 10.12).

Psalm 51: There are many penitential prayers in Scripture. This psalm stands out among them and commands our attention. It walks us through the process of judgment to the victory of restoration, and it is intensely personal.

In the cry 'have mercy upon me, O God' (v. 1) David uses a legal term for mercy. By this he recognized his own culpability to judgment under terms of the law of God. He also sensed his own personal estrangement from God.

David follows this petition with the use of the term loving kindness, which emphasizes the covenant that stood between God and David. It is for this grace that believers trust the Lord: 'How excellent is thy loving kindness, O God! Therefore, the children of men put their trust in the shadow of thy wings' (Ps. 36.7).

As this psalm shows, repentance and confession reach the depths of human emotional experience, and this strikes a chord with God's feelings for His people; so David appeals to the 'multitude of thy tender mercies' (v. 1). To understand God in this fashion is to see in Him deep emotional ties to His people: 'Like as a father pitieth his children, so the Lord pitieth them that fear him' (Ps. 103.13). The New Testament ascribes the same emotional union with believers in their weaknesses; He is 'touched with the feeling of our infirmities' (Heb. 4.15).

We are not cheapening the grace of God because sin requires a clear confession of sin: 'For I acknowledge my transgressions: and my sin is ever before me' (51.3). His struggle is described in Ps.

32.3-5a: 'When I kept silence, my bones waxed old through my roaring all the day long. For day and night thy hand was heavy upon me: my moisture is turned into the drought of summer. Selah. I acknowledge my sin unto thee, and mine iniquity have I not hid.'

We sometimes pass off the personal impact of David's confession by restricting the sin involved to David's sin in the matter of Uriah and Bathsheba. So we can depersonalize the application by placing it all on David and such egregious sins as this. The confession shown here reveals a pattern of repentance. We cannot escape the obligation of confession by disclaiming this particular sin.

The real impact of confession is the realization that sin is always against God: 'Against thee, thee only have I sinned' (51.4). It is true that David had committed atrocities against Uriah and Bathsheba and he had corrupted his God-ordained kingship; but the actual act of sin was against God. This is always the case for David and for us.

All sin is against God. It is more than a violation of a legal code or document. It is a personal attack on God and an alienation from Him. Joseph understood this because he feared sinning against God more than he feared violating Potiphar's trust in him (Gen. 39.9).

Though there are degrees in the heinousness of sin, there are no degrees in the fact that every sin is against the holiness of God. This is absolute. It is an attack on divine nature, a rupture of our personal relationship with Him, a defilement of His holiness and a spurning of His love. We destroy our peace, because 'There is no peace, saith the Lord, unto the wicked' (Isa. 48.22; cf. Isa. 26.3).

Conviction and confession of sin demonstrate the righteousness of God. David acknowledges this in his words, 'That thou mightest be justified when thou speakest and be clear when thou judgest' (51.4; cf. 3.4).

Confession not only involves confession of acts of transgression, but it also involves the confession of the root of sin, sin in the heart. David acknowledges his proclivity to sin in these words: 'I was shapen in iniquity, and in sin did my mother conceive me (51.5); but this proclivity is never used in Scripture as a ground for tolerance for sin or an excuse for it. This text shows that what had been done was the outworking of carnality. Hebrews 12.15 warns that the root of bitterness may spring up and trouble and defile the individual. To excuse sin as inescapable because of this condition fails to take into account the holiness of God and the sinfulness of our deeds. In these sins David demonstrated the truth of Christ's words; 'For out of the heart proceed evil thoughts, murders, adulteries, fornications, thefts, false witnesses, blasphemies: These are the things that defile a man…' (Mt. 15.19, 20).

The answer to the issue of temptation and victory over sin is threefold. The first ingredient in this victory is inner truth: 'Thou desirest truth in the inward parts' (51.6). The term 'inward parts' refers to all the immaterial nature of humankind. This is where truth is to dwell; it is the fabric of the heart. This indwelling of truth produces a pattern of behavior in which an individual lives a life of integrity and holiness. 'Happy are those whose strength is in you, in whose heart are the highways of Zion' (Ps. 84.5 NRSV). This is borne out in speech and actions. The first quality of truth speaking is accuracy, but it is accuracy that is born out of love for the truth—delighting in the truth.

Truth is also a matter of emotional integrity and purity. The quality of truth that makes it a spiritual virtue is love. Only when truth is spoken in love does it participate in wholeness of truth (Eph. 4.15). It is God's will to give believers hearts that are pure in the love of the truth. This is reinforced by the parallel line in 51.6, 'and in the hidden part thou shalt make me to know wisdom'. Spiritual knowledge of the truth is experiential knowledge, a thorough and intimate knowledge of truth and a bonding with truth so as to become one with it. This is love of the truth.

The second ingredient in victory over temptation and sin is to be cleansed within: 'Purge me with hyssop, and I shall be clean' (51.7).[9] This prayer for cleansing is correctly translated, 'De-sin me with hyssop, and I shall be clean'.[10] The Psalmist's assurance 'I shall be clean' comes from the fact that this is a petition to God, and not a resolution of the psalmist. The purifying of the heart is an atonement provision and is an act of God. It is not an act of human will. Verse 7b uses poetic repetition to intensify and explain the prayer: 'And I shall be clean: wash me and I shall be whiter than snow'. David shows by this confession that the provision and promise of a clean heart is a realizable experience.[11]

---

[9] Hyssop is a plant that was used in ceremonial cleansing: Lev. 14.4-6, 49-57; cf. Heb. 9.18-23.

[10] Derek Kidner, *Psalms* (TOTC; D.J. Wiseman (ed.); Madison, WI: InterVarsity Press, 1973), I, p. 191.

[11] The theological and experiential difficulty with the Reformed doctrine of sanctification is that it claims 'positional' sanctification, but defers the experience

The third ingredient of victory is joy: 'Make me to hear joy and gladness' (51.8a). Joy is essential to spirituality: 'For the joy of the Lord is your strength' (Neh. 8.10). In victory God gives joy (Neh. 12.43).

The chastening of the Lord does wound (Heb. 12.5-13; Prov. 3.11, 12), but in joy God heals the wounds that He has inflicted by His chastening. David's prayer is, 'that the bones which thou has broken may rejoice' (Ps. 51.8). Healing follows forgiveness and purging; in fact there is no ground for healing as long as there is a root of bitterness remaining in the heart. The removal of that root of bitterness is the provision that God has made in order to heal our smitten consciences. If it were not for this grace, we would spend our lives under inescapable condemnation.

The psalmist describes the experience of restoration in three terms: forgiveness, purity of heart and restoration of the Holy Spirit (51.9-12, which are parallel with vv. 6-8). Forgiveness, in particular, deals with the theology of judgment: 'Thou art of purer eyes than to behold evil, and canst not look on iniquity' (Hab. 1.13a). The terminology of forgiveness depends heavily on the concept of atonement as covering for sins and an advocacy for the sinner (Lev. 17.11; 1 Jn 2.1, 2). Forgiveness causes David to pray, 'Hide thy face from my sins, and blot out all mine iniquities' (Ps. 51.9). Blot is an extreme word; it is more like erase; blot out/expunge and do not leave a trace.[12]

The grounds upon which God will answer this prayer of David (and all others who come in the same way) are the name of the Lord, and the nature of God as holy, just and full of love. He forgives for His name's sake: i.e., for the honor of His name and the faithfulness that it stands for: 'I, even I, am he that blotteth out thy transgressions for my own sake, and will not remember thy sins' (Isa. 43.25; Pss. 25.7; 79.8).

---

of entire sanctification until the death (hence glorification) of the believer. This theology places on the death of the believer the work that God provided in the death of Christ. The result is that sanctification is never achievable as long as one is in the mortal body. This implies that the mortal body is itself sinful which the Scriptures deny.

[12] The radical nature of this word is illustrated in Moses' request that God would 'blot me out of thy book'. God responded that it is the evil doer that He will blot out of His book (Exod. 32.32, 33). The same Hebrew word is used in each of these occurrences. The prayer of David is that God would blot out his sin and its defilement in the same way.

The second aspect of restoration is the purifying of the heart; so David prays 'create in me a clean heart' (Ps. 51.10a). The word 'create' here is the same as in Gen. 1.1 (original creation) and Isa. 65.17 (the new creation). Throughout Scripture the language of creation and redemption coincide. The ground of each is the goodness of God, not the goodness of the created or the redeemed. Both creation and redemption bring about an entirely new thing. The agents of both are the divine Word and the divine Spirit, and in each case the product of God's action reflects His nature.

These creation-redemption considerations place the believer in an entirely different environment. This is such a radical change that the believer can no longer live as a citizen of this world order. Believers must live as citizens of the new heavens and the new earth (Phil. 3.20, 21). So, it is appropriate, even necessary, that David pray for a pure heart. This purity is both act and process. In initiation it is act.[13] In continuation it is process; that is, it is the pursuit of holiness as a way of living in Christ (Heb. 12.14; 2 Cor. 7.1). It is a way of life that is always open to God for conviction and correction.

That which is to be created here is a clean heart, which is the purification of the entire inner nature of the believer: intellect, emotions and volition. When man and woman were originally created, they were pure in heart. Redemptive creation also provides for purity of heart. The origin of this purity in each case is God's likeness imparted to the creature (Eph. 4.24).

The language of renewal in this psalm shows that David is seeking restoration after personal failure. It also shows that David recalled an earlier experience in which he had enjoyed purity of heart. He now seeks its restoration. He describes this experience with parallel terms: 'right spirit' and 'clean heart'. Paul describes this experience in New Testament fulfillment. It is a spirit given wholly to God 'by pureness, by the word of truth, by the power of God, by the armor of righteousness on the right hand and on the left' (2 Cor. 6.6, 7; cf. Rom. 12.9; 1 Pet. 1.22).

There were many tragic physical and social consequences of David's sin, but he does not complain to God about them. He did, however, seek respite from the spiritual judgments. So he prayed,

---

[13] All the petitions for the sanctification of believers in John 17 are aorist tense verbs. This tense emphasizes the punctiliar nature of that which is described. This does not deny continuation, but it does show that the beginning experience of sanctification is specific and definite.

'Cast me not away from thy presence; and take not thy Holy Spirit from me' (51.11). It is in the presence of God that David experienced judgment (Ps. 68.2), redemption, the fullness of joy (Ps. 16.11), refuge and protection in God (Ps. 31.19). This is where the upright dwell (Ps. 140.13)).

In parallel David prayed, 'Take not thy Holy Spirit from me' (51.11b). David and all Israel had seen the consequences of the withdrawal of the Spirit of God from Saul: 'But the Spirit of the Lord departed from Saul and an evil spirit from the Lord troubled him' (1 Sam. 16.14).

The third step in restoration is the return of the joy of the Lord and the presence of the Holy Spirit; so David prayed, 'Restore unto me the joy of thy salvation' (51.12). It is God's will to restore this joy, even though we have failed Him miserably as David had. David further describes this spiritual restoration as 'thy free spirit' (51.12b). A free or steadfast spirit is the willingness of the human spirit to obey God by the power of the Holy Spirit. These are the antidotes to temptation. Temptation that is resisted apart from joy in the Holy Spirit is barely resisted, if it is resisted at all (Jas 1.2).

The restoration of joy and gladness in the Lord produces results in others (51.13). David envisions that sinners will be converted to the Lord and that prayer and praise will characterize the believer's life.[14] There is an important insight here; a defeatist witness is no witness at all. Only a witness of joy and of a steadfast spirit can give a clear invitation or an attractive example of discipleship (Jn 17.20-23).

How does God respond to this statement (whether prayer or declaration)? Kidner (who treats this as a petition) notes that the 'psalm itself is the richest answer to the prayer, since it has shown generations of sinners the way home, long after they had thought themselves beyond recall'.[15] As a statement this psalm gives the same assurance.

The crushing weight of David's sin is reflected in his prayer, 'Deliver me from blood guiltiness, O God, thou God of my salvation'

---

[14] Kidner (*Psalms*, I, p. 192) treats v. 13 as a prayer: 'Then let me teach transgressors thy ways'. This is an interpretation judgment concerning punctuation, but the fundamental impact of the verse remains whether it is a petition or a statement of result. It seems better to treat it as a statement of result as in the KJV translation.

[15] Kidner, *Psalms*, I, p. 193.

(51.14a). David did not attempt to reduce the despicability of his sins with euphemisms and rationalization. He could not have expressed the heinousness of his deeds more graphically than in these words.

The result of such a clear confession of sin and break with sin is that 'my tongue shall sing aloud of thy righteousness' (51.14b). The forgiveness of sin looses the tongue to praise God. David knew that God's righteousness had been demonstrated in every step of restoration from Nathan's accusation (2 Sam. 12.1-14) to this moment of joy.

The joy of sins forgiven breaks out in the praise of God: 'Open thou my lips and my mouth shall show forth thy praise (51.15). When God opens the lips in this way, the restored believer can offer to God the sacrifice of praise, the fruit of the lips (Pss. 107.22; 116.17; 119.108; Jer. 33.11; Hos. 14.2; Jon. 2.9; Heb. 13.15).

In the Old Testament sacrifices of the heart superseded the prescribed ceremonies. Moses declared this (Deut. 10.12-16) and the later prophets kept this message before Israel (Isa. 1.10-17; Mic. 6.8). David's words describe spiritual worship: 'For thou desirest not sacrifice; else would I give it' (51.16a). The sacrificing of an animal or many animals is of little consequence to a king; it is less so to God who made the heavens and the earth, and owns the cattle of a thousand hills (Ps. 50.10).

One animal or all the animals of the earth cannot purchase anything from the righteousness and holiness of God. They can never become an adequate substitute for true sacrifice. 'The sacrifices of God are a broken spirit: a broken and contrite heart, O God, thou wilt not despise' (51.17). These are essential to confession. A heart or spirit that is not shattered by its own sinfulness has not seen the glory of God, and has not seen its defilement in the light of God's holiness. If there is no Sinai experience (Heb. 12.18-24) or temple altar experience (Isaiah 6), there is no contrition. Hear Jeremiah's description of his own contrition: 'Surely after that I was turned, I repented; and after that I was instructed, I smote upon my thigh: I was ashamed, yea, even confounded, because I did bear the reproach of my youth' (Jer. 31.19).

God knows the contrite heart and will honor it by receiving the worship offered. He makes a special promise to the broken hearted: 'For thus saith the high and lofty One that inhabiteth eternity, whose name is holy: I dwell in the high and lofty place, with him also that is of a contrite and humble spirit, to revive the spirit of the humble, and to revive the heart of the contrite ones' (Isa. 57.15).

Verses 18 and 19 provide the conclusion of the psalm, and give application to the petitions and pledges of this hymn. These verses also represent a transition of the psalm from the individualistic nature of vv. 1-17 to the corporate applications in these statements. By this transition the nation is incorporated into the prayer of the individual.[16]

This is the kind of solidarity that Ezra felt with all the congregation of the returned exiles. Even though he was personally uncompromised, he still cried, 'O my God, I am ashamed and blush to lift up my face unto thee, my God, for our iniquities are increased over our head, and our trespass is grown up unto the heavens' (Ezra 9.6).

The body of Christ must not become divided between those who consider themselves free from sin and those who have sinned. Whenever this happens, pride and animosity rend the spiritual body. Even in matters of discipline, which are necessary to the purity of the body of Christ (1 Cor. 5), the church must act with the sense of everyone's vulnerability to sin and union with the offender (Gal. 6.1-3).

This prayer introduces the metaphor of building the walls of the holy city: 'build thou the walls of Jerusalem' (51.18b). As it is with the individual in repentance and restoration, so it is with the whole body. Only God is able to restore 'the years that the locust hath eaten' (Joel 2.25). David put it in these words: 'Except the Lord build the house, they labor in vain that build it' (Ps. 127.1).

This metaphor of the city is important because the holy city is the site of the temple; these stand for the testimony of YHWH, the throne of judgment, the blessing of the Lord and redemptive peace (Psalm 122). The order of repentance, restoration, judgment and the descent of God upon the tabernacle of the wilderness and the

---

[16] Biblical interpreters refer to this transfer as the principle of corporate solidarity. This reflects the biblical understanding that there is union between individuals in a spiritual body and the entire body. Each is represented in the other. We see this in the understanding of rulership; the king is the nation, and all individuals in the nation have representation in him. This is also demonstrated in the role of the high priest who went into the most holy place for the whole nation. All the tribes were represented by having their names on the ephod of the high priest. Spiritually the whole nation went into the most holy place with and in the high priest. As individuals and as a nation they stood before the mercy seat and received atonement by the priestly acts of the high priest.

temple of Jerusalem are the paradigm of redemption. The assurance of restoration enables David to conclude, 'Then shalt thou be pleased with the sacrifices of righteousness, with burnt offering and whole burnt offering: then they shall offer bullocks upon thine altar' (51.19). When repentance is fulfilled, God will look upon and receive the physical sacrifices of true worship—offerings which He would have despised if they had been given without repentance and contrition. He will inhabit the praises of Israel (Ps. 22.3) in the restored temple as He did the original temple. This is the wonder of the grace of God.

Conclusion: In Psalm 51 the psalmist moves from the particular and individual to the nation. He transforms individual repentance to corporate repentance. We have attempted to reflect that in the exposition above. Earlier in the prayer of Ezra we noted that the prophet took the corporate sins of the leaders of the nation on himself as if he were personally involved in the compromises of which he repents. In the dedicatory prayer of Solomon, the king deals mostly with corporate sins and the need of repentance.

There is New Testament corollary to this sense of corporate solidarity. This is especially observable in the letters of our Lord to the seven churches of Asia (Revelation 2, 3). This understanding of the unity of the individual with the body comes from the organic character of the body of Christ. There is mutual identity in weakness and strength, sin and obedience and the confession of sin and the forsaking of sin.

In this identity we personalize the chastisements of the Lord, the sense of shame for sin, the call to heart searching and the commitment to confession and repentance. The converse is true. We can personalize the divine promises of forgiveness and restoration. The letters to the churches contain commendation and rebuke, and blessing and judgment.

Five times in these letters Christ calls on the church to repent. Even where the precise word 'repent' is not used these letters are weighted with the chastening of the Lord, and He never chastens without also offering to heal the wounds of His rebukes. The scourge of the Lord is always dipped in the balm of Gilead before He uses it to chastise His people (Jer. 8.22).

John assures us of this truth: 'I am writing to you my little children that you should not sin; and if anyone sins, he/she has an intercessor [παράκλητον, Advocate] who is Jesus Christ the righteousness One. And He is the atonement [covering, mercy seat] for our sins, and not for ours only, but also for the whole world' (1 Jn 2.1, 2).

Think about this: a penitential spirit is a quality of godliness and purity. Notice the remorse of Isaiah (Isa. 6.5), Ezra (Ezra 9.6), the penitential psalms of the godly psalmist and John the Apostle (Rev. 1.17). To profess godliness and holiness is a good profession when affirmed by Scripture, by the witness of the Holy Spirit and by valid spiritual experience; it is not haughty. However, it is remarkable that those who are the most godly are also the most sensitive to their unworthiness when they see the glory of God.

'Purge me with hyssop, and I shall be clean: wash me, and I shall be whiter than snow…. Create in me a clean heart, O God; and re-new a right spirit within me' (Ps. 51.7, 10).

3

JUSTIFICATION

Introduction

Justification is an act of God's grace in which the sins of the penitent believer are pardoned, and he/she is accepted in Jesus Christ (1 Cor. 1.30, 31; 2 Cor. 5.21; Rom. 4.5-8). As an act of grace, this redemptive benefit is the gift of God; therefore, it is not based in the merit of the recipient, but in the merits of Jesus Christ 'who is made unto us wisdom, and righteousness, and holiness, and redemption' (1 Cor. 1.30).

The redemptive provision for this gift of God is the Person of Jesus Christ who in His life, death and resurrection fulfilled the righteousness of God (Mt. 3.15; Rom. 10.4). Christ fulfilled the law, satisfied its judgments and presents Himself to God as the propitiation (i.e., the atonement covering) for our sins (Rom. 3.24-26; 1 Jn 2.1, 2; Heb. 9.14, 15). As the atonement covering for our sins, He provides protection from judgment by the fulfillment of the law for those who believe on Him (Jn 3.16; Rom. 1.16, 17; 10.10).

The divine agents for justification (both in provision and application) are the Word of God and the Spirit of God. The Word of God consists of both law and promise, but more particularly the Word is the Person of Jesus Christ (Jn 1.1-18). The Spirit of God is that Member of the Holy Trinity who is the Power of God. He both reveals the nature of God and executes His will (1 Cor. 2.10-16).

The definition of justification above deals with the following issues in salvation. First, it deals with the individual's guilt. This is the core of Paul's argument in Rom. 1-3. His statement that 'all have sinned and are coming short of the glory of God' (Rom. 3.23) is the climax of Paul's demonstration of human sinfulness.

The second issue in justification is the forgiveness of sin. This is an act of divine judgment, and the place of its occurrence is the tribunal of God.

The third issue is the individual's acceptance before God in Christ. This involves the forgiveness of sin, peace with God and the transmission of righteousness of God to the believer (Rom. 1.17; 4.5, 5.1-11; Hab. 2.4; Ps. 32.1, 2).

Since justification is an act of divine grace, it follows that the only avenue for appropriating this redemptive benefit is faith in Jesus Christ as He is revealed in Scripture.

Justification is a forensic act; that is, it is a judicial declaration. This act changes the legal standing of an individual from condemnation to forgiveness. This act of God occurs along with a complex of other redemptive experiences in the initial experience of salvation.

In this study we will follow the order of reasoning shown in Rom. 3.1-5.11. In chapter 3 the Apostle develops the doctrine of justification as a declaration and demonstration of the righteousness of God. In chapter 4 he defends the doctrine of justification by faith. Certainly the necessity of faith is imbedded throughout this discussion by Paul, but he collects his arguments on the subject especially in Romans 4. In 5.1-11 he shows the relationship of justification to other experiences in the transformation of the believer. In the course of the study we will incorporate texts from many other books of the Bible in order to show that this doctrine is consistently represented throughout Scripture.

The study which follows will attempt to take each of these issues into account in the explanation of the doctrine and experience of salvation.

Justification is the Fulfillment and Demonstration of the Righteousness of God

God is faithful in all His Judgments

All classes of humanity are sinful: Jew or gentile, rich or poor, sophisticated or unsophisticated, wise or foolish. This especially includes the great dividing marks of Jews and gentiles shown in Scripture. God has created all humankind, and He did not bestow a greater presence of the image of God on any race. Conversely, He did not withhold from any race any of the advantages of being in the image of God. God intervened against the sinfulness of the human family in order to reveal Himself to all (Tit. 2.11, 12). In relation to the distinction of Jew and gentile, God gave advantages to both. The Jews had the oracles of God in the law and the prophets. Though the gentiles did not have the written law, they 'showed the work of the law written in their hearts' (Rom. 2.14, 15). Whatever revelation either Jews or gentiles had, neither Jews nor gentiles had escaped the fact of sin. Though the Jews had the honor of receiving the tablets of the law (Rom. 3.1, 2; 9.4, 5), that advantage had not kept them from sinning as terribly as the gentiles (Rom. 2.1-5). Though the gentiles had a noble heritage of philosophical sophistication, that advantage had not kept them from producing a degraded society (Rom. 1.18-32). In their nature both Jews and gentiles are depraved; in their behavior they are sinners.

These facts would lead some to make terrible accusations against God as if He were unjust to condemn sin since all had fulfilled their fallen nature. Does their nature and the universality of sinfulness make 'void the faithfulness of God? It cannot be so!' (Rom. 3.3, 4a). Paul's suggestion is that this remark is so far from the truth as to be blasphemy.[17]

God is faithful to His own nature of righteousness even when He justifies the ungodly. Even in His forgiving sin, God confronts evil and the sinner. This confrontation is with the individual sinner and with universal unbelief and wickedness. None can escape the righteous judgment of God even if he/she can show that all the world is in darkness. At the same time universal unbelief cannot frustrate God in His will to save because where sin abounds grace much more abounds (Rom. 5.20).

The detractors of the gospel of grace attempt to press the doctrines of sin and grace to the point of absurdity. These enemies of grace would like to slander God and deny His righteousness since His righteousness is magnified by the universality of sin. So they vainly argue that since our unrighteousness commends the right-

---

[17] The KJV has the words 'God forbid' where we have used the exclamation 'It cannot be so!' Neither is an exact translation of the Greek text. Paul's exclamation is in the Greek optative mood which is the strongest exclamatory mood in Greek. The words 'God forbid' (though not a translation at all) do convey Paul's sense of the blasphemous character of the accusation against the judgment of God.

eousness of God, God is unrighteous when he judges (Rom. 3.5, 6). Such a conclusion would destroy any basis for righteousness and justice. If God cannot judge the world for its sin, there is no right or wrong in the world (Gen. 18.25b, 'Shall not the judge of all the earth do right?'). No one can offer any excuse for continuing in sin, and there is no possibility of escaping judgment.

By the nature of the case justification is an act of divine judgment. On the judgment to forgive sins, Scriptures use the legal metaphor of pardon. In the KJV the word pardon appears only in the Old Testament. There the Hebrew word סלח is the word most frequently translated with the word 'pardon'. However, this word is translated in the LXX with the Greek word ἀφίημι, which is translated in the New Testament with the words 'pardon' and 'forgive' in various contexts. As legal metaphors this terminology evokes the notion of a court of law in which the guilty are held accountable for their misdeeds. Whether they are pardoned or punished, the disposition is a legal decree. This is the way God disposes of the accusations of sin which are brought before His judgment. The sins of those who believe are forgiven. The sins of those who do not believe are not forgiven. Either decree is a declaration of judgment.

The biblical process by which sins are forgiven is through atonement, typologically and prophetically presented in the Old Testament by atonement sacrifices and fulfilled in the New Testament by the perfect life, sacrificial death and resurrection of Jesus Christ. The heart of this understanding is a covering for the sinner and for the sins he/she has committed. God accepts the covering as adequate for pardon, the establishment of peace and the extension of the benefits of righteousness.

This places justification in the realm of the forensic; that is, it is a legal declaration. It is a declaration that frees the believer from accusation before the tribunal of God, but it does not free him/her from guilt. Transgressions that have been forgiven are a part of the individual's personal history; these events cannot be undone. Justification relieves the believer of the penal consequences of prior sins as if he/she had never committed those sins. For this fact the believer is guiltless before the court/judgment of God. Those sins can never be the ground of punishment from God.

Justification goes beyond the negative act of removing judgment; it declares the believer righteous in Christ's merit. Paul enlists the witness of David to enforce this idea: 'Even as David also describeth the blessedness of the man unto whom God imputeth righteousness with out works' (Rom. 4.6,7; cf. 1 Cor. 1.30, 31; 2 Cor. 5.21).

The declaration of which we speak is a judgment concerning past sins and not future sins. Future sins will be forgiven as they are confessed and forsaken (1 Jn 1.9; 2.1, 2; Prov. 28.13; Ps. 66.18), but they are not already declared forgiven in the initial experience of justification.[18]

The experience of justification occurs in the believer along with a complex of other experiences in initial salvation: saving faith, repentance, regeneration, adoption and the witness of the Holy Spirit that we are the children of God. Though one may establish a logical order for discussing these experiences, it is unwise to attempt a chronological order for these experiences except to say that faith in Christ is prior to and fundamental to all experiences in grace. They occur in the order of salvation along with each other, and are dependent on each other in the economy of salvation and the fullness of redemption.

The sinfulness of the human race is a presupposition of the teaching of justification by faith. Any doctrine of salvation by works/merit assumes the inherent goodness of people. It claims

---

[18] Pentecostal preaching is being flooded with doctrines that are more in harmony with evangelical Reformed theology than with holiness Pentecostal theology. It is frequently said that justification covers all our sins: past, present and future. This is a perfect foil for the doctrine of eternal security (the perseverance of the saints). Eternal security is an inevitable conclusion from such a theology of salvation. Eternal security is inextricably tied to other doctrines in the Reformed tradition, particularly the doctrine of unconditional election. This corruption of Pentecostal theology robs faith of its component of obedience (the 'obedience of faith', Rom. 1.5). It renders all acts of obedience as unnecessary to salvation. It reasons that since all obedience is less than absolutely perfect, it is defective and therefore sinful. This reasoning drives a wedge between the experiences of regeneration and justification. Some of these theologians claim that one must be regenerated before he/she can repent or even believe. This is a contradiction of the biblical doctrine of justification by faith. If one is saved/regenerated before he/she believes, faith has nothing to do with salvation. It is an event after the fact. Imbedded in this theology is the teaching that believers continue to practice sin even after they are saved. It has become a mark of 'proud humility' to say, 'All our righteousnesses are as filthy rags' (Isa. 64.6). Even a superficial look at the Isaiah text will show that this application is not what the prophet had in mind. If this is what he meant, even our faith is sinful. All obedience is counterproductive because it is less than perfect, and therefore, sinful. This is not biblical teaching and it does not contribute to holiness, but to antinomianism.

that even though there is evidence of some degree of fall in the human race, fallen men and women are able to satisfy the demands of the holy God. Whatever God demands is deemed to be within the creature's ability. It is further argued that whatever is beyond the creature's ability is simply 'absorbed' in the goodness of God.

The Scriptures very specifically reject these presumptions, and require all to come before God in faith because justification is given to the one who 'worketh not, but believeth on him that justifies the ungodly' (Rom. 4.8; cf. Rom. 8.33). The intercessory work of Christ presupposes the unworthiness of those for whom He intercedes. Note Paul's question and answer in Rom. 8.34, 'Who is he that condemneth? It is Christ that died, yea, rather, that is risen again, who is even at the right hand of God, who also maketh intercession for us'. Christ is Judge (Jn 5.22-29; Acts 17.30, 31), but He is also Mediator (1 Tim. 2.5). So, in His intercession, He also establishes the sinfulness of those who come to God by Him (Heb. 7.25). Jesus tells us exactly that in Lk. 5.32: 'I came not to call the righteous but sinners to repentance'.

The Universality of Sin
It is necessary that the fact of sin be proved in order for the doctrine of justification to make sense. This is the burden of argument in Romans 1-3. In the fact of being sinful (by deed and by depravity) there is no difference between Jew and gentile: 'What then, are we better than they? No, in no wise: for we have before proved both Jews and gentiles, that they are all under sin' (Rom. 3.9).

The depth of this condition of depravity is described in Rom. 3.10-18. Paul draws from several passages of Scripture to create this description of human sinfulness.[19] This catalog of human sins is designed to show that having the law in written form did not make the Jews righteous. It also shows that having the law in their consciences did not make the gentiles righteous (Rom. 2.14-16). In this demonstration Paul has shown that all grounds for human merit have been destroyed and that humankind is without righteousness before God.

Neither the law nor conscience can bring righteousness; they can provide only a measure for the definition of sin. They cannot produce the righteousness necessary for the fulfillment of the right-

---

[19] Pss. 14.1-3; 53.1-3; Eccl. 7.20; Pss. 5.9, 10; 140.3 [LXX 139.4]; 53.4; 10.7 [LXX 9.28]; 59.7, 8; 36.2 [LXX 35.2].

eousness of God or for the decree of remission (Gal. 3.21). There are two purposes of the law in this relationship. First, it designed to stop the mouth of those who would accuse God (the 'gainsayers'). Second, it is designed to hold the whole world (Jews and gentiles) guilty and accountable to God: 'Now we know that what things soever the law saith, it saith to them who are under the law, that every mouth may be stopped, and all the world may become guilty before God' (Rom. 3.19). Clearly the Jews are included in these purposes because they have the oracles of God (Rom. 3.2). The gentiles are included. Though they do not have the law as delivered by Moses, they 'do by nature the things that are contained in the law. These having not the law are a law unto themselves: which shew the work of the law written in their hearts, and their conscience also bearing witness, and their thoughts the mean while accusing or else excusing one another' (Rom. 2.14, 15). In the light of these considerations we must conclude that neither the law nor conscience can justify. They give the knowledge of sin and wrath but not the knowledge of forgiveness. Neither law nor conscience can bestow righteousness.

The Fulfillment of the Righteousness of God in Justification
This view of God's righteousness was described in both the law and the prophets. The righteousness which the law described is now being manifested in God's provision of righteousness in justification: 'but now the righteousness of God without the law is manifested by the law and the prophets' (Rom. 3.21; cf. Gal. 3.21, 22). In this way the Apostle answers his critics who interpret forgiveness as a compromise of justice and holiness. The law has been fulfilled (both in terms of perfect obedience and complete judgment) in Jesus Christ. God in grace is sharing that fulfillment with all those who believe in Christ. So, it is not simply one person who is displaying the righteousness of God; an uncountable host of believers in Jesus Christ becomes the display of the righteousness of God in time and eternity. These are drawn from all nations and ethnicities and from all ages from Adam to the end of the age.

Such a view of the righteousness of God places all people in the same position of judgment. Since they are all depraved, since they all have the same spiritual inabilities and since they have all actually committed sins, there is no difference between Jews and gentiles. So the righteousness demonstrated in justification cannot be the righteousness of human achievement or the righteousness of works. It can only be the righteousness of God fulfilled in Jesus Christ. The term 'the righteousness of God' has a twofold meaning. First, it is the righteousness that matches the perfection of God. Second, it is the righteousness that comes from God; which was and is fulfilled in Jesus Christ.

Having stripped the creature of any ability to provide his/her own righteousness, Paul now presses the point that righteousness can come to an individual only by faith. Having been driven from any hope in his own accomplishments the sinner is driven to one route, and only one, 'For by grace are ye saved through faith' (Eph. 2.8). Faith is the believer's way of appropriating to himself/herself the righteousness of God. Since both Jews and gentiles are driven to the same inability, they are driven to the same solution. There is only one answer to the sin question: the grace of God; and it is the answer that God always gives (Rom. 5.20, 21).

Paul brings his demonstration of the sinfulness of the human race to a head in Rom. 3.23, 'For all have sinned [Greek aorist tense] and are coming short [Greek present tense] of the glory of God'.[20] It is this condition of unworthiness and inability that God addresses in His provision for justification.

The Atonement

The ground for the provision and application of justification is the atonement. The Scriptures use several words to describe the grounds of justification in the atonement. Prominent in this list are two specific words: redemption and propitiation. The word redemption (from the Greek word ἀπολύτρωσις) means the deliverance which comes when a forfeiture has been repurchased—when a debt has been satisfied.[21]

---

[20] There are those who use this text and the translation above as a proof to claim that everyone (believer and unbeliever) continues to commit sin. If this is the case, Paul stands in contradiction of 1 Jn 2.1; 3.4-10; 5.18.

[21] This Greek word is often translated as 'ransom' which is a good translation if properly understood. I have chosen the phrase 'repurchase of a forfeiture' as a better understanding of the word. This is not a criminal's ransom (viz., a kidnapper's ransom), or the ransom paid to a captor (viz., satan). It is the restoration of the benefits which God gave in creation and which Adam forfeited when he sinned (Rom. 5.12-21). The benefits of the covenant of life (all the benefits and privileges of the original state of humankind) returned to God who had given them to humankind in the covenant of life. The benefits which had returned to

The word 'propitiation' (from the Greek ἱλαστήριον) appears in the New Testament only in Rom. 3.25 and Heb. 9.5 (translated with the words 'mercy seat' in the KJV and RSV).[22] The intention is to describe a covering provided by God to protect the sinner from the judgment of God. We usually describe this covering as the blood of Jesus, but in actuality Jesus is the propitiation—the atonement cover over the believer. According to 1 Jn 2.2, Jesus is the propitiation (The Greek word here is ἱλασμός, a cognate to ἱλαστήριον). John uses this word again in 1 Jn 4.10, 'Herein is love, not that we loved God, but that he loved us, and sent his Son to be the propitiation for our sins'. Jesus is the covering provided by God to be the protecting cover for the sinner and the forgiveness of his/her sins.

These facts make the death and resurrection of Christ equally necessary for our justification (Rom. 4.25) because the covering at the heavenly altar requires that the Redeemer be alive eternally (Rev. 1.8, 17, 18; Heb. 7.25).[23] By seeing the atonement as a Person—Jesus Christ—we join together the Sacrifice and the Priest (Heb. 9.14). In this way we see the necessity of the eternal nature of both the Sacrifice and the Priest. God has provided everlasting covering and everlasting intercession.

In the Person of Jesus Christ God has declared His righteousness for the remission of sins. Justification is forgiveness, but it is

---

God on the occasion of human sin are now restored under terms of Christ's atonement.

[22] NIV translates this word with the term 'atonement cover'. NEB uses the translation 'place of expiation'. All of these are attempts to describe the atonement in the sense of covering the sins of the offender so that they are not subject to further judgment by God. This also has the effect of covering the offender so that he/she is protected from divine wrath. The OT sacrifice of atonement is explained in Lev. 17.11 in terms of the blood of the sacrificed animal: 'For the life of the flesh is in the blood: and I have given it to you upon the altar to make an atonement (covering) for your souls; for it is the blood that maketh an atonement [covering] for the soul'.

[23] Some in the Reformed tradition have placed all requirements for justification in the death of Jesus; they have treated the resurrection of our Lord as unessential to justification. This comes out of an extreme application of the penal substitution theory of the atonement. This implies (some of these authors actually state it.) that all requirements for justification were fulfilled in the Cross. This is an evisceration of the doctrines of Christology and soteriology. This view treats salvation as if it were totally contained in the satisfaction of judgment. One of the main faults of this teaching is that it leaves no logical reason for the continuing ministry of Christ as high priest, and it ignores the biblical statements concerning that ministry.

more than that. Forgiveness alone would give the believer a state of innocence. There is another essential of justification; it is that God declares the believer to be righteous (Rom. 4.5; Gen. 15.6; Rom. 1.17).[24] It is Christ's righteousness, not just His blood, that is declared for the remission of sins.

There are three necessities for this righteousness. The first is the perfect fulfillment of righteousness in the life of our Lord. The second is the atoning death of Christ for our sins. The third is the victory over sin by Christ's resurrection. God fulfills these requirements by giving His Son to be made sin for us in order that we may be made the righteousness of God in Him (2 Cor. 5.17-21). The believer becomes beneficiary of the righteousness of our Lord, inheriting the name of God, the righteousness of God, the kingdom of God and eternal life. These benefits are not simply juridical and forensic. They are actual.

The remission of sins provided in Christ's death and resurrection covers the sin of past ages (that is, Old Testament believers) in which God exercised forbearance: 'Whom (i.e., Christ) God has set forth to be a propitiation through faith in his blood, to declare his righteousness for the remission of sins that are past through the forbearance of God' (Rom. 3.25). The term 'forbearance' (from the Greek word πάρεσις) means to let go unpunished. The term is used here to show that God withheld final judgment on the sins of the believers in the Old Testament until their redemption was completed in the atonement which Christ provided.

The sacrifices of the Old Testament did not take away sins; neither could they give righteousness (Heb. 10.4). They were, however, God's provision for delaying judgment (hence the word forbearance) until the coming of Christ and His fulfillment of all righteousness in His life, death, and resurrection. Those sacrifices were prophetic of Christ's fulfillment of righteousness in which He becomes the atonement: i.e., the covering for our sins.

---

[24] By declaring the believer to be righteous God is declaring (i.e., making a judicial decree) that the believer is in actual fact righteous. God is not engaging in a judicial fiction. He is declaring that a transfer of the righteousness of Christ to the believer has occurred. This truth is stated in these words by the Apostle Paul: 'For he hath made him [i.e., Christ] to be made sin for us, who knew no sin that we might be made the righteousness of God in him' (2 Cor. 5.21). This declaration gives the believer the benefits of Christ's perfect life, His death and His resurrection. In this transfer the believer is placed in the position of acceptance by God and is made to be the righteousness of God in Christ.

The author of the epistle to the Hebrews joins the promise and the fulfillment in these words: 'and for this cause He [Christ] is the Mediator of the new testament, that by means of death, for the redemption of the transgressions under the first testament, they which are called might receive the inheritance' (Heb. 9.15).

Both Paul and Hebrews show the unity of the old covenant and the new covenant. This also unites the believers in both ages. They are so closely joined in covenant and faith that the writer of Hebrews concludes his review of the heroes of faith with these words: 'And these, all having obtained a good report through faith, received not the promise: God having provided some better thing for us, that they without us should not be made perfect' (Heb. 11.39, 40).

This pattern for the remission of sins, far from being a compromise of divine righteousness, is the supreme declaration of God's righteousness: 'To declare, I say, at this time his righteousness: that he might be just, and the justifier of him that believeth in Jesus' (Rom. 3.26). So God makes no compromise with sin when He forgives. He does not merely overlook sin, and He does not set aside His justice. Forgiveness of sins which have been confessed before God is a matter of the fulfillment of the justice of God (1 Jn 1.9), and a declaration of His righteousness—a declaration that will stand in the day of judgment and for eternity.[25]

Such a doctrine of justification and divine righteousness is universally applicable. It cannot be exclusive to any race, whether Jew or gentile. Righteousness fulfilled through the law assumes a superior position for the Jews. Righteousness through any kind of works assumes a superior position for those who are 'morally fit'. They can achieve righteousness on their own. These distinctions and superiorities are not allowed in the doctrine of grace. So we are driven to a doctrine of justification through the grace/gift of God received by faith. Any system other than faith gives the 'righteous' a ground for boasting, but no one can boast of righteousness as if it were his/her own achievement. Boasting is excluded by the law of faith which is free to all humankind (Rom. 3.27, 28).

This follows from the fact that God is the God of all humankind without any racial distinction. So God works by faith among the

---

[25] Forgiving sin does not represent a contest between the justice of God and the mercy of God. It is a harmony of divine perfection in the love of God.

Jews and the gentiles: 'Seeing it is one God, which shall justify the circumcision by faith, and the uncircumcision through faith' (Rom. 3.30).

Justification by faith does not void the law, as the Jews feared. It really confirmed the law. Neither Jews nor gentiles had been able to show a display of the righteousness of God (Rom. 3.23). Now, however, it is being displayed by Jews and gentiles as they are presented in the righteousness of God in Christ. This demonstration of righteousness is by the rule of faith: 'Do we then make void the law through faith? God forbid! Yea, we establish the law' (Rom. 3.31).

There are those who challenge the doctrine of justification without works as if it were a compromise of the righteousness of God. However, any challenge to the truth of God—even in His act of forgiving the ungodly—renders the one who makes the challenge a liar, even if everyone in the world is shown to be a liar (Rom. 3.4). God's judgments demonstrate His righteousness and sovereignty in judgment: 'That thou mightest be justified in thy sayings, and mightest overcome when thou are judged' (3.4b). God's judgments show Him to be a righteous judge whether He judges by retribution or by forgiveness, or by the reward of righteousness

Justification by Faith

The Covenant Argument for Justification by Faith

The history of justification by faith extends to the Old Testament. There the understanding of justification is that it includes the forgiveness of sins and the establishment of righteousness for the believer: 'Abraham believed God and it was counted to him for righteousness' (Gen. 15.6). In His description of justification David included both forgiveness of sins and the transfer of righteousness to the believer (Ps. 32.1, 2).

These texts show that God's declaration of forgiveness and communication of righteousness go together. They do not allow that there can be a state of forgiveness that does not carry with it a state of righteousness. So a declaration of forgiveness is accompanied with a declaration of righteousness. The statement from which Paul begins his reasoning is Gen. 15.6 (Rom. 4.3; Gal. 3.6). Though the Genesis text does not mention forgiveness, it does say that Abraham was accounted to be righteous; and this is the point that

Paul presses. There is no 'blank slate' of innocence here. Romans 4.11 refers to the righteousness which Abraham had by faith, and v. 13 describes it as the righteousness that comes by faith.

In his address at Pisidian Antioch (Acts 13.14-41) the Apostle brought these two aspects of justification into a single promise. He declared that through Jesus Christ 'is preached to you the forgiveness of sins' (Acts 13.38). Then he explained, 'And by him all that believe are justified from all the things, from which they could not be justified by the law of Moses'.

This text is in line with Paul's phrase 'without works'. Righteousness is accounted to the believer even though he/she has no prior record of good works (as Abraham and David show). One does not come before the tribunal of God with a list of good deeds. Witness the rich young ruler who went away from Christ lost (Mt. 19.16-24 and parallels). All his professed fulfillment of the law did not gain him the kingdom or divine approval. Paul describes his own obedience to the law as nothing more than dung, even though concerning the law he was blameless (Phil. 3.3-9).

The blessing of justification comes to those whose lawlessness has been pardoned. In Col. 2.15 Paul describes this as a cancellation of charges: 'Blotting out the handwriting of ordinances that was against us, and took it out of the way, nailing it to his cross'.

By the terminology of covering Paul reflects the promise of Lev. 17.11, where the blood of the atonement is given on the altar as a covering. Paul speaks of the sins of the past as having been placed under an impenetrable shield so that they can never be recalled in accusation (cf. also Ezek. 18.21, 22).

Faith is a gift of God's grace (Eph. 2.8, 9) by which the penitent appropriates to himself/herself the covering for sins provided in Jesus Christ. This faith claims the promise of God, but it does not claim a falsehood (i.e., that one is justified while still remaining a sinner). It lays a claim on what God has done in His Son Jesus as personal benefit and experience. God has provided a covering for sins (an atonement; a propitiation). God has provided the pardon of sins and a shelter from His wrath. Faith takes us into that shelter.

Faith claims acceptance before God (even at the judgment bar of God) in Jesus Christ. This acceptance places the believer in a position to receive the reward of Christ's righteousness which is eternal life. Faith also abandons all attempts to achieve eternal life except the saving name of our Lord (Jn 14.6; Acts 4.12).

Biblical faith is described by the Apostle Paul with the expression 'the obedience of faith' (Rom. 1.5; 16.26). Faith always operates in the context of obedience especially the obedience of repentance and confession (Rom. 10.8-10). James joins faith and obedience in these words, 'You see that faith worked together with his [Abraham's] deeds, and out of works faith was fulfilled' (Jas 2.22). James follows this statement with the same quotation of Hab. 2.4 that Paul used in Rom. 1.17, 'The righteous person lives out of His faith'.[26] James goes on to make the bold statement, 'You see that out of works [by works] a man is justified and not out of faith alone' (Jas 2.24). Any other interpretation of faith is antinomian; that is, it is an attack on the law of God and a rejection of obedience.

Faith as a gift of grace has its origin in God and has God as its Object of belief. From the human standpoint, it is an abandonment and repudiation of any form or claim of human merit. It rejects any notion of the inherent goodness or worthiness of the creature.[27] The vocabulary of worthiness is the vocabulary of obligation; such language implies that God owes forgiveness and righteousness to the creature. Such is the language of contract between equals. God establishes covenant with the creature, but never contract.

Faith rejects any notion that the individual can make himself/herself righteous by any form of good deeds or other claims of worthiness, whether defined by law or human culture.

Faith is an acknowledgement of human inability; this inability is the result of four teachings of Scripture. The first is the creature status of humankind. The human creature is limited as to ability and as to time. It is impossible for the creature to break the barrier from

---

[26] The meaning of Hab. 2.4 is that the manner in which the righteous live is by keeping on believing. This sense appears clearly in the reading of the Hebrew text; it is this sense in which both Paul and James cite this Old Testament text. This text is often quoted as if it said that if one believes on Christ at any point, he/she is forever saved. There were Gnostics in the early Christian community that taught that; it is this error that James is addressing in his epistle, and that the Apostle John addresses in His epistles, especially 1 John.

[27] The critical word here is 'worthiness', and worthiness should not be confused with worth. To imply that the sinner is worthless is to say that God sacrificed His Son (the greatest treasure of heaven: Rom. 8.32) for a prize that had no value. The death of Jesus Christ is God's most profound statement of the worth of humankind.

finite to infinite. He/she cannot satisfy the demands of infinity of which eternity is one facet. That which is temporal cannot generate anything of eternal value.

The second limitation is the sinfulness of human beings. This sinfulness is represented by the total depravity of humankind, by death in trespasses and sins and by the record of personal transgressions. These conditions are universally true of humankind, as Romans 1-3 show. Humanity as sinner is the offender; as the offender he/she cannot determine the grounds of reconciliation. Only the offended can set the terms of reconciliation and the offended is God.

The third limitation is the inadequacy of the law. The law can only define sin and announce judgment/condemnation. It cannot give life or generate righteousness 'because the law worketh wrath…' (Rom. 4.15a).

The fourth obstruction to humanly generated righteousness is the infinite glory of God. This is the overarching condition that qualifies the preceding three limitations on human ability.

Over against the inability of humankind, we note the ability of God which is the result of four facts. First, God is infinite in glory and power. He can provide all righteousness, holiness and power necessary to justify for time and eternity. Second, God is perfect in love, mercy, power and justice. All that He does is consistent with perfect righteousness and judgment. Third. He is the offended party, and He alone can set terms of reconciliation. Fourth, He is sovereign in His authority to judge; therefore, He is sovereign in His authority to reconcile.

The Historical Sequence Argument for Justification by Faith
Justification by faith has been Paul's presupposition from the beginning of the epistle to the Romans. In Romans 4 he makes his climaxing argument for justification by faith.

Paul uses two Old Testament characters to demonstrate that justification is by faith: Abraham and David. We have earlier taken into account the description of justification as David described it and as Abraham experienced it. In this mention of these Old Testament believers, we are interested in the temporal sequence of faith and justification. These are critical choices. Abraham is the father of the covenant. David is the covenant king of Israel. It is also worthy of note that the author of the record of Abraham's justification is

Moses, the lawgiver. Paul's purpose is to show that the doctrine of justification by faith is established in the Scriptures. He shows this by a quotation from Gen. 15.6, 'Abraham believed God and it was accounted to him for righteousness (Rom. 4.3).

First, the Apostle establishes that a doctrine of justification by works contradicts and voids the entire doctrine of grace. If Abraham had been justified by works, the rewards of righteousness would have been his as a matter of debt. The patriarch would have been able to boast that he was righteous on his own account. Paul quickly adds, 'but not before God' (4.2). Certainly, the creature cannot lift himself before God the Creator and Judge of all the earth (Gen. 18.25).

Second, Paul argues that grace and works are mutually exclusive systems. Works produce wages, and wages represent debt. This is the language of merit: 'To the one who works the reward [wages] is not accounted according to grace' (Rom. 4.4). So any system that allows the offender to reconcile by his/her own works is a system that achieves reconciliation by obligation.

Paul reasons in the same way, and even more deliberatively when he discusses the calling of the righteous remnant. The remnant, which represents the Israel of faith (true Israel), is a remnant according to grace: 'Even so then at this present time also there is a remnant according to the election of grace. And if by grace, then is it no more of works; otherwise grace is no more grace. But if it be by works, then is it no more grace: otherwise work is no more work' (Rom. 11.5, 6). In Israel's call there can be no mixture of grace and merit. These systems are mutually exclusive. What is true of the covenant body is true of the individuals in the covenant; one system of grace is applied to all; and grace contradicts every doctrine of merit.

Third, Paul uses David as witness to his argument. In Ps. 32.1, 2 David describes two aspects of justification: the imputation of righteousness and the forgiveness of sin: 'Even so David also describeth the blessedness of the man unto whom God imputes righteousness without works. Saying blessed are they whose iniquities are forgiven, and whose sins are covered' (Rom. 4.6, 7).

David describes this experience in the legal terminology of accounting: 'Blessed is the one to whom the Lord will not account (impute) sins' (4.8). The double negative (in Greek) gives this statement the force of saying that God will not under any circumstances allow an accusation of sins that are past to be brought against the person whom He has justified.

In continuing his argument of justification by faith Paul reviews the sequence of events in the Abrahamic covenant (4.9-12). He shows that the provision of justification is not limited to the Jews.[28] He asks the question, 'Does this blessedness come on the circumcision only, or upon the uncircumcision also?' (4.9a). It is a rhetorical question, and the Apostle anticipates the answer. This blessing comes 'both to the Jews and to the gentiles'.

The order of events in the life and covenant of Abraham also answers the question. Paul repeats his contention that it is faith that is accounted for righteousness, not circumcision. So he asks the question, 'Did God declare Abraham justified after he was circumcised or before he had been circumcised?' (4.10a). He answers his own question, 'Not in circumcision but in uncircumcision' (4.10b)[29] So Paul argues that it is faith that accounts for the Patriarch's justification and not circumcision. Circumcision is secondary and not primary; as a secondary consideration, the rite is a sign of justification already declared and accomplished. It is a sign of the righteousness that God had already made a fact by divine declaration. So circumcision is not righteousness and it does not produce righteousness. It is clear that righteousness can be declared of an individual who believes even if he has not been circumcised; therefore, circumcision is never a condition of being justified.[30]

This is important for Paul's argument to the Romans and all believers. He wants to establish that justification is a provision for all

---

[28] Paul uses the term 'the circumcision'. By this term he intends to identify all those who use circumcision as if it represented the entirety of the law and the proper identification for the elect or the Jews. Conversely, Paul identifies the 'uncircumcision' as those who are not the children of Abraham according to the flesh; hence, gentiles.

[29] The historical order in Genesis shows that God declared Abraham justified in Gen. 15.6. Circumcision was not a factor in the Abrahamic covenant at this time. It was not introduced into the covenant until Genesis 17 when God reaffirmed the covenant and changed the name of the patriarch from Abram to Abraham. Abraham was justified by God's declaration before the rite of circumcision was a part of the covenant order.

[30] Paul's argument here is not limited to the rite of circumcision. He is using this one rite as symbol of the legalism for which his opponents were contending. They had poured the entire law and all righteousness into this one sign. What they conceived to be their greatest argument Paul shows to be their weakest point.

those who have faith in Christ: Jews or gentiles; circumcised or un-circumcised. The most important consideration is that being Jew or gentile has nothing to do with being justified. The Abrahamic covenant continues by the rule of faith and not by the rule of genetics. At the end of chapter 3 Paul concludes this aspect of his argument. He asks if God is the God of the Jews or the gentiles: 'Is he the God of the Jews only? Is he not also of the gentiles? Yes, of he gentiles also' (Rom. 3.29). The fact that God is the God of both Jews and gentiles means that He created both and He loves both; so He provides for and seeks the salvation of both. He is not willing that anyone should perish (Jew or gentile; circumcised or uncircumcised; 2 Pet. 3.9). The justification which God offers to all is justification by faith, not justification by genealogy or sacramental rite (4.30).

Justification and Spiritual Transformation

In the earlier portions of this study the emphasis has been on justification in terms of the atonement. This is not the complete biblical picture of this experience. Justification is one of several experiences in salvation which we have designated initial salvation. By this term we mean those experiences in grace in which the saved person is transformed from death to life, from darkness to light, from being ungodly to being godly, from being unrepentant to being repentant and from being a child of satan to becoming a child of God. It is necessary to emphasize these experiences as occurring along with each other and as being in unison with each other. If we do not have this emphasis, justification becomes a juridical act alone and a forensic falsehood. Here we emphasize those transformations of nature and standing that accompany reconciliation and freedom from condemnation.

Paul introduces these changes with his statement, 'Therefore, having been justified by faith we have peace with God through our Lord Jesus Christ' (Rom. 5.1). This is the climax of all that Paul has been saying in this book since Rom. 1.16, 17.

Peace with God

The first result of our justification is peace with God. This is the peace of knowing that our sins have been forgiven. There are no charges against us at the tribunal of God. This does not mean that the justified are innocent. Our misdeeds have not be made non-existent; they are still a part of our personal history, and many of the social, physical and emotional results remain. It means that our sins do not exist in God's record of our lives. The accusations have been nailed to Christ's cross, and the charges have been satisfied before the judgment of God: 'And you being dead in your sins and the uncircumcision of your flesh, hath he quickened together with him, having forgiven you all trespasses; blotting out the handwriting of ordinances that was against us, which was contrary to us, and took it out of the way nailing it to his cross' (Col. 2.13, 14). The word picture in this text is that our bill of emancipation has been put on public display by having been nailed to the cross of our Lord.

The ground of this peace is the access that we have to God through Jesus Christ by faith; we stand in the grace of God.[31] The position that is described here is experienced by believing in Jesus Christ. We are not placed under the burden of having to maintain our place before God by works. Having begun in faith, we will be perfected in faith (Gal. 3.1-5).

The result is that we are at peace with God; we are no longer angry with God. Enmity has been removed because all accusation by God has been removed. We no longer labor under the sense of the judgment of God: 'There is therefore no condemnation for them that are in Christ Jesus' (Rom. 8.1). This is peace which comes from having been restored to our rightful relationship with God. Humankind was made for communion with God, and a sense of fellowship. This fellowship was interrupted by sin and the consequent divine judgment. When God removed His charges against the believer, he established the peace of which we speak. He also removed from the believer the sense of enmity which every condemned person feels toward the source of his/her condemnation.

In this way the believer becomes a peaceable person. Though the text before us does not go further in elaborating that peace, peace with God is fundamental in any harmonious relationship with other persons. Peace having been established with God we are free to

---

[31] This verse is a very strong statement because of the frequent use of the Greek perfect tense. 'We have [perfect tense] access by faith in this grace in which we stand [perfect tense]' (5.2). The sense of this Greek tense is that it describes a present condition based on a past accomplishment or event. So the standing described here is one of previous establishment and of current experience.

pursue peace with all others, even our enemies (Heb. 12.14). If God can provide peace with us while we were still enemies, we can and must live peaceably with our enemies (Rom. 12.18-21). Even if they persist in animosity, this must not provoke animosity in us. This is an outgrowth of peace with God.

Rejoicing in the Hope of the Glory of God
The next transformation provided in our being justified is that the believer rejoices in the hope of the glory of God. As long as there is a sense of condemnation from God, the prospect of the appearance of divine glory is terrifying, and it shatters any hope of peace with Him. This peace goes beyond being relieved of terror; the believer is able to rejoice in the hope of seeing the glory of God. Imagine, if you can, Israel shouting with joy before Mt. Sinai. In the light of the fiery mountain they could only cringe in terror afraid to touch and afraid to look. In justification the believer has come to the glory of God in the face of Jesus, and we move toward the revelation of His glory in His return and in His manifestation in the mountain of His glory, the Holy City (Heb. 12.22-24). We can rejoice in the hope of the glory of God because that glory has already been implanted in the heart as the firstfruits of the Spirit (Rom. 8.23-25). It is this rejoicing that is the incentive for holiness of life in the prospect of Christ's appearing (1 Jn 3.1-3; Heb. 9.28).

Patience in Tribulation
The believer also has peace with life. He/she has a changed relationship with tribulation; we are able to glory in tribulation (5.3). Tribulations are going to occur in a sin cursed world order whether or not we believe in Christ. Believing in Christ does not provide immunity to trials; it views trials as contributions to the 'eternal weight of glory' (2 Cor. 4.15-18).

For those do not know Christ in faith, tribulation provokes fear, animosity and anger; often that anger is directed at God. Before coming to faith, we interpreted tribulation as being evidence of God's anger toward us. We could see only injustice in the fact of tribulation. We were angry with those around us because it was easy to blame them and their self-centeredness for our distress. Tribulation was to be avoided at all costs; if it could not be avoided, we cursed the day and often cursed God to whom we attributed the difficulty. Under these circumstances tribulation created bitterness, disbelief, cynicism and impatience.

Now that we are in Christ and have all the evidences of the love of God, tribulation works patience. The word for patience here carries the meaning of endurance, steadfastness under trial, and the ability to wait confidently for the fulfillment of God's purposes for us and in us. The glory of this promise is that God turns the tribulations around in such a way that the tribulations themselves produce patience (Jas 1.2-4). The very things that satan throws against us to destroy us, God transforms as instruments of grace and spiritual growth: 'For we know that for the ones who love God—the ones who are the called according to His purpose—He works all things together for good' (Rom. 8.28).[32] If we know these things we can be at peace with life—even life that is filled with trials.

Patience developed under these conditions produces other spiritual benefits. One of the most important (and the one Paul mentions here) is that patience demonstrates genuineness of spiritual character. The word translated experience uses the analogy of the testing of metal to determine what kind of metal it is and to determine if it is pure. Patience developed out of tribulation is evidence of the genuineness and purity of the believer's character—his/her likeness to Christ.

This demonstration of character produces hope (5.4, 5). Hope is a confident trust in God for those things that have not yet been fulfilled: 'For we are saved by hope: but hope that is seen is not hope: for what a man seeth, why doth he yet hope for?' (Rom. 8.24). This hope has confidence that those things which we do not now see will be fulfilled by God in the perfecting of our experience in redemption (Heb. 11.1). This aspect of spirituality looks especially at the fulfillment of redemption in the last days; in fact, it anticipates the vindication and reward for the believer in the final day of judgment. Though that day has not yet come, and that vindication has not yet occurred, this hope is not ashamed to make the claim of vindication in the promise of God. It is confident in claiming that God can and will do what He has promised. The strength of this hope is not in the tenacity of the believer, but the believer's understanding of God 'who quickeneth the dead, and calleth those things which be not as

---

[32] The translation used above is not based on the Textus Receptus, the text that stands behind the KJV. It is based on a text with better documentation when other Greek texts are compared.

though they were' (Rom. 4.17; cf. Heb. 11.3).[33] The believer is not afraid that he/she will be confounded or refuted when he/she lays claim on the promises of God. This is truly an emulation of the faith of our father Abraham who 'against hope believed in hope' (Rom. 4.18). He was not afraid to set aside the deadness of his own body and the deadness of Sarah's womb, because He knew that God could and would produce the child of promise in spite of the physical obstructions.

The New Testament believer is especially confident in the promise of the return of Christ and the fulfillment of salvation. Though we do not now see the fulfilled kingdom, we have learned to hope in the glory of God. We can now anticipate with joy the glorious appearing of our God and Savior (Heb. 9.28; 1 Jn 2.28-3.3).

Earlier we noted that the believer has come to peace with life. These are the things that we mean by peace with life. The believer does not try to escape life; there is no denial of its tribulations. Yet the faithful can already enjoy the victory of the day of the Lord's appearing, knowing that He is faithful who has promised (Heb. 10.23).

The Love of God Poured out in the Heart

God establishes peace with other people—even enemies—because of 'the love of God which has been poured out in our hearts through the Holy Spirit who has been given to us' (Rom. 5.5). This love is the strength of our hope, and it has been and remains poured out (perfect passive verb) in the hearts of the believers. The extent to which God loves us is demonstrated in the sacrifice of His Son (5.6-11).

We know that God loves us because when we were yet without strength, Christ died for us: the godly for the ungodly. Paul shows

---

[33] There is a popular corruption of the use of this text that encourages believers to call those things that are not as though they were. This is not what the text says, and it is not in the power of the believer to do in his/her faith the things that only God is able to do. There are many dangers to this misunderstanding. It imputes to the believer a power that he/she does not have. It makes claims that are not true, and a lie cannot be transformed into truth simply because it is uttered 'in faith'. To say that one is not ill when clearly he/she is ill is not faith. It is falsehood. On the other hand to be confident that God will supply needs in His own order, even when we still labor under the burden of those needs is genuine faith (Phil. 4.19); this faith is able to remain confident even in the presence of scoffers. The response of Job to his wife's scoffing remark is exemplary (Job 2.9, 10).

the marvel of this love in the reasoning that follows. Hardly anyone would die for a righteous person; though some might, it would be rare. God goes beyond all that and commends His love toward us while we were still sinning. In the midst of our sinning God gives the greatest gift of His heart, His Son (Rom. 8.31, 32).[34] The most awful of sins in the history of all creatures is the crucifixion of God's Son. Even while we were doing this, God loved us and heard the prayer of His Son to forgive us in the very act of our murder of Jesus (Lk. 23.34).

The way Paul describes this love shows that love becomes in the believer what it is in God: the ground of existence. God loves because He is love (1 Jn 4.8). In Christ, God has transformed the character of the believer so that love becomes the ground of his/her existence; so the believer lives out of love. It is not only the ground of existence for the justified; it is also the ground of thought, word and action. They live and act out of love as God lives and acts out of love.

The knowledge of this love and the hope that it undergirds are the most fundamental elements in our living out of love. To be confident that God loves us and that He has given us hope in spite of our sinfulness sets us free to love others even if they offend and persist in offending (Eph. 4.32). Only in this way can the believer be at peace with others. Any other basis for peace produces only a tenuous 'cease fire'.

The formula for fulfilling this love is for the Holy Spirit to pour out this love in the heart—the entire inner nature of those who are justified by faith. It is not the product of discipline, though it cannot be realized without the spiritual disciplines of holiness. It cannot be achieved by mimicking Christ; on the other hand it cannot be achieved except by 'beholding in a glass the glory of the Lord [by

---

[34] The New Testament doctrine of sacrifice is unique in the history of religions. Even in the provisions for sacrifice in the Old Testament, the lesser was sacrificed for the greater. It was better to sacrifice a lamb at the Passover than to sacrifice a child (in this case the first born son). All of the sacrifices operate on this level. In the New Testament God reverses this order and sacrifices the greater for the lesser, the sinless for the sinful, the pure for the impure, the Creator for the creature. It is a challenge to the so-called history of religions school to show how this doctrine could evolve out of any of the existing religions at the time of Christ's coming and the writing of the New Testament. It is a challenge which liberal theology has never met.

which we] are changed into the same image from glory to glory, even as by the Spirit of the Lord' (2 Cor. 3.18).

4

BORN OF THE SPIRIT

The most comprehensive single statement on regeneration in the Scriptures is Jn 3.1-21, though this text does not use the word 're-generation'.[35] Aside from its historical purpose, it is recorded in Scripture in order to explain the nature of regeneration.

The story of Nicodemus represents the character of unregenerate humanity, the character of regeneration, and the character of regenerate humanity. What is said concerning these things to Nicodemus is universally true. Nicodemus as an individual stands for all human beings under these relationships.

The character of regeneration is set forth by John in a description of the disparities between light and darkness, life and death, and flesh and spirit. These contradictions exist in the clash between the kingdom of this world order and the kingdom of God. They exist in personal and individual crises in the question of being born again. The crisis which Nicodemus faces is a crisis of conflict between the kingdom of satan (darkness, death, and flesh) and the kingdom of God (light, life, and, Spirit).

The natural origin of humankind and the spirituality of the kingdom of God are incompatible. Therefore humankind cannot enter or even see the kingdom of God by his/her natural origin.

---

[35] The Greek word παλιγγενεσία appears in the New Testament only twice: Mt. 19.28 and Tit. 3.5. It is a compound word from πάλιν (again) and γένεσις (beginning).

In the Matthew text it is used eschatologically to refer to the restoration of all things in presence of Messiah. It is not used in this text to refer to personal redemptive experience. The disciples had followed him and were participants with Him in the restoration of all things. This is a new genesis.

Titus 3.5 refers to the 'washing of regeneration and renewal of the Holy Spirit'. Here the word is used soteriologically to refer to personal redemptive experience in which the individual is radically changed in all the faculties of personal nature: mind, emotions and will. Though this word is not used in John 3, the birth of which Jesus speaks represents this kind of change.

The Conflict of Nature

The first point of incompatibility lies in the nature of humankind and the nature of God and His kingdom. Humankind is in darkness because this is the nature of this world, which is humanity's origin. The kingdom of God has its nature in Christ, the eternal Word (Jn 1.1). 'In Him was life; His life was the light of men' (Jn 1.4). 'He was the true Light which enlightens everyone who comes into the world' (Jn 1.9).

The darkness of the world was of such a nature and was so deep that the people of the world did not see the Light (which is life) shining in the world. John emphasizes this by three bold statements. The first is 'And the light in the darkness shines, and the darkness did not take hold of (claim as its own) the light' (Jn 1.5). Darkness could not receive the Light.

The second statement is, 'He was in the world and the world did not know Him' (Jn 1.10). In view of the progression of thought in this passage and in the light of vv. 4 and 5, this statement refers to the Word's preincarnate and invisible omnipresence in the world. That world of humankind to which He is both light and life did not know Him.

The third statement is, 'He came into the things which were His own, and the people who were His own did not receive Him' (Jn 1.11). The omnipresence of the Word is apparently still in the mind of John. In His omnipresence He indwelt all that was His: even the people of that world which belonged to Him as Creator and by divine presence did not know Him.

The darkness of the world was such that it did not—it could not—perceive the Light shining. The world still sought the kingdom of God, but it sought it from the standpoint of its own darkness. This was the position of Nicodemus even in the presence of Jesus, the incarnate Word. Therefore, Jesus said to him, 'Verily, verily, I say to you, unless someone has been born again,[36] it is not possible to see the kingdom of God' (Jn 3.3).

---

[36]The predominant use of this word in the New Testament is in the sense of 'above' or 'from above' (Mt. 27.51; Mk 15.38; Jn 3.31; 19.11, 23; Jas 1.17; 3.15, 17). The word does have temporal applications however (Lk. 1.3; Acts 26.5; Gal. 4.9). The context of this appearance of this word seems to favor the latter meaning: Hence 'again' in the translation above. Nicodemus responded to this understanding of the word with his question in v. 4. This is apparently the meaning of the word in v. 7.

The Conflict of Understanding

The world and its citizens clash with the kingdom of God in their perception. The natural person is unable to understand the kingdom of God. Nicodemus reveals this incomprehensibility by the questions which he asks of Jesus. He asks, 'How is it possible for an old man to be born? It is not possible, is it, to enter the womb of his mother a second time and to be born?' (Jn 3.4). These are puerile responses to Jesus' statement. Such ignorance is especially reprehensible for a Jewish religious leader. As such Nicodemus should have known similar terminology from the Scriptures and from rabbinic literature.

Even after Jesus' explanation of the nature of the Spirit and the flesh (Jn 3.5-8), Nicodemus asks, 'How is it possible that these things come to be?' (Jn 3.9). The appalling thing is that Nicodemus could ask a basically pagan question.[37]

In another way, however, this is understandable. Nicodemus looked for the kingdom of God in purely human terms. The pagan could do no better or no worse.

We meet this same lack of understanding in the Samaritan woman. To Jesus' promise that He would give 'living water' (Jn 4.10) she protests, 'Sir, You have no bucket and the well is deep: whence, therefore, do You have the living water?' (Jn 4.11). This spiritual intellectual density is summed up by Paul: 'But the natural man does not receive the things which are of the Spirit of God' (1 Cor. 2.14).

The Conflict of Origins

The natural person and the kingdom of God clash with each other because of an incompatibility of origins. This is epitomized in Jesus' statement to Nicodemus, 'That which is born of the flesh is flesh; and that which is born of the Spirit is spirit' (Jn 3.6). This statement is designed to explain Jesus' immediately preceding statement: 'Unless someone is born out of the water and the Spirit, it is not possible (for him/ her) to enter into the kingdom of God' (Jn 3.5).

There are two origins of existence. On the one hand there is the natural, that which is begotten of natural seed. Because it is of this

---

[37] C.K. Barrett, *The Gospel according to St. John* (London: S.P.C.K., 1962), p. 174.

world order, it partakes of darkness, death, and the carnal nature of this world order. The flesh can only produce flesh with its basic sinful character—a character that cannot see or enter the kingdom of God.

It should be carefully noted that John is not using the terms flesh here to describe the human physical body. The Scriptures do not treat the constitutional nature of flesh, blood and bone as evil or as the enemy of the immaterial nature (soul and spirit) of human beings. The term flesh is used here to refer to an order of existence which has its origin and identity in darkness and death.

On the other hand, there is the spiritual order of existence, that which is begotten of the water and the Holy Spirit. That which is begotten of the Holy Spirit by virtue of its origin and nature rejects, forbids, and condemns the darkness, death, and evil of the fleshly order. There is such a contrast between these two worlds of origin and nature that the presence of Christ in the world is both condemnation and salvation for the world. In a derived sense, the presence of even one believer in the world is a condemnation of the world and an offer of salvation.

The essence of Christ's message is that human beings must have a totally new beginning if they are to enter the kingdom of God. It must be a beginning that rejects and takes the place of the old order. It is a beginning that is not of the bloodlines of man, nor of the will of the flesh, nor of the will of man (Jn 1.13). These are the ways that human systems understand continuity, inheritance, power and rights of place. They are totally foreign to and antagonistic to the values structures, continuity and power in the kingdom of God.

Jesus climaxes His statement with the words, 'Stop marveling that I said to you, "It is necessary for you to be born again" ' (Jn 3.7). Two things stand out in this statement. First, Jesus emphasizes the moral necessity of the new birth. Second, He makes the command personal by telling Nicodemus that he personally had to be born again.

The Apostle Paul describes the old order—that which is born of the flesh—in Rom. 3.9-18. This passage, in effect, presents in summary all that we have established from John. Humankind is totally evil in his/her actions: 'We have before charged both Jews and Greeks that they are all under sin, just as it is written there is not one righteous' (vv. 9, 10; cf. Pss. 14.1-3; 53.1-3). Humanity is depraved in his/her mind: 'There is none that understands' (v. 11).

His/her will is in darkness; he/she pits his/her own will against God's will: 'There is not one that seeks God; all have turned aside; every one of them has been made useless, There is not one that does right, not even one' (vv. 11, 12). Humankind is depraved emotionally: 'An open grave is their throat; with their tongues they have deceived. The venom of snakes is under their lips, whose mouth is full of cursing and bitterness' (vv. 13, 14). The unbeliever's relationship to society shows the evil nature of the unregenerate by a murderous and destructive manner of life: 'Swift are their feet to shed blood. Ruin and misery are in their ways, and the way of peace they have not known' (vv. 15-17). Humanity climaxes his/her evil nature and behavior by acting as if God did not exist and did not see: 'There is no fear of God before their eyes' (v. 18).

The important point to be made here is that in John and in Paul, the descriptions of unregenerate humanity are universally applicable. Paul begins by saying that both Jews and Greeks stood accused (Rom. 3.9). John records Jesus' statement in a direct charge to Nicodemus, a ruler of the Jews, 'It is necessary for you to be born again' (Jn 3.7). Both the Jew with his high moral standards and the Greek with his culture and worldly wisdom came before the same necessity: 'It is necessary for you to be born again'. The 'good moral person' and the debauched person face the same moral necessity, the new birth. In the narrative of John, both Nicodemus, a teacher in Israel, and the Samaritan woman, an outcast, showed the same misunderstanding and spiritual blindness.

The Necessity of a New Origin

From these considerations it is evident that men and women from the standpoint of natural origin cannot inherit the kingdom of God. The origin of the Kingdom is heavenly. The origin of the natural is worldly. The nature of the Kingdom is light; sinful humanity is in darkness. The rule of the Kingdom is the Word of God written; the ruler is the Word of God incarnate. In contrast, humankind is carnal in word and wisdom. The personal agent of the Kingdom is the Holy Spirit. Humanity is possessed of 'the spirit which is now working in the sons of disobedience' (Eph. 2.2). The King of the Kingdom is the Lord of glory. Unregenerate people give lordship to the 'god of this world' (2 Cor. 4.4).

The kingdom of God stands opposed to the kingdoms and the course of this world. Therefore, the kingdom of God by its existence is a condemnation of the kingdom of darkness. It is not possible to be a partaker and subject of both kingdoms.

The experience of the new birth is an experience that establishes a totally new relationship of life. This relationship is based on a new origin of life.

The Agents of the New Birth

The agents of the new birth are the Word and Spirit of God. The Word of God is the seed of the conception of the new nature. 'Being begotten again not from perishable seed but from imperishable seed—through the living and abiding Word of God' (1 Pet. 1.23).

In its written and proclaimed form, the Word of God consists of both law and promise. The law reveals the holiness of God and hence our own fallenness and condemnation. The promise reveals the grace of God and the light of the gospel of redemption. It is by the 'great and priceless promises' that we become partakers of the godly nature' (2 Pet. 1.4).

Written and proclaimed Word is the very nature of Christ. So that which is written in law and promise is the revelation of the eternal nature of the Son of God—the eternal, personal living Word of God Jn 1.1-12. So to be born of the Word is to be born of the nature of Christ.

The Spirit of God is the personal administering Agent of redemption. The Spirit's association with the redemptive work of God is grounded in His divine nature and His Trinitarian relationships. He is divine person, an equal person and member of the holy Trinity with the Father and the Son. He is the inspiring Author of the written Word of God. He is the begetting Agent (Mt. 1.20) and the overshadowing Agent (Lk. 1.35) of the incarnate manifestation of the personal and eternal Word of God. He is the eternal Spirit by whom our Lord Jesus Christ offered Himself as a flawless sacrifice to God (Heb. 9.14). He is the Spirit of holiness who declared our Lord to be the Son of God by the resurrection from the dead (Rom. 1.4). He is the Paraklete whom the world cannot receive 'because it neither sees nor knows Him' (Jn 14.17), and who will prove the guilt of the world in relation to sin, to righteousness, and to judgment (Jn 16.8).

The New Birth: A Radical Change

The new relationship requires a drastic change of nature. This radical change is provided in the new birth, which is by the Holy Spirit. The radical nature of this experience is represented by two changes: a change of origin and a change of nature.

The new nature is heavenly in its origin. The seed of the earthly is according to the flesh and can produce only carnality. The seed of the heavenly is spiritual. It is of the Word and the Spirit. It can produce only that which is spiritual.

That which originates in the basis of the worldly existence must share not only the nature of the world but also its destiny. The destiny of this world is already set. Its condemnation is announced in the ministry of the Holy Spirit (Jn 16.7-11). By its nature and by divine judgment it passes away (1 Cor. 7.3 1). The judgment that is set for this world order is destruction (2 Pet. 3.7). Paul eloquently declares this common destiny: 'For the mind of the flesh is death' (Rom. 8.6). Those who are of this world order are already participating in its destiny; as they move toward destruction, they are already participating in that divine judgment (Jn 3.18).

That which originates in the basis of the heavenly must share not only the nature of the heavenly but also its destiny. John represents the heavenly as Christ's order of existence. He is from above (Jn 3.13). He is God's gift sent from heaven (Jn 13.16). To those who believe on Him, He gives the status and the character of the children of God (Jn 1. 12), and they are born of the will of God (Jn 1. 13). He imparts to them everlasting life (Jn 3.16), and He delivers them from the condemnation of this world order (Jn 3.16, 17; Rom. 8.1a). These also are already participating in their destiny because the Holy Spirit is the firstfruits of the resurrection (Rom. 8.23).

The change of nature is produced by the new origin. This is the new birth—born again—and regeneration. A new principle of life has been infused; a new nature is born. The believer becomes a new person in Christ Jesus. He/she becomes a child of God begotten of the will of God (Jn 1.12, 13) not one of the children of disobedience and wrath (Eph. 2.2, 3). Believers are born of the Spirit of

God (Jn 3.5) and indwelt by the Spirit (Rom. 8.9) and not by 'the spirit that is now working in the sons of disobedience' (Eph. 2.2). The believer is a new person in Christ (Eph. 4.24; Col. 3. 10).

The heart of stone has been broken up and removed, and in its place is the heart of flesh. This is the covenant promise of God. This new heart is produced by the new Spirit in the people of the covenant and is the ground upon which they are identified as the people of God and He is their God (Ezek. 11.19, 20). This heart becomes the 'epistle of Christ written not with ink, but with the Spirit of the living God, not in tablets of stone but in tablets of the heart of flesh' (2 Cor. 3.3).

The producing of this new heart is a creative act of God. In this act of God's grace a new seed of life is implanted and the governing disposition of the soul is made holy. From this new principle of life the fruit of the Spirit (love, joy, peace, long-suffering, gentleness, faith, meekness, self-control) is implanted.

The new birth is the restoration of the spiritual essence of the image of God in the believer, though it is not the final perfection of that image. The 'old man' (the nature of the earthly origin) has been put off (Eph. 4.22). The new nature (the nature of the heavenly origin) is the product of the renewal of the mind: 'to be renewed in the spirit of your mind' (Eph. 4.23). This is the putting on (to be clothed with) of that which 'according to the character of God has been created in righteousness and holiness of truth' (Eph. 4.24). Paul further defines the new person as 'the one who is being renewed in knowledge in accordance with the image of the One that created him' (Col. 3.10). The central point of both these references is the image of God. The old origin cannot bestow spiritual things—a spiritual mind, righteousness, and holiness. It remains for the new nature to bestow these and to renew the image of God in the believer.

The experience of the new birth answers in every respect the problem raised by Paul's description of the unregenerate (Rom. 3.9-18). It is the renewal of the mind that was once depraved and had no understanding of God. It is the renewal of the will that was once pitted against God's will and would not seek God. It is a renewal of the emotions that were once embittered and produced cursing. The love of God is shed abroad in the heart by the Holy Spirit (Rom. 5.5).

The Effects of this Change

This change of nature also produces a change in the manner of life. The first change to be expected of the new life is to stop sinning; this is John's exhortation 'My little children, these things I am writing to you in order that you should not sin' (1 Jn 2.1). In chapter 3 of this epistle John shows the basis of this expectation. Being in Christ and abiding in Him prohibits sin (1 Jn 3.6). Christ's redemptive purpose is to take away sin (1 Jn 3.8). Being born of God and having the seed of that birth in one stops sin in practice: 'Everyone who is born of God does not sin, because His seed remains in him: and it is not possible to sin, because out of God he is born' (1 Jn 3.9).

Reformation theology has consistently and from its inception insisted on the perpetuation of sinning even after conversion. Wesleyan holiness theology offers a correction: 'The very first effect of the new birth on human character is that God enables whoever has experienced it to avoid committing sin'.[38]

Wesley notes a second effect of the new birth: 'The second effect of the new birth on human character is that God gives to whoever has experienced it a new motive of life. That motive is the motive of love.'[39] The love of God has been poured out in our heart through the Holy Spirit, who has been given to us.

This love is not merely our love for the brethren, or even our love for God, or beyond that God's love for us. It is specifically that God has implanted His godly nature in us, that love is in us as it is in God —the motive of thought, word, and action—the totality of our existence.

There are certain applications of these principles that are necessary. Four are of particular importance. If this new nature is not of this world, it cannot be cultivated by the devices of this world order. The fellowship of this world cannot cultivate the new life which is not of this world. The worldly wisdom of human philosophy cannot produce, explain, or improve the quality of the life that is from God. The pattern of life of this world order—its value systems, its standards of achievement and happiness—cannot repre-

---

[38] William R. Cannon, *The Theology of John Wesley* (New York: Abingdon-Cokesbury, 1946), p. 131.

[39] Cannon, *The Theology of John Wesley*, p. 133.

sent spiritual living. Therefore for those who have been born again, there must be a separation from the world in life, separation from its company (i.e., fellowship), and conduct.

If this new nature is begotten of the incorruptible Word God, it must be nourished by its source of life—the divine Word. There is a direct continuity between the begetting seed and the growth of the new life and the new nature. The attempt to nourish this new life from any other source is impoverishment.

If this new nature is of the Holy Spirit, it must be perfected by walking in the Spirit: that is, to walk in a line with the nature of the Spirit of God (Gal. 5.25). Herein lies the necessity of being filled with the Spirit. The baptism and infilling of the Holy Spirit are called for by this experience of spiritual birth. The Spirit is the element of life in the new nature as the flesh was the element of life in the old nature. Walking in the Spirit is the natural expectation of being born of the Spirit.

If this new nature is of heavenly origin, it must set its affections on things above (Col. 3.1-3). The chief ambitions of the new life are to be realized in relation to the heavenly origin and destiny. The relationship to the heavenly kingdom is of prime importance to the new nature. To be born from above—born again; born of the Spirit—makes the believer already a participant of the goal of the new life. That goal is heaven; if one is not now participating in heaven, he/she is a foreigner to the kingdom of God.

Think about This.

The new birth required Nicodemus to repudiate and abandon his first birth and all the privileges and power that it bestowed on him. These endowments included status, security, pride and many other 'adult' trappings. These are not inherent in birth, but are added by others as if they were the rights of birth. They are not.

The new birth would place Nicodemus in the position of an infant born to poverty and powerlessness. This position is one of dependency and the absence of all the endowments of one's adult status. We generally call these birthrights, but they are not.

This teacher in Israel had to become the student of Jesus, a Galilean itinerant preacher/teacher from Nazareth—a despised town. The wealthy ruler had to become the powerless beggar. The proud had to be humbled. The man had to become a newborn.

He had to follow the steps of Jesus' advent

Who was rich, who became poor;
Who was the Teacher come from God who had to learn obedience through suffering;
Who was the righteousness of God,
Who had to be made sin;
Who was the prince of life who had to die;
Who was the Commander of twelve legions of angels,
Who had to yield to a petty Roman governor and an insignificant centurion.

Jesus' condescension to death is the paradigm and provision for our abdication of adulthood to become a newborn. It is our kenosis—the emptying of ourselves.

Being born again or becoming like a child is not some romantic notion of innocence of children or their beauty. It is the idea of total dependency and impoverishment. Being a newborn is humanity at its irreducible minimum. The wealthy child is not born wealthy exactly as the slum born child is not born of wealth. Both are impoverished and dependent. To be born again is to be reduced to dependency and impoverishment in the same way.

`The rich young ruler' could not accept this; so, he walked away from the kingdom of God, a wealthy pauper. He could not take his wealth through the womb of the new birth exactly as a camel cannot go through the eye of a needle.

Is being born again repeatable? No, not in the strict sense of the word. However, we must remain in this mentality and spirituality of infancy. We do not like the idea; so, we seek 'maturity' or 'mature status'. When we do that, we must ask the Lord, 'Bring me back to my infancy, for I have lost it. Let me be born again; let me be a child again'.

When one accepts this infancy, impoverishment and dependency, contentment is the spiritual result. This emptiness makes room for the flood of Light to bathe the soul within and without. It gives room for the love of God to be shed abroad in our hearts by the Holy Spirit who is given to us. It opens us up to the uninhibited joy and laughter of babyhood. This is joy unspeakable and full of glory.

5

THE SPIRIT OF ADOPTION AND FREEDOM

There are two families of humanity: the satanic and the godly. Each is known by its allegiances, character, conduct, and spirit. The members of each family bear the character of their father.

The Family of Satan

The Bible does not teach that all people are children of God. Some people are of their father, the devil (Jn 8.44). The children of Satan reflect and exhibit, in varying degrees, the nature of their father, which is the nature of sin. They are in bondage to the law as transgressors (Gal. 3.19). They are bound by and condemned by the whole law (Jas 2.9-11). They are bound by the law which is spiritual and good and they are carnal (Rom. 7.14).

Disobedience to the law is no proof of freedom from bondage to it; it is of no consequence. The disobedient are bound by the law in its condemnation of them. As long as a person is condemned by the law, he/she is bound by it. One may sear the conscience so that sin can be committed without apparent pain. The searing itself is evidence of bondage; for if the sinful course of conduct were right, there would be no need for the unnatural searing of the conscience.

This continual condemnation (though just and inevitable in view of divine law) leads to other evils in the nature of the children of sin. Condemnation produces fear and enmity. The fear is manifold—fear of death, of hell, of other people, of 'blind forces', of demons and spirits, even of life. This is not the reverential fear of God, which the Scriptures command; it is the fear that comes from terror and rebellion.

Enmity is the inevitable companion of condemnation and fear. The condemnation is just, but the human nature is such that condemnation (though just) breeds animosity. There is contempt for the One who condemns. Though there is in some social climates a certain respectability of speaking great things of God, this cannot hide the enmity against Him and contempt for Him. The primary evidence of this enmity is disobedience or sin.

Bondage to sin and its manner of life is characteristic of Satan's family. To be a child of satan is to be his slave; it is an inheritance of bondage. It is not one of free access to the father or of loving communion with him. Satan's ways are tyrannical and enslaving. They are hate filled even toward those who serve him.

In Romans 8 Paul gives special attention to one of the instruments of this enslavement—the carnal mind. This mind is the seat of the restlessness, bitterness, and death of the children of sin. This restlessness is perpetual and proceeds from the futility of human existence without communion, union, and peace with God. The human race was created by God, in God's image, and for union and communion with Him. Until these conditions are met, only restlessness can result.

This turmoil takes many forms. It is expressed in the gap between humanity's aspirations and humanity's capabilities. The inner person is thwarted by its own sinfulness and the body of flesh. The body exhibits in every breath and in every pulse of the heart the approaching death. At the same time, the soul cries out for eternity for which it was made. The body is shaped for and adapted to time and would like to be perpetuated in time. Still the soul cries out for true immortality. The carnal nature finds its pleasure in physical satisfaction. The soul is dominated by this kind of physical nature and becomes aware of and troubled by its own dictation. Here the soul has a dual conflict—the conflict with the body and its own inner clash of desires. The body is self-seeking and finds its satisfaction in its own pleasure and self-centeredness. The soul cries out for spiritual satisfaction. The soul is enslaved to the flesh.

The soul is also filled with inner conflict. There is the conflict of its own sinfulness and love of sinning with its sense of a call to a higher realization. The only way for the soul to be at rest is for men and women to be restored to their original nature and purpose. The soul that is dragged down from that purpose cannot be at peace. The soul was made for freedom and it is in bondage. 'But the wicked are like the troubled sea, when it cannot rest, whose waters cast up mire and dirt. There is no peace, saith my God, to the wicked' (Isa. 57.20, 21).

To this point we have discussed men and women in sin from the standpoint of their darkness, death, carnality and condemnation. The sum of all of these conditions is that humankind in sin is distorted. Humanity was made for light not darkness. When God created the human being he/she was alive in holiness and not dead in sins. He/she was holy in body and spirit, and not carnal. God created the human being for union and harmony with Himself. God did not create the human being to be condemned.

Sin is a foreign element in humanity. It is unnatural for human beings to be sinful. It is a false fatherhood for a person to be a 'child of wrath'. Immortal life in Christ is the goal for humanity, not mortality.

The promise of the gospel, then, is the promise of a return to natural order, which is holiness. Life in the Spirit is freedom and not bondage because this is the way of holiness.

The Family of God: the Grace of Adoption

The other family of humankind is the family of God. These are those who have been justified by faith, who have peace with God (Rom. 5. 1), who no longer fear the judgment of God but 'rejoice in hope of the glory of God' (Rom. 5.2), who learn patience and glory in tribulation (Rom. 5.3), and whose character is proved (Rom. 5.4). Their sins have been remitted and the righteousness of Christ has been given to them (Rom. 4.5-8).

The family relationship is emphasized in Scripture under the concept of adoption. Adoption is an appropriate term, because persons born in this world order are not by nature the children of God. Human beings are by nature children of disobedience and of wrath (Eph. 2.3).

The redemptive act of adoption is God's gracious act in which He receives as His children those who were born as children of another. He gives them His name and the privileges of His household. God draws those men and women who are so adopted into the same intimacy as if they were by nature His children.

This experience is properly a redemption experience because it changes the status of the believer. Further, it is a work which rests on the authority of Christ as Word of God and as the Redeemer; He gives believers the right to become children of God (Jn 1.12). It is redemptive because we come to this right through Him. It is redemptive because it is received by faith (Jn 1.12).

It is this experience that we wish to discuss, especially as it relates to the Person and work of the Holy Spirit.

The life of the child of God is marked by specific characteristics. The first of these is that it is a governed life. In this there are three principles of government: freedom from condemnation, the law of the Spirit of life in Christ Jesus, and the spiritual mind.

The first principle of government in Christ is our freedom from condemnation. This is the freedom of justification (Rom. 5.1). This is the freedom of peace that has been established by God in reconciliation and received by faith in justification.

The freedom of reconciliation is expressed by Paul in Rom. 5.10: 'For if while we were still enemies [of God] we were received into the favor of God through the death of His Son, much more now that we are in His favor we shall be saved in His life'. Reconciliation (the favor of God) sets us free from the fears and enmity of the old life.

The act of faith, which receives justification, lays to rest all condemnation and gives the sense of peace with God. The peace toward the sinner that has already been established in God's mind by the death of His Son is transferred to the heart and mind of the believer.

The sum of it is that 'there is therefore now no condemnation to the ones who are in Christ Jesus' (Rom. 8.1).[40] This freedom from condemnation is the status of life for those who are in Christ. There is no basis for enmity against God because the condemnation has been removed. There is no reason to live under a sense of condemnation because that does not represent one's true status. You may continue to berate yourself for past sins and their consequences. You may condemn yourself for the struggle which you have with temptation. None of these condemnations represents your true status before God. These condemnations do not issue from the

---

[40] The best textual evidence closes this statement as it is quoted above. The conditional clause 'who walk not after the flesh, but after the Spirit' is not properly a condition of the believer's freedom from condemnation.

throne of divine judgment. They issue from the accuser of our brethren.

The exhortation that resounds from this truth is, 'Live on the level of your true status—free from condemnation!' If you had been acquitted by a trial judge and the decree had gone out from the judge's bench, would you be intimidated because your accusers continued to quarrel with you? Certainly not! Then you must not continue to live in condemnation; God has set you free from condemnation.

The second principle of government as a child of God is that 'the law of the Spirit of life in Christ Jesus has set you free from the law of sin and death' (Rom. 8.2). Two terms must be established here: the law of the Spirit of life and the law of sin and death. 'Law' is used in each case as a principle of operation, not of a written code. Though the laws may become codified, their fundamental existence is in divine nature and is carried out in loving relationship.

The 'Spirit of life' is the Holy Spirit. He is the divine Person by whom Christ is raised from the dead and declared to be the Son of God (Rom. 1.4). He is the Spirit that raised, Christ from the dead and who will also raise us from the dead (Rom. 8.11). He is the Spirit who brings about the new birth (Jn 3.5, 6). 'Spirit of life' is, therefore, an appropriate title for the Spirit of God.

The 'law of sin and death' is the principle of sin, which Paul has designated by various terms in Romans 7. It is the 'sin dwelling in me' (v. 17). It is the 'law in my members' (v. 23). It is the 'body of this death' (v. 24). It is the 'law of sin' (v. 25).

The important declaration of Rom. 8.2 is that submission to and being indwelt by the law of the Spirit of life in Christ Jesus frees us from the law of sin and death.

We come under the law of the Spirit of life in Christ Jesus in order to fulfill the law of God by the Spirit of God. This is a higher manner of living than the old legalism. Legalism says, 'Thou shalt not hate'. Grace says, 'Thou shalt love'. Legalism says, 'Thou shalt not kill' and leaves the moral duty at that level. Grace says, 'Thou shalt give life'. Legalism says, 'Thou shalt not steal'. Grace says, 'Give to him that asketh thee, and from him that would borrow of thee turn not thou away' (Mt. 5.42). Legalism says, 'A tooth for a tooth'. Grace says, 'Avenge not yourselves' (Rom. 12.19). Legalism exacts its pound of flesh, but the law of the Spirit of life in Christ

Jesus exhorts, 'And be ye kind one to another, tenderhearted, forgiving one another, even as God for Christ's sake hath forgiven you' (Eph. 4.32).

In this manner of life and rulership, the nature of the believer is brought into conformity to the nature of the law of God. This is the secret of fulfillment. To be filled with the divine person who is the Author of the law (the Spirit of obedience) is the route of fulfillment without bondage. It is freedom from the law within law. We receive the freedom of Christ's yoke and enter rest under His burden (Mt. 11.29, 30).

The third principle of government for the child of God is the spiritual mind (Rom. 8.6). The carnal mind cannot be allowed to govern the child of God. First, 'to be carnally minded is death' (Rom. 8.6). Second, 'the carnal mind is hostile toward God' (Rom. 8.7). Paul's conclusion is that 'the ones who are in the flesh are not able to please God' (Rom. 8.8). The mind that feeds itself on this condemned world order, partakes of the condemnation and judgment that have already been passed on this world. Such a mind feeds on selfishness, lust, pride, haughtiness, strife, vainglory, manipulation for one's own advantage, hatred, covetousness, murder, drunkenness—all the works of the flesh. The mind that feeds on these things feeds on death. To set one's mind on worldly things and values is to be damned with the world.

'To be spiritually minded is life and peace' (Rom. 8.6). As the eye that beholds Christ transforms the beholder from glory to glory (2 Cor. 3.18), the mind that feeds on the nature of Christ (love, joy, peace, long-suffering, gentleness, goodness, faith, meekness, temperance) partakes of the life of Christ. Such a mind cannot but issue in life and peace. To feed on life everlasting is to partake of life everlasting. The thoughts of such a mind are characterized by Paul's exhortation in Phil. 4.8: 'Finally, brethren, whatsoever things are true, whatsoever things are honest, whatsoever things are just, whatsoever things are pure, whatsoever things are lovely, whatsoever things are of good report; if there be any virtue, and if there be any praise, think on these things'.

Spiritual living is a cultivated relationship. It is realized in a pattern of spiritual nurture. All of the provisions of grace that we have discussed to this point are gifts of God. The potential of joy and freedom which these benefits offer us can be realized only by cultivation and nurture.

This means that the old life must be rejected by a deliberate act. Victory over it is a claim of faith. It also means that the status and privileges of the new life must be claimed by faith.

This faith of which we speak is not faith in oneself, but faith in Christ as He is presented in the Word of God.

The Bases of the New Life

The life of the child of God is a new life. It has a new legal status: adoption. It has new bases (or origins) of life: the indwelling of the resurrected Lord and the indwelling of the Holy Spirit.

The first basis of the new life is the presence of the resurrected Lord Jesus Christ. By His resurrection, our Lord 'became a life-maker unto the Spirit' (1 Cor. 15.45). His presence requires the crucifixion of the flesh: 'If Christ is in you, the body is dead because of sin' (Rom. 8.10). By His presence we are not only alive, but also nourished by Him. We partake of His life—His body and blood.

These things are essential to Christ likeness. If we would be Christ like, He must be formed in us by faith (Gal. 4.19).

The converse of Christ's being in us is our being in Him. To be in Him is to sit with Him in heavenly places; where Christ sits as Redeemer we sit in redemption (Ephesians 1). Christ, our Lord, is seated at God's right hand (Heb. 1.3); God has so exalted Him and has lifted Him 'far above all principality, and power, and might, and dominion, and every name that is named, not only in this world, but also in that which is to come' (Eph. 1.21). If we are in Him, we also have been so exalted. All that He has conquered in the act of redeeming He has conquered for us in the experience of redemption.

The second basis of the new life is the presence of the Holy Spirit. This is in fact the route to the fulfillment of the law. This fulfillment depends on our being 'made free from the law of sin and death' (Rom. 8.2). Secondly, this fulfillment depends on our walking 'not after the flesh, but after the Spirit' (Rom. 8.4). The Holy Spirit's presence forbids our being in the flesh and joins us to Christ in life. This lifts the plane of living from the earthly to the heavenly, and from the fleshly to the spiritual. The Holy Spirit enlivens our hope, because He is the earnest (the foretaste and guarantee in kind) of the purchased possession.

The Obligations to the New Family

There are certain obligations, which result from this new status and new life. We are no longer debtors to the flesh that we should live in accord with its nature (Rom. 8.12). Fleshliness (carnality) has no further claim upon those who are the children of God.

The obligation of life that is now owed is the obligation to live in the Holy Spirit. This obligation arises from the fact that the child of God is indwelt of the Spirit that raised Christ from the dead (Rom. 8.11.). He is the Spirit of life in Christ Jesus.

Therefore, we must put to death the deeds of the flesh (Rom. 8.13). It is not possible for us in ourselves to 'mortify the deeds of the body.' To attempt to do this by self-will is to return to legalism. The various forms of self-imposed piety employed separately from the leading and empowerment of the Holy Spirit simply substitute one form of carnality for another.

There is another positive obligation: we must accept and live in the privileges of our new status as the children of God. It is grievous to any father when his children neglect to claim his provisions for their happiness and well being. It is no less so for our heavenly Father.

The Evidences of Adoption

The Evidences of Being Children of God

The next consideration in the life of the child of God is the evidence that we are children. How may we know that we are the children of God?

The first evidence of being a child of God is that we are led by the Spirit of God: 'Whoever is being led by the Spirit of God, these people are the children of God' (Rom. 8.14). This evidence of sonship rises above the tests that are so often used to affirm or deny sonship: emotional liberty and exuberance, success or failure, depression, discouragement, chastisement and a host of other human-made tests.

The sure persuasion that we are the children of God is the presence of the leading of the Holy Spirit. I do not refer here to an indescribable, mystical experience that has no goal other than an emotional release. Such experiences, standing isolated in an otherwise fruitless life, tend simply to confirm as right, our present condition. They tend to sanctify our shortcomings. They allow us to avoid soul search by convincing us that we are acceptable with God despite our carnality. They are a salve to a guilty conscience and they dodge the rebukes and corrections, which the Holy Spirit would give us out of the Word of God.

Instead of these substitutes for the witness of the Spirit, I refer to the guidance of the Holy Spirit to holiness of life. This is His guidance which is our confirmation that we are the children of God. The Spirit of adoption is by name and nature the Holy Spirit. It is His character to be pure and it is His work to lead the child of God to purity. There is no acceptable definition of purity except that which is prescribed in Scripture. The Holy Spirit leads within that standard and He cultivates holiness by Scripture exhortations and standards.

By the nature of our being the children of God, we are led by the Spirit of God in chastening. That which satan would use to deny that we are children is in fact assurance: 'If you undergo child training (chastisement, discipline), God is dealing with you as children' (Heb. 12.7). The aim of this discipline is that we may share in His holiness (Heb. 12.10). It yields the 'Peaceable fruit of righteousness' (Heb. 12.11).

If there is any point at which we are aware of the Spirit's leadership, we know that we are the children of God. By the authority of God's Word, we can make this claim against any accusation, in spite of all temptation, even in the throes of depression and in the midst of terrible reversals. Though all these other things assail us, and though it seems that we are the sole target of satan, if God's Spirit is leading us, God is saying to us that we are His children.

The second evidence of our being children is the witness of the Holy Spirit. This is a twofold witness: the cry 'Abba, Father' and the mutual witness of God's Spirit with our spirit.

The spirit that now works in the children of disobedience is the spirit of bondage and fear (Eph. 2.2, 3). But 'you have not received the spirit of bondage unto fear, but you have received the Spirit of adoption' (Rom. 8.15). The term adoption means the 'status of a child.' The Holy Spirit is the Spirit of adoption; that is, He is the Spirit who makes us children of God who are not by original nature children of God.

The intimacy of this status of adoption is shown by the cry, 'Abba, Father'. It is in the Holy Spirit that we pray. These two words (אבא in Aramaic, the native tongue of Jesus, and πατηρ in Greek) both mean 'Father'. It has been suggested that the word 'Abba' is used because of its intimacy—that of a child calling 'Daddy'. On the other hand the term 'Father' is a more majestic address. There is probably good reason for this claim. However, there is yet a more intimate significance; these are the words that Jesus himself used in His agony of Gethsemane (Mk 14.36). These are the prayer words of the only begotten Son of God; they were uttered in the depth of His trial in Gethsemane. This prayer is the most critical and profound prayer recorded in Scripture. We, though children by adoption, are invited into the heart of that prayer and into the same intimacy as that enjoyed by Jesus Christ, our Lord.

The mutual agreement between the Spirit of God (the Spirit of adoption) and the human spirit of the child of God is witness that we are children: 'The Spirit himself bears joint witness with our spirit that we are children of God' (Rom. 8.16). He is the Spirit of God; we are the children of God. So the Spirit of God leads the children of God and testifies by that leadership that they are God's children.

The Spirit's leading is unique and distinct from the spiritual guidance given by the spirit that works in the children of disobedience. God's Spirit leads to obedience, to repentance when there has been disobedience, to the cry 'Abba, Father' when there have been estrangement and chastisement, and to holiness of life. If there is any degree to which this leading can be detected, we know that we are the children of God.

The Heritage of the Family of God
The family identity always raises the question of the family's heritage. So we now consider the heritage of the child of God.

The first fact of a family's heritage is to bear the name of the family. Though the name of God as family heritage is not emphasized in Romans 8, it is inherent in the cry 'Abba, Father'. The real significance of that name for the believer is shown in 1 Jn 3.1, 2.

The bestowal of God's name upon a child is the bestowal of His love: 'Behold what wonderful love the Father has given us that we should be called children of God; and we are (children)' (v. 1a).[41]

The name of God does what any name does; it distinguishes one family from any other family. So John notes, 'On account of this (name and love of God), the world does not know us because it did not know Him' (v. 1). To bear the name of God is to be alienated from the world.

To bear the name of God is to anticipate the glory of Christ's return: 'Beloved, now we are the children of God, and it has not yet been made known what we shall be. We know that when He is made known (manifested) we shall be like Him (Christ), because we shall see Him just as He is' (v. 2). To bear the name of God now is to be identified with what we shall be when Christ appears in glory. As God has placed His name upon His only begotten Son and redemptively upon us, He will share with us the glory, which He has placed on His only begotten Son.

The second aspect of the heritage of the child of God is the family inheritance: 'And if, as it is true, we are children, we are also heirs' (Rom. 8.17). To be a child is also to be an heir. This heritage is made even more glorious by Paul's explanation: 'We are heirs of God, and joint heirs with Christ' (Rom. 8.17). Christ is the only begotten Son of God; He is the only heir by nature. He is the only Son who has pleased God the Father in all respects of His being and actions. He is, therefore, the beneficiary of all that belongs to the family of God. By the grace of adoption we become beneficiaries with Him.

The heritage is a twofold legacy; it includes both suffering and glory. In this we are also joint heirs with Christ. His glory came through His suffering and was dependent on that suffering in the pattern of crucifixion and resurrection. Yet the glory of His resurrection has such an effect on His death that even His death is His glory; it is His being lifted up (Jn 3.14; 12.32, 33). So the early church looked upon the privilege of suffering for Christ's sake as a

---

[41] This glorious exclamation 'And we are!' represents the realization in experience. The reality of the status comes home and we shout 'We are God's children!' This reading of the text is supported by most of the oldest and most reliable Greek manuscripts.

gift of God (Phil. 1.29). To suffer for Christ's sake is to inherit the legacy of Christ with Him.

Consider also Paul's example of suffering and the assurance that it gave him. He relates his sufferings in the following terms. Five times he was beaten with thirty-nine stripes by the Jews. Three times he was beaten with rods by the Romans. He had been stoned, shipwrecked three times, and had floated in the sea (the deep) for a night and a day. He summarized his other perils: of the water, of robbers, of his own countrymen, in the city, in the wilderness, in the sea and of false brothers. The burden which he carried drove him to hunger and thirst, to fasting and to exposure to the cold. He carried in his heart the burden of the churches (2 Cor. 11.23-28).

Paul can still say of all his afflictions that they are light and only of short duration compared with the eternal weight of glory which they accomplish (2 Cor. 4.16-18). In Rom. 8.18, he concludes, 'The sufferings of this present time are not worthy to be compared with the glory which is about to be revealed unto us'.

In this suffering God gives witnesses of the glory which is to be revealed. These witnesses are a foretaste and guarantee of the glory of Christ in which we shall share. There is an expectation in creation that anticipates the day in which the children of God will be manifested (Rom. 8.19). The present sin-cursed world order is an order of suffering and turmoil, but even this anticipates and testifies to glorious liberty of the children of God in which all creation will participate (vv. 20, 21). We ourselves, though having the firstfruits of the Holy Spirit, are suffering; but this suffering is testimony and proof of resurrection of the body (v. 23). This is the essence of salvation by hope (v. 24). What the world sees as evidence of denial of glory the child of God sees as evidence and affirmation of glory.

God gives us a foretaste of the glory that is to come in the ministry of the Holy Spirit. He is the firstfruits of the harvest (v. 23). In this ministry to our suffering, the Holy Spirit 'takes hold of our infirmities'. When we do not know how to pray about these infirmities, the Holy Spirit himself intercedes for us with unutterable groanings (v. 26).[42] We may know that these intercessions are in perfect accord with the will of God (v. 27).

---

[42] Note: The text does not say inaudible or non-verbal groanings, but 'unutterable groanings:' that is, groanings of the human soul and body, which are beyond the ability of cognitive speech to express (cf. 1 Cor. 14.14, 15).

In the continuation of our heritage, God our Father daily provides for us. We know that God works all things together for our good. The highest good that He has established for us is that we should be conformed to the image of His Son (vv. 28-30).

In order to show the implication of these truths, Paul asks, 'What, therefore, shall we say to these things [i.e., vv. 28-30]? If God is for us, who can be against us?' (v. 31). This assurance is further strengthened by Paul's next question. Let us expand this question: 'If God did not spare His own Son [the dearest treasure of His heart] why should He withhold from us any of the lesser treasures; how shall He not with Him give us all things?' (v. 32). If God has given us His Son, the streets of gold are paltry beside that gift, and the gates of pearl are only trinkets.

So it follows that God will give us freely all the benefits listed in vv. 33-39. He protects us with His decree of our justification (v. 33). This is assured us by the intercession of Christ, our elder brother and high priest. This protection prevails against all the assailants that are mentioned in vv. 35-39. The weakness of all the enemies is that they are temporal. The strength of our protection is that He is eternal; it is the love of God. The child of God has inherited an everlasting protection—the love of God (v. 39).

6

SANCTIFICATION: REDEMPTIVE PROVISION AND CLAIM OF FAITH

Distinctions in Salvation Experiences

It is important to establish the priority of the conversion experiences both from a logical standpoint and from the standpoint of temporal sequence.

The conversion experiences deal with the individual as she/he is found in sin—condemned by God's judgment and dead in trespasses and sins. The scripture appeals to him/her to repent, to accept the reconciliation of God, and to come alive from the dead. These are addressed to the person in the condition of sin. It is the ungodly whom God justifies (Rom. 4.5). Justification is the legal ground upon which God deals with the believer. Prior to this act of God, the only relationship possible between God and the sinner is one of condemnation.

Regeneration is promised to those (such as Nicodemus) who are not yet born again; they are still dead in trespasses and sins. They do the things of the flesh; 'that which is born of the flesh is flesh' (Jn 3.6). In this person there is no ground of obedience. Regeneration is the creative ground upon which God deals with the believer. Prior to this act of God, the only relationship possible between God and the sinner is to treat the sinner as one who is not of the kingdom of God and cannot see it (Jn 3.3-6).

Adoption is promised to the individual while there is still a need for a change of family status: that is, while he/she is still accounted as a child of wrath. This experience answers the problem of alienation from the household of God. Prior to this, the only relationship that the individual could have toward God was that of a subject to a monarch. This experience meets that problem and by the grace of inheritance in Christ makes believers heirs of God and joint heirs with Christ.

Though these experiences all differ in definition, in accomplishment, and in need addressed, there are certain common points to them.

1. They are all crisis experiences; they change the individual's relationship to God or they change the nature of the individual.
2. They are atonement based and produced experiences.
3. They are acts of God accomplished by His Word and Spirit.
4. They are all addressed to the needs of humankind while they are still in their sins.

This last point, together with other considerations, leads us to conclude that these experiences (justification, regeneration, and adoption) are concomitant experiences. They are logically and temporally prior to all other aspects of God's dealings with the individual. We refer to them as experiences in initial salvation.

The experience of sanctification has common ground with these experiences. It is a crisis experience. It is an atonement based and produced experience. It is an act of God and not a work of humankind. As separation, it is concomitant with these experiences; that is, the moment one belongs to Christ, he/she is separate from the world (Jn 17.6, 9, 10).

On the other hand, the experience of sanctification is distinct from these experiences by definition, by accomplishment, and by need addressed. It is addressed to the needs of those who are already in Christ. It is, therefore, logically and temporally subsequent to justification, regeneration, and adoption.

To argue for sanctification fully accomplished in the initial experience of believing (the 'finished work' theory) is to ignore the circumstances of Christ's prayer for His disciples in John 17, Christ's witness of their having followed Him in 'the regeneration' (Mt. 19.28), and the exhortations to holiness in life and experience indicate that these people are already in Him.

Christ prayed for the sanctification of His disciples (Jn 17.17), even though they were already separate from the world (Jn 17.16). He based their sanctification on His own sanctification (Jn 17.19). Christ's sanctification was His suffering without the gate (Heb. 13.12); the suffering outside the city gate clearly places the provision of sanctification in the atonement. Therefore, the believer is exhorted to 'go forth…unto him without the camp, bearing his reproach' (Heb. 13.13) in order to appropriate personal sanctification by faith.

The provisions and exhortations of Romans 6 are especially pertinent to this discussion. This chapter must be seen in context. Romans 5 has laid the groundwork in justification and the relationship which the entire human race has with Adam and Christ. Romans 6 deals with the believer and his/her responsibility to live a holy life. Romans 6 consists of the atonement provision for holiness and the exhortation to holy living.

Atonement Provision for Sanctification

In Rom. 6.2, Paul asks the question which he anticipates answering: 'How shall we that are dead to sin, live any longer therein?' He then draws the analogy of the spiritual experience of baptism into Christ and crucifixion with Christ. He concludes this analogy with the statement: 'Knowing that our old man was crucified (aorist or a past tense verb) with Him that the body of sin might be destroyed, that henceforth we should not serve sin' (Rom. 6.6). In the crucifixion, atonement provision is made. The purpose of this provision is that the 'body of sin' ('the old man', the sin that dwelleth in me, the law in my members, the body of this death) might be destroyed and that we should not serve sin.

From this point Paul is concerned with showing the believer how to make personal and experiential this atonement provision for the crucifixion of 'the old man'.

In Rom. 6.1 Paul deals with the question of presumption upon the doctrine of grace that has been set forth in chapter 5. The presumptuous world asks, 'Shall we remain in sin in order that grace may increase?' Paul's answer is twofold. The first is the resounding 'Let it not be so!' (v. 2). The second answer is another question: 'We that have died in relation to sin: how shall we still live in it?' (or in relation to sin) (v. 2). It is totally out of character for those who have been forgiven their sins to continue in the practice of sin.

Romans 6 is designed to show the believer how to claim and live in the new estate in Christ. Justification by faith anticipates holiness of life to follow that experience. Holiness is the only appropriate lifestyle for those who are in Christ. This problem is addressed from two points of view. The first is the redemptive provision in Christ's atonement. The second is the faith claim of the believer.

To be baptized into Christ Jesus is to be baptized into His death (v. 3). This is the position of the believer in Christ (cf. 1 Cor. 12.13). Since the believer's death to sin is in Christ's death, the believer is also buried with and in Christ. The death of Christ is overcome by His resurrection through the glory of the Father. The believer's death and burial in Christ have the same result: 'We have been buried with Him through baptism into death, in order that exactly as He was raised up out of death through the glory of the Father, thus we also should walk in newness of life. For if we have been buried together (with Him) in the likeness of His death, we shall also be raised up' (vv. 4, 5). Christ's resurrected life became the pattern of the believer's new life.

To this point, Paul is talking about the death of the believer to sin. This is a provision of Christ's redemptive work. The next step in Paul's reasoning is the death of sin in relation to believer. Christ's crucifixion provides the crucifixion of the believer in relation to sin. It also provides the crucifixion of sin in relation to the believer.

This is the thrust of v. 6: 'Knowing this, that our old man has been crucified in order that the body of sin might be destroyed for the purpose that we should not serve sin as our master any longer'. This verse contains three key segments. The first is the redemptive provision ('our old man has been crucified'). The second is the result, the redemptive experience ('in order that the body of sin might be destroyed'). The third is the purpose: 'that we should not serve sin as our master any longer'.

This verse contains two key terms: 'the old man' and 'the body of sin'. The expression 'old man' appears only here, in Eph. 4.22, and in Col. 3.9. In Eph. 4.22, 'the old man' relates to the former pattern of life; it is described as corrupted according to deceitful lusts; it stands in contrast to 'the new man' (Eph. 4.24). In Col. 3.9, 'the old man' also stands in contrast to 'the new man' (Col. 3.10); Paul declares that the believers have discarded 'the old man' with his practices (Col. 3.5-8).

The closest parallel to the expression 'body of sin' appears in Col. 2.11 where Paul represents the believers as having received spiritual circumcision in Christ by which they had put off 'the body of carnality'.

We judge that these phrases all define the same thing: the carnal nature. There are amplifying expressions in Romans 7 and 8 that aid our understanding. These terms are the 'motions (affections) of sin' (7.5), the 'sin which dwells in me' (7.17, 20), the 'law in my members' (7.23), the 'law of sin' (7.23, 25), the 'body of this death' (7.24), the 'law of sin and death' (8.2) and the 'deeds of the body' (8.13). These are all terms used to define the term 'our old man' and 'body of sin'. Christ has crucified our 'old man', in order that we should no longer serve him. The 'old man' is a figure of speech, which designates the principle of sin in fallen human nature: the Adamic nature. It is the physical body and its emotions as they are governed by sin.[43]

The Appropriation of this Experience

From this point on (Rom. 6.6), the Apostle Paul is concerned with showing how this redemptive provision can be personally experienced. The heart of what follows is that this crucifixion becomes personal experience by faith in Christ. It is a specially directed faith, which lays hold on a specific provision and promise: namely, the provision and promise of sanctification.

From v. 6 the apostle discusses the redemptive consequence of Christ's crucifixion of our 'old man'. The first consequence is that we have been made free from sin: 'For the one who has died has been set free (and remains free) from sin' (v. 7). The second consequence is that we are to live by Christ's life: 'If we have died with Christ, we believe that we shall also live with Him' (v. 8). Verses 9 and 10 elaborate this consequence. The fact that Christ has been raised from the dead means that He is no longer under the power of the sin for which He suffered death. That is the consequence in His life (v. 9). By this redemptive provision, it is our experience in

---

[43] Many quibbles are raised on this question about the death of the 'old man'. Some ask, 'If he dies, can he be resurrected?' This kind of question attempts to make literal a figure of speech. Nowhere in Scripture is the human body represented as being inherently sinful; it is not the 'lower nature' implying that the spirit is the 'higher nature'. The body is not that part of our constitution that keeps us from being holy. Indeed, we are called on to be holy in body, soul and spirit (1 Thess. 5.23).

redemption that our life in Christ frees us from the sin to which we have died in Him: 'For the one who has died has died in relation to sin once and for all; and the one who lives, lives in relation to God' (v. 10).

The claim of this relationship is a specific claim of faith. As a consequence of the truth of vv. 6-10, 'we account ourselves to be dead in relation to sin and living in relation to God in Christ Jesus' (v. 11). The word which we have translated by the words 'we account ourselves' means 'to look upon ourselves as ...', 'to claim ourselves to be ...', 'to consider ourselves to be ...' and so forth. This is a faith claim. It is not possible for any person to put himself/herself to death in relation to sin or to make oneself alive unto God. This is a benefit of divine grace, which is received by faith. The specific claim of faith is to deny any subordination to sin and to claim a life (and living) unto God.

In vv. 12-14, Paul elaborates on this claim of faith. The first application is that we are not to allow sin to rule: 'Therefore (i.e., as a consequence of the faith claim of v. 11), do not let sin rule in your mortal body unto the obedience of its lusts' (v. 12). The verb 'do not let sin rule' has a continuative force. This is not a faith claim that can be made once and left in the past. It is a continuing (a perpetual) denial of the rulership of sin. The rulership of sin manifests itself and is evidenced in the fact that one obeys its lusts in the mortal body. Sin in the mortal body may be only inward (i.e., not acted out in physical action); lust, covetousness, and hatred are all sins of obedience to the lusts of the mortal body even if they are never fulfilled outwardly. Our faith is to deny sin this rulership.

The second application of this claim of faith is v. 13: 'Neither are you to be yielding the members of your body to become instruments of unrighteousness in relation to sin, but you are to yield yourselves to God as alive from the dead and the members of your body as instruments of righteousness in relation to God'. The two verbs here change tenses. The first ('you are not to be yielding') has the same continuative force that is seen in v. 12. The second ('you are to yield yourselves') does not imply this need for repetition of the claim. The temptation to sin is a continual assault; consequently, it is necessary to deny the rulership of sin repetitively. The claim of life and living unto God is a settled claim. The threats to life must be continually denied, but life is itself an established reality: 'and do not go on, as you have been doing, putting your members at the service of sin, but put them once for all at the service of God'.[44]

The third application of this faith claim is the believer's status in relation to law and grace: 'For sin shall not be ruler over you, for you are not under law but under grace' (v. 14). To be under the law is to be under sin in the position of the transgressor (Rom. 7.5, 6; Gal. 3.19). By the act of faith the believer is to deny the sin this rulership. He does this by recognizing that he is a partaker of grace.

The New Way of Life Resulting From This Experience

This act of faith opens to the believer an entirely new way of life. Paul warns against presumption; being free from the law does not give freedom to sin: 'What is it therefore? Shall we sin because we are not under law but under grace? God forbid!' (v. 15). This question brings a severe warning; you are a slave to whomever you give yourself in obedience (v. 16). If you continue to sin, you are the slave of sin. The proof of it is that you obey sin. If you live a righteous life, you are the servant of righteousness. The proof of it is that you obey righteousness. Bondage to sin is no longer the believer's condition: 'But thanks to God you were the servants of sin' (v. 17), but you are not now servants of sin. The true position of the believer is that he has already obeyed God: 'But you obeyed from the heart the form of teaching into which you were delivered' (v. 17). The new teaching (doctrine) takes the place of the old bondage to sin and law.[45]

This is the position in grace. Paul applies this in v. 18: 'But since you have been made free from sin, you have been made servants to righteousness'. This holiness of life, however, does not come automatically. It comes by the claims of faith in which the believer gives himself/herself to purity of life. There is a hint of rebuke in v. 19: 'I speak in human terms because of the weakness of your flesh'. The weaknesses of the people pressed Paul to speak to them with the exhortation that follows: 'For just as you yielded your members as

---

[44] James Denney, "St. Paul's Epistle to the Romans", in W. Robertson Nicoll (ed.), *The Expositor's Greek New Testament* (Grand Rapids: Eerdmans, 1961 printing), II, p. 634.

[45] Law as such is not a slaveholder. It is the element of sin in the individual that gives to the law its enslaving nature. The obedient (though they obey the law) are not in bondage to it. The disobedient are the ones who are in bondage.

servants to impurity and to lawlessness unto lawlessness, now in the same manner yield your members as servants to righteousness unto sanctification' (v. 19).

Faith makes a specific claim and that claim is twofold. The first is that it denies the way of sin; sin can no longer have its way. You have no obligation to sin because it is no longer your master. The second is that it lays a claim on freedom and holiness of life. Paul illustrates this in the analogy of the lordships: 'When you were the servants of sin, you were free from righteousness' (v. 20). You accounted sin to be your lord; so, you (in that reasoning) had no sense of responsibility to obey righteousness as if that were your lord. It was a fruitless life as the present consciousness of the believer knows: 'What fruit did you have then in the things of which you are now ashamed? For the end of those things is death' (v. 21).

The new lordship takes the place of the old and creates a new way of life. It is freedom from sin and enslavement to God: 'But now, since you have been freed from sin and since you have been made servants to God you have your fruit unto sanctification to the end of everlasting life' (v. 22). Paul's concluding statement reemphasizes this truth: 'For the compensation of sin is death' (v. 23). The choice of the word 'compensation' shows that death is an earning—a just desert of the way of sin. On the other hand 'the gift of the grace of God is everlasting life in Christ Jesus our Lord' (v. 23).

Sanctification as it is discussed in Romans 6 consists of the redemptive provision in Christ's atonement for sin and in the redemptive experience, which is claimed by faith. This experience consists of the following acts of grace: the crucifixion of 'the old man', the destruction of the body of sin, deliverance from the body of this death, the cleansing of the heart, and being set free from the law of sin and death.

The person of the Holy Spirit is the personal Agent by whom this grace is given. He does this by an application of the atonement provision of Christ's death and resurrection.

Baptism with the Holy Spirit is the infilling of the Person and power of the Spirit of holiness. This is not specifically an atoning experience, though it is a provision and application of the atonement.

The appropriate and biblical order of experience is that sanctification is the appropriate preparatory experience for the baptism with the Holy Spirit. It is the cleansing of the vessel for the infilling of the Holy Spirit. It is the destruction of the body of sin for the cultivation of the fruit of the Spirit by the personal dwelling of the Spirit within us.

7

SANCTIFICATION: THE PROVISION OF CHRIST'S INTERCESSION

Sanctification in the Order of Salvation

Sanctification properly occupies a place in the order of salvation. It meets all the criteria for that position. It is God's act. It is provided in Christ's work of atonement. It is a critical experience that changes the nature of the individual. It is appropriated by faith, and its agents of application are the Word and Spirit of God.

There are those who relegate sanctification to the level of separation and consecration. They, therefore, take this experience out of the order of salvation. Separation from the world takes place at the same time and as a result of being joined to Christ. Consecration is an act of the human will in submission to God. Though both of these experiences are biblical and necessary, they are not to be understood as events in the order of salvation. Neither should they be confused with the full meaning of sanctification.

Sanctification by design deals with the corruption of the sinful nature. It is a purging act of God provided to cleanse the nature of the believer and to set him free from the law of sin and death (Rom. 8.2). Some will object that there is no need for such cleansing if an individual has been born of the Spirit. This conclusion ignores significant statements of Scripture. Paul declares of some of the Corinthians (apparently so many that this was a characteristic of most of this congregation) that they were not spiritual, but that they were carnal. At the same time, he regards them as infants in Christ (1 Cor. 3.1).

Paul describes his own experience of struggle with two contrary inward drives. He declares, 'I delight in the law of God according to the inward man; but I see another law in the members of my body warring against the law of my mind' (Rom. 7.22, 23). He also declares a dual bondage: 'Therefore I myself in the mind serve the law of God; on the other hand, in the flesh (I serve) the law of sin' (Rom. 7.25).

This order of emphasis in Scripture takes into consideration the dual nature of sin. Sin exists in both the specific transgression of God's law (either by omission or commission), and in the corruption which sin brings. The first problem is addressed by the believer's change of judicial position by the forgiveness of sin. The second is met in the believer's purifying of nature in sanctification.

There are several passages of Scripture to which we may appeal in this study. We limit ourselves to two: John 17 and Romans 6.

Christ's High Priestly Role

We begin the study of John 17 with a presupposition. It is that Christ is acting as our high priest in this intercession; so His petitions are based on atonement provisions and applications. This is essential if we are to understand certain petitions in the prayer.

This prayer should also be seen in its context in John's Gospel account. There are two focuses of this context. The first is the relationship to the promise of the coming of the Holy Spirit (John 14-16). The second is Christ's imminent departure (Jn 14-16; 17.11, 12). This prayer and its answer are preparatory to each of these events. The opening of Christ's prayer (Jn 17.1-5) shows the atonement and high priestly relationship of the prayer. In His initial address to the Father, Jesus declared that His hour had come (v. 1). He explained that His hour was the hour of His being offered up in sacrifice; it is the hour of His glorification of the Father and His being glorified by the Father (v. 1). This is the terminology of Jesus in John for His crucifixion (Jn 3.14, 15; 8.28; 12.30-34). The petitions that follow are premised on these words about Christ's death.

It is in this light that the Father had given the Son power over all flesh and had given Him the disciples (v. 2). The Son had given them eternal life (vv. 2, 3).

Christ had glorified the Father upon earth. Now He has come to the point of His own glorification, which will culminate in His return to the glory that He had with the Father before the world came to be (v. 5). This is the high point of Jesus' exaltation in the priestly role.

Those For Whom Christ Prayed

There is in this opening address and in the petitions which follow an identification of the ones for whom Christ offers this prayer. These are three identifying marks of those for whom Christ prayed. First, He prayed for those whom the Father had given Him. Second, He prayed for those to whom He had already given eternal life. Third, He prayed for the ones who had known the Father and His Son Jesus Christ (vv. 2-4).

This identification is strengthened by other statements as the prayer proceeds. Jesus had manifested the Father's name to these men; they were by that fact God's (v. 6). They had kept God's Word (v. 6), even the words that the Son had given them from the Father (vv. 7, 8). They had believed on the Son whom the Father had sent (v. 8).

Jesus specifically delineated those for whom He prayed from the world: 'I am praying for them; I am not praying for the world, but for those whom You have given Me because they are Yours' (v. 9). Christ extends the boundaries of this identification in v. 20: 'I am not praying for these alone, but also for the ones who believe on Me through their word'. We may conclude, then, that this prayer was offered for all believers of all ages of gospel proclamation.

Christ prayed for those who were in the world, but were not of the world. He specifically said of them 'they are in the world' (v. 11). Their distinction from the world rests on the following facts: they are to be kept by the name of the Father (v. 11); they had been kept by Christ's carefulness over them and presence among them; and He had kept them by the Father's name (v. 12). Christ had bestowed the Father's Word upon them (v. 14). They were in the world as Christ was, but they were not of the world, exactly as He was not of the world (vv. 11-16). The name of God is not only an identification of these believers. It is also the seal of His ownership and the agent by which His grace is conveyed to the believer. The Word of God is also a means of grace.

Christ's imminent departure may imply to the disciples that they also would escape the world. Christ clarified this in v. 15: 'I am not praying that You take them up from the world, but that You should keep them from the evil one'.

Of this evidence we may offer the following applications. The prayer of Christ was offered for those who were in a saved relationship to Him and His Father. The prayer was not designed to give them escape out of the world, but to keep them as Christ had kept them. They were to remain in the world, kept by the intercession of Christ. Therefore, if this prayer is to be fulfilled, it must be answered in a temporal relationship. 'The disciples are left in the world, in the position that He himself occupied. They, now with the Holy Spirit, must bear witness to the world, and endure its hostility.'[46]

The Petitions of This Prayer

Our Lord makes a series of petitions in the course of this prayer. These are to be considered in continuity with each other so that they culminate in a single idea and experience. We consider this culmination to be expressed in vv. 17-19.

The first petition in the series is, 'Holy Father, guard them as a treasure by means of Your name the ones whom You have given Me in order that they may be one just as We are one' (v. 11). This unity is explained more fully in vv. 21 and 22 where Christ has expanded His prayer to extend beyond the apostolic body. He prayed that all may be one (v. 21). The example and pattern of unity are shown in the unity of the divine Father and the divine Son. It is the unity of the Father's being in the Son and the Son's being in the Father; the believers are then to be in the Father and the Son: 'That all may be one, as You, Father, are in Me and I am in You, in order that even they may be in us' (v. 21). This unity of Redeemer with the redeemed is represented in Heb. 2.11 in these words: 'For the One who is sanctifying and the ones who are being sanctified are all of one'. This is a redemptively established unity which produces in the redeemed a unity of nature and a submission of the will and mind to the will of God. It is the grace of becoming possessed of the mind that was in Christ (Phil. 2.2-5).

The second petition is for the fulfillment of Christ's joy in the disciples: 'And now I am coming to You, and these things I am saying in the world in order that My joy may be fulfilled in them' (v. 13). This and the following verses tell us the circumstances of that joy. First, it originates in Christ; it is His joy. It is the joy, which He has in being in the Father and in doing the Father's will in the world. Second, the agent of this joy is Christ's Word and the Fa-

---

[46] Barrett, *The Gospel According to St. John*, p. 423.

ther's Word: 'These things I am saying … in order that My joy may be fulfilled in themselves. I have given them Your word' (vv. 13, 14). Third, this identification with Christ's joy and with the divine Word separates and alienates the believer from the world: 'I have given them Your word, and the world hated them because they are not of the world just as I am not of the world' (v. 14). Finally, these words are witness to the fact that these disciples do not have their origin in and of the world; they have been born of the Spirit. Jesus repeats this emphasis in v. 16.

The third and culminating petition is, 'Sanctify them in (with) the truth; thy word is truth' (v. 17). The grammar and vocabulary of this petition are important. First, the prayer 'sanctify them' is specific in terms of the result and the fulfillment. The result expected is the purifying of the believers. Purification is more prominent in this petition than separation, because Christ has already established that these people are separated from the world (v. 16). Purging (cleansing) is the prominent anticipation. The nature of the fulfillment (or answer) of this prayer is represented by the kind of verb used in the prayer. This verb anticipates action at a specific point as distinct from process, progression, or graduation.

The Agents for the Fulfillment of this Prayer

The instrument for the realization of this prayer is the Word of God. Christ by this petition excludes human contribution as the basis of this experience. It is the Word of God ('thy word is truth', v. 17) which is God's person and power to sanctify His people. It is, as is the name of God, a means of the application of the grace of God. Throughout the Scriptures the Word is assigned various functions which are related to purification. The Word is the instrument of enlightenment because of its own purity (Ps. 19.8); it is incisive (Heb. 4.12); it is the pruning agent in the vine (Jn 15.3), and it is the sanctifying agent appealed to in Pauline theology (Eph. 5.26). This function is an application of the Word as the power of God—unto salvation (Rom. 1.16, 17).

This prayer is directly related to the mission of the disciples in the world. Christ had specifically prayed that these should not by this experience be taken out of the world (v. 15). Now He relates their mission in the world to His. The Father had sent Him into the world and now Jesus has sent them into the world (v. 18). As Jesus' separation and purity were essential to His mission, the sanctification of the disciples is essential to their mission assigned to them by Jesus.

The ground upon which sanctification is provided is redemptive: 'And on behalf of them, I am sanctifying Myself in order that they may be sanctified by truth' (v. 19). Christ's own sanctification must be more than simply His dedication and submission to the crucifixion. The meaning of 'sanctify' here must be the same as the meaning in v. 17. So if we understand the term in v. 17 to refer to a redemptive experience, the term here must refer to a redemption-providing experience: a work of atonement. So, we take the word sanctify here to mean 'purging' as in the earlier verse.

Some will question how this can be so if Christ is sinless. Scripture provides an analogy in Heb. 13.11, 12. The bodies of the sacrificial animals were burned without the camp because the sin, which had been placed upon them for atonement must be purged (v. 11). For the same reason Christ suffered outside the gate: 'Wherefore also, Jesus in order that He might sanctify the people with His own blood suffered outside the gate' (v. 12). Christ was made to be sin by imputation, but this act placed on Him and to His account (His answerability) both the acts of sin and the corruption of sin: 'The One who had not known sin, He (God) made sin for us' (2 Cor. 5.21).

These things are essential to the provision of sanctification as an atonement benefit; He died, so we die in Him. In His death, He crucified our old nature: 'Knowing this, that our old man was crucified in order that the body of sin might be destroyed' (Rom. 6.6). It is this redemptive act that is the basis of Christ's intercession. He also demonstrates that He or God can destroy sin and sanctify believers.

This atonement concept is further enforced by the fact that sanc-tification is by the truth. This is not a progression in sanctification as one progresses in the knowledge of truth. The Word is the agent of sanctification as it is the agent of regeneration and justification.

This prayer and its provisions are universally applicable. For this reason, Jesus said, 'I am not praying for these alone, but also for the ones who believe in Me through their word' (Jn 17.20). This petition shows that the prayer of v. 17 is more than dedication to the Cross. It is a redemptive provision for all the ages of human need.

Our Lord repeats for these future believers the provisions that He had named for the apostles. He prayed that all believers should be one, in the same way that the Father and the Son are one: 'In order that they may be one, just as You, Father, are in Me and I am in You, and in order that they may be in Us' (v. 21). This is not the unity of a single visible body. It is the harmony that is appropriate to indwelling. It is also the unity which is created by the common glory which is upon Christ and His disciples: 'And I, the glory which You have given Me (and still rests upon Me) I have given them (and it still rests upon them) in order that they may be one even as we are' (v. 22). This glory cannot be dissociated from Christ's cross. So the Cross is for Christ both His sanctification and His glory. The Cross has the same necessity for the disciples. Christ bestowed upon the disciples that glory which the Father gave Him.

This is the concept of perfection in spiritual life. In a spiritual and real sense, the presence of Christ provides a twofold pattern. First, as He indwells the Father the believers are to indwell Christ. Second, as Christ indwells the believers, they are to indwell each other. This is the biblical pattern of unity, which is the experience and practice of holiness.

Earlier (v. 13) Christ had included in His petitions a prayer for His joy to be in the disciples. This is the joy of His indwelling the Father, the Father's indwelling Him and His fulfillment of the Father's will. This is the pattern of the believer's joy.

In sum, these things are the epitome of sanctification. It consists of purging (vv. 17-19), of unity (vv. 11, 21-23), the joy of Christ fulfilled in the believer (vv. 13, 22, 23), and the glory of Christ resting upon them (v. 22).

It is clear that Jesus intended that the petitions of this prayer be fulfilled among the disciples in this life. His concluding words define these terms. There is evangelistic purpose in the sanctification of the disciples of Christ; such a purpose can be served only if the experience occurs while the believers are still in the world. Those purposes are set forth in terms of witness.

The first witness that this spiritual excellence is to provide is that 'the world may believe that You sent Me' (v. 21). The holiness of the believer is witness to the commission of the Father upon the Son.

The second witness intensifies the first by adding the witness of love. This witness of love is associated with the oneness of the disciples—the perfection of the disciples in one: 'In order that they might be perfected in one' (v. 23). This indwelling of God in the believers and the believer in God through Christ will make the world 'know that You sent Me and that You loved them just as You loved Me' (v. 23). Believers living in the unity of God are testimony of God's shared love in the world. There can be no greater evangelistic impact.

There are eschatological goals for this experience in Christ. Christ prayed the Father that those whom the Father had given Him might be where He (i.e., Christ) is, and is to be: 'Father, that which You have given Me, I wish that they may be where I am and that they may be with Me' (v. 24; cf. Jn 14.1-4; Heb. 12.14). Holiness of life is the appropriate stance of those who will be where Christ is. John enforces this in his exhortation to holiness based on the hope of the return of Christ (1 Jn 3.2, 3).

The second eschatological goal is that the believer may behold Christ's glory. This is the second part of the petition begun in v. 24: 'In order that they may behold My glory which You have given Me because You loved Me before the foundation of the world' (v. 24). The relationship of this glory to the eternal love of God for the Son shows that the glory here is His eternal glory (cf. v. 5). To behold that glory is the eternal destiny of those who are here called to holiness.

The seal of all of this prayer is the name of God. Christ had declared that name to the disciples (v. 26). This is fundamental to the experience of holiness. The name of God is the person, power, and presence of God. It is the conveyance of His life and love. It is the means of the reception of His grace. It is His love in a word—His name. Christ will declare His Father's name to the disciples in order that the love in which His Father loved Him may be in them and He himself in them: 'And I have made known to them Your name, and I will make it known, in order that the love with which You loved Me may be in them and I in them' (v. 26).

8

BAPTISM WITH THE HOLY SPIRIT: A DEFINITION

Terminology: Baptism with the Holy Spirit

Two questions confront us. The first is the question of the terminology. In Bible study and theological literature the term 'baptism in the Holy Spirit' is probably the most frequently used term to describe Spirit baptism. In the introductory chapter this issue was addressed. There we chose for this study the term 'baptism with the Holy Spirit'. We will offer further reasons for this decision shortly. We have attempted to use this expression or its equivalent consistently throughout this study, without being slavishly bound to it.

The second question relates to the order of salvation. Is the baptism with the Holy Spirit to be placed among the experiences of redemption?

In relation to the first question, the Greek verb βαπτίζω (or variants of the form) is used of the gift of the Holy Spirit in six places in the New Testament (Mt. 3.11; Mk 1.8; Lk. 3.16; Jn 1.33; Acts 1.5; 11.16). All of these refer to John the Baptist's promise that the Messiah would baptize with the Holy Spirit. In each case, the Messiah's baptizing with the Holy Spirit is contrasted with John's baptism with water. In each case, except Mk 1.8, the Greek prepositional phrase 'in the Holy Spirit' is used to describe the experience. In Mk 1.8, the Greek dative ('with' or 'in') is used designating the baptism of the Holy Spirit. The two forms of expression are equivalents in Greek. Either may be translated 'with'[47] or 'in'. The term

---

[47] F. Blass and A. DeBrunner, *A Greek Grammar of the New Testament* (trans. and rev. Robert W. Funk; Chicago: University of Chicago Press, 1961), §195. These authorities list several passages including Lk. 3.16 and Acts 1.5 as using the Greek preposition 'ἐν' in the instrumental sense.

'baptism with the Holy Spirit' is adequate and appropriate to describe the experience of Spirit baptism as it is represented in the book of Acts, and as it has been experienced in subsequent ages.

In each of these cases the administrator of baptism is Christ. The element of baptism is the person of the Holy Spirit.

A number of scholars consistently translate the passages as 'to baptize in the Holy Spirit'. They feel that the intention is to emphasize one's immersion in the Holy Spirit as one is immersed in water in water baptism.[48]

There is certainly no objection to the emphasis on the totality of experience expressed here. However, it does not seem to be grammatically necessary or primary. The practice consistently followed by the King James Version, the Revised Standard Version, the New English Bible,[49] and the New International Version ('to baptize with the Holy Spirit') seems to be preferable. Immersion is not the primary emphasis here; this would also seem to be confirmed by the consistent description of the Holy Spirit as being poured out on believers (Acts 2.17, 18; 10.45), as coming upon the believer (Acts 1.5; 19.5, 6), and as falling upon believers (Acts 10.44; 11.15). The primary emphasis in all of these instances is that the Holy Spirit is the element of baptism.

A more critical issue is whether the expression 'baptism with (or in) the Holy Spirit' is a term to be restricted to Acts 2.[50]

---

[48] Stanley M. Horton, *What the Bible Says About the Holy Spirit* (Springfield, Missouri: Gospel Publishing House, 1976), p. 84. 'But John adds a new thought not mentioned in the Old Testament. The Spirit is not only to be poured out upon them; they are to be immersed in Him, saturated with Him.'

[49] NEB translates Jn 1.33 'to baptize in the Holy Spirit'.

[50] This has become a favorite argument among non-Pentecostals and particularly among dispensationalists. This argument is used to show the discontinuance of tongues as a manifestation of the experience of being filled with the Spirit. These scholars argue that tongues accompanied the initial gift of the Holy Spirit because this was the baptism with the Holy Spirit. This baptism (and so also tongues) came upon the Gentiles when the gospel formally spread to them. The baptism with the Holy Spirit came once to the Jewish believers (Acts 2) and once to the Gentiles (Acts 11) According to this argument it is not proper to speak of the baptism with the Holy Spirit as continuing in personal experience. It is proper to speak of being filled with the Spirit in personal experience.

We cannot agree with this line of reasoning because it cannot be defended in Scripture. It seems also that it is a distinction, which was tailor-made to attempt to prove that tongues do not continue in church and personal experience. We shall give our arguments in the body of the above text.

In order to answer this question, it is necessary to determine the significance of the baptism with the Spirit. John the Baptist contrasted this baptism with the baptism that he administered. He used the contrast to show that he was a human Agent of baptism and that the Messiah would be a divine Agent of baptism. The contrast also shows that John's baptism was with a temporal element (water) and that the Messiah's baptism would be with an eternal element (the Holy Spirit). Water, the element of John's baptism, was an impersonal and impotent element. The Spirit, the element of Christ's baptism, is a personal and an omnipotent divine agent as well as element. Water is effectual in a sacramental sense. The Holy Spirit is effectual by personal divine nature and authority. The Holy Spirit is personally active in the fulfillment of divine grace in those upon whom He comes, and into whom He enters. Water is not a personal agent of salvation but the Holy Spirit is.

These baptisms contrast the two ages to which each applies: The age of promise and the age of fulfillment—the age of preparation and the age of consummation (eschatological age). The proclamation of John, 'Behold the Lamb of God who takes away the sin of the world' (Jn 1.29), is the pinnacle of the Old Testament revelation and prophecy; likewise John's baptism is the pinnacle of Old Testament ceremonies. Each of these stands in the nature of promise and preparation.

The appearance of the Lamb of God is the fulfillment of all of the prophetic messages of the Old Testament in general and of the proclamation of John in particular. In these two events (John's proclamation and Jesus' appearance) the program of God moves from promise to fulfillment—from preparation to eschatology.

John is the baptizer of preparation; Jesus is the baptizer of consummation. Water is the baptizing element of promise; the Holy Spirit is the baptizing element of personal fulfillment.

John's promise that the Messiah would baptize with the Holy Spirit is the promise by which this experience is introduced to biblical terminology. In every place where this promise is referred to it is either in the words of John the Baptist or in an allusion to him.

The manner in which Jesus referred to this promise in Acts 1 is instructive. The prediction of John is the promise of the Father which the disciples had heard from Jesus himself (Acts 1.4; cf. Jn 14.16, 17; Lk. 11.13). The receiving of this promise is the fulfillment of John's prediction and the day of its fulfillment is at hand: 'You shall be baptized with the Holy Spirit not many days hence' (Acts 1.5). Jesus repeated this promise in v. 8: 'But you shall receive power after the Holy Spirit has come upon you'. The baptism with the Holy Spirit (v. 5) is used interchangeably with the Holy Spirit's coming upon the believer (v. 8). Similar or exact terminology is used in other references: the Holy Spirit's being upon Simeon (Lk. 2.25), the promise of Christ that the Holy Spirit would come upon the disciples (Lk. 24.49), the Spirit's coming upon the Ephesian believers (Acts 19.5, 6), and the Spirit of glory and of God resting upon believers (1 Pet. 4.14).

The fulfillment of this promise on the Day of Pentecost describes baptism with the Holy Spirit as the filling of the believers with the Holy Spirit: 'And all were filled with the Holy Spirit and they began to speak with other tongues because the Spirit was giving to them inspired utterance' (Acts 2.4). Since this is the fulfillment of the promise of baptism, it is appropriate to refer to the experience of being baptized with the Spirit also as the experience of being filled with the Spirit. This terminology is used prior to Pentecost in certain special cases: of John the Baptist (Lk. 1.15), of Elisabeth (Lk. 1.41), and of Zacharias (Lk. 1.67). After the Day of Pentecost, it is used of Peter in his defense before the Jewish rulers (Acts 4.8), of the band of disciples in prayer (Acts 4.31), of Paul (Acts 9.17, 13.9), and of a group of disciples (Acts 13.52). The Ephesians are exhorted to 'keep on being full of the Spirit' (Eph. 5.18). The condition of being full of the Holy Spirit is referred to in the following instances: of the seven chosen to minister to the needs of the widows (Acts 6.3, 5), of Stephen in his being stoned (Acts 7.55), and of Barnabas in Antioch (Acts 11.24).

From these references we may draw the following conclusions. First, the term 'baptism with the Holy Spirit' is used exclusively of the experience in the age of fulfillment. It is not used of the Old Testament economy. Second, in the period of fulfillment we may conclude that baptism with the Holy Spirit may also be described as being filled with the Spirit. However, baptism refers to the initial experience, and being filled with (or continuing to be full of) the Holy Spirit refers to a continuing spiritual condition and way of life.

Peter on the Day of Pentecost also refers to the coming of the Holy Spirit as an outpouring of the Spirit by citing the words of Joel

2.28-30 (Acts 2.17, 18). The coming of the Holy Spirit upon Cornelius and his household is referred to as the falling of the Holy Spirit upon them (Acts 10.44) and as the pouring out of the Spirit upon them (Acts 10.45). Peter later described this experience: 'And when I began to speak the Holy Spirit fell upon them, just as also upon us in the beginning' (Acts 11.15). We judge that it is appropriate to refer to baptism with the Holy Spirit as the pouring out of the Spirit upon believers. In this figure, the continuing spiritual condition is appropriately referred to as the Spirit's resting upon the believer (1 Pet. 4.14).

In summary, the following conclusions are justified. References to the baptism of the Holy Spirit, being filled with the Spirit, and the Spirit's being poured out may all be used interchangeably. To limit the use of the term 'baptism with the Holy Spirit' to the Day of Pentecost and to Cornelius' experience is not justified. Baptism with the Holy Spirit is an initiating experience for the believer. Being filled with the Spirit is a continuing experience. Baptism with the Holy Spirit is not intended to be a repetitive experience for the individual believer; being filled with the Spirit is to be continuous.

Baptism with the Holy Spirit and the Order of Salvation

Our second question relates to the order of salvation; is baptism with the Holy Spirit to be placed in the experiences of salvation?

The term 'order of salvation' is a theological term designed to describe specific experiences in God's redemptive work. This term allows us to distinguish specific experiences in redemption from the ongoing process of life in redemption: that is, such designations as consecration, dedication, separation, and growing in grace. If the term 'order of salvation' is to serve this purpose, it must be defined carefully. The experiences that are to be placed in the order of salvation must meet certain requirements.

The first standard of definition is that the experience is God's act in the believer. We establish this in order to distinguish these experiences from human actions. When we say that these experiences are God's act, we mean that these experiences are accomplished by the agency of God's Word and of the Holy Spirit. They are not the product of human achievement. Even those who believe on Christ are not contributors to such works or acts. Believers are recipients by the act of faith. The Word of God's power is the effective cause of the experience of redemption.

The second standard of definition is that the experiences in the order of salvation are based on the redemptive activity of Christ in the atonement. The fundamental facts of Christ's redemptive activity are the perfection of Christ's life, the satisfaction of divine judgment in His death, and the provision of redemptive life in His resurrection. For an experience to be in the order of salvation, it must be an atonement-based experience.

The third criterion of the order of salvation is that the experiences in it are provided by Christ's high-priestly work. The experience is the result of Christ's intercession before the Father. This condition is related to the atonement, for such is a priest's work. The work is done in this fashion because the one for whom intercession is made does not have access to the Father and has neither the ability nor the assets to meet the Father's terms.

The fourth standard of our definition is that the experiences in the order of salvation provide a critical change in the status of the individual before God or a radical change of nature in the individual. These are crisis experiences. They represent redemptive changes in and for the believer.

These are crisis experiences in the fact that they are pivotal and determinative. They are pivotal because they represent a turning point in life. There is a radical difference in the nature and position of the individual before and after the experience. These experiences are determinative. They represent a change of direction, which change is determinative of the individual's eternal destiny.

The fifth requirement of the *ordo salutis* is that the experiences in it are received by faith. First, faith is a denial of human contribution to the experience of salvation. Second, it is a declaration of the believer's complete dependence on God. Third, it recognizes the essential nature of the agents of redemption which God has provided: namely, His Word and His Spirit. Faith so understood is the gift of God's grace and is the instrument of reception from God.

Louis Berkhof cites a summarization of the order of salvation, which incorporates the experiences, the atonement, and the redemptive offices of Christ. The sinful condition is represented by the terms 'guilt, pollution, and misery'. The plan of salvation must deal with each of these problems of sin. Christ's redemptive offices are fulfilled in His suffering and victory. Guilt represents a wrong relationship to God; this need is met in the order of salvation by reconciliation, justification, peace with God, adoption, and liberty in Christ.[51]

Pollution represents a defect in human nature. Redemptive provisions meet this need by the change of nature through regeneration, sanctification, and glorification.

The way of salvation addresses the problem of human misery by the alteration of the believers' direction and status, by setting them free from the law of sin and death and by the assurance of everlasting life.

The believer's direction is altered not only in the experience of repentance, but also by the call of the Holy Spirit to holiness of life. In this pursuit of holiness, the believer is dependent on being made free from the law of sin and death by the Spirit of life in Christ Jesus (Rom. 8.2). The assurance of everlasting life is the work of the Holy Spirit who is the earnest of the eternal inheritance and the seal of God upon the believer.

The Redemptive Heritage

We must now determine how these conditions relate to baptism with the Holy Spirit. A critical beginning text for us is Jn 20.19-23. Atonement provision and application are central to this passage. The scene is an appearance of the resurrected Jesus; His words are atonement words, and He displays the physical wounds from His crucifixion. In the display of His wounds Jesus demonstrates that the crucifixion body and the resurrection body are one and the same. There is, therefore, continuity of person and redemption from the crucified Jesus to the resurrected Jesus. All that He was and gained in His humiliation He is and bestows in His glory.

His first words, 'Peace to you' (v. 19), are words of atonement. They are the announcement of peace with God. Jesus had earlier defined this peace as His peace, which He would bestow through

---

[51] Louis Berkhof, *Systematic Theology* (Grand Rapids: Eerdmans, 1959), pp. 418-19. 'The blessings of Christ consist in the following: (a) He restores the right relation of man to God and to all creatures by justification. (b) He renews man in the image of God by regeneration, internal calling, conversion, renewal, and sanctification. (c) He preserves man for his eternal inheritance.' These fundamentals provide the bases on which this discussion is extended in the text above.

intercession (Jn 14.25-27). It is not the peace that the world bestows, but it is the peace that saves from turmoil and fear (14.27). In Jn 16.33, He based the peace which He bestowed on the promise He had given. From these uses of the word 'peace' we judge the meaning of the term in this case. Christ here announces peace with God. This is the peace of God's reconciliation and the believers' reconciliation in justification and regeneration.

Jesus repeated His announcement of peace and gave the apostles His commission: 'Peace to you. Just as the Father has sent Me, I also send you' (20.21). There is a fundamental connection between the peace that Christ announced and the commission, which He gave. It is a redemptive union. The witness of Christ's redemptive work can go forth as Christ went forth only if the witness is redemptively in Christ and at peace with God and the rest of humankind (cf. Heb. 12.14).

Following this commission, our Lord 'breathed on them and He says to them, 'Receive the Holy Spirit'' (v. 22). His breathing is the symbol of His bestowal of the gift of the Holy Spirit and a symbol of the procession of the Holy Spirit from His divine person. His words are the command of receptivity. This act of Christ is foundationally unified with the bestowal of peace and the giving of the commission. There is still the same continuity here between the crucified Christ and the risen Christ. What He had purchased in His crucifixion He now bestows in His resurrection. This is atonement. Our conclusion is that the Holy Spirit is bestowed as a product of Christ's atoning work and in the fulfillment of His intercessory work. The Apostle Peter proclaimed this truth on the Day of Pentecost (Acts 2.33). This declaration certainly relates baptism with the Holy Spirit to the high priestly work of Christ.

We have concentrated on Jn 20.19-23 because this text answers several questions of our inquiry. It shows that the gift of the Holy Spirit is based in the atonement of Christ. It is bestowed by a divine act. It is provided in the priestly function of Christ.

In addition to these considerations, the gift of the Holy Spirit is the promise of God as His act of outpouring (Joel 2.28-30; Acts 2.16-21). It is the gift of the Father (Lk. 11.13; Jn 14.16). The Holy Spirit is received by faith (Gal. 3.2). The Holy Spirit's coming is the promise of God (Word of God) and comes in the ministry of the Word (Acts 10.44; 11.15).

The Holy Spirit is directly related to our redemptive calling, way of life, and destiny. The Holy Spirit's function in relation to salvation is as earnest, firstfruits, and seal. In Eph. 1.13, 14, Paul suggests a relationship between baptism with the Holy Spirit and the order of salvation:

> In whom (i.e., Christ) after you had heard the word of truth, the gospel of your salvation, in whom also after you had believed you were sealed (i.e., marked and guaranteed by an official seal) with the Holy Spirit of promise, who (the Holy Spirit) is the pledge (guarantee in kind) of our inheritance unto the redemption of the purchased possession unto the praise of His glory.

The figure of speech appealed to here is a guarantee in kind. It carries the connotation of a foretaste of the glory that shall come; that foretaste is also assurance. It is the guarantee of God of the final accomplishment of that which is now experienced in foretaste.

The figure of speech that speaks of the 'firstfruits of the Spirit' is parallel to the 'earnest' (Rom. 8.23). 'It is the foretaste of heaven, the heaven begun in the Christian, which intensifies his yearning'.[52]

The word 'earnest' is also associated with the work of the Holy Spirit in sealing the believer (Eph. 1.13, 14; 1 Cor. 1.22). The giving of the earnest of the inheritance is God's authenticating and protecting seal upon the believer.

All of these symbols have a common point: they relate the work of the Holy Spirit to the total experience of redemption.

The reasoning that we have followed above and the Scripture witness establish a case for identifying baptism with the Holy Spirit as one of the experiences in the order of salvation. Clearly we have established the following points which are pertinent. First, the giving of the Holy Spirit is the provision of Christ's atoning death and of His high priestly intercession. Second, baptism with the Holy Spirit anticipates and gives a foretaste of final redemptive glory. Third, baptism with the Holy Spirit is received by faith, and life in the Spirit is a walk of faith. Fourth, the agents of this baptism are the Word and the Spirit of God.

---

[52] Denney, "St. Paul's Epistle to the Romans", p. 650.

Be Filled With the Holy Spirit

There is an important exhortation in Eph. 5.18: 'Do not be drunk with wine, in which is excess, but keep on being full of the Spirit'. We cannot escape the nature of command here; it is God's expectation that His children live a Holy Spirit-filled life. This expectation is clear in the words of Christ's bestowal: 'He breathed on them and He says to them, 'Receive the Holy Spirit'' (Jn 20.22). There is both commandment and endowment in these words.

We have earlier established a connection between baptism with the Holy Spirit and being filled with the Spirit. One is the initiating experience (baptism) and the other refers to the manner of life: a spiritual life, one characterized by remaining full of the Spirit of God.

So when we use Jn 20.22 and Eph. 5.18 together we emphasize the initiating experience (the baptism) and the continuing way of life (filled with the Spirit). The union of these verses gives us a background of command and provision. God's provisions for the believers represent His expectations of them.

There are certain conclusions that must be drawn from these considerations. First, the experience of receiving the Holy Spirit (His baptism) and the life of being filled with the Holy Spirit are essential to the New Testament concept of Christianity. This is shown by the expectation of Christ that the disciples tarry in Jerusalem until the Holy Spirit comes (Lk. 24.49). It is further shown by the relative inactivity of the church from the day of Christ's ascension to the Day of Pentecost. The church was not prepared to fulfill Christ's commission of proclamation and discipling without first having the equipment of baptism with the Holy Spirit (Acts 1.8).

The church was not fully prepared for its existence as church without the descent of the Holy Spirit. The Holy Spirit is the Spirit of worship and witness; hence, His presence and baptism are fundamental in the functions of the church.

It is significant that the New Testament attitude toward baptism with the Holy Spirit is that this experience is the normal expectation of being in Christ. The idea of being a Christian could not be separated from being baptized with the Holy Spirit.

It is unfortunate that the Pentecostal experience became a basis for denominational distinction. Pentecost is Christianity and Christianity is Pentecostal.

The Significance of Baptism with the Holy Spirit

The significance of baptism with the Holy Spirit rests in the person of the Holy Spirit. To be baptized and filled with the Holy Spirit is to be indwelt of a divine person—a member of the Trinity. The full significance of this must be seen in perspective. We were sinners by nature. Our bodies had been the temples of the spirit of this world—'the spirit that now works in the children of disobedience' (Eph. 2.2). In material significance, we are but clay. In spiritual significance, we are creatures.

The Person who fills the Spirit-baptized believer is the divine Holy Spirit. He is that divine Person who moved upon the face of the waters in creation (Gen. 1.2), who searches the deep things of God (1 Cor. 2.10), who knows the depth of His will and heart (Rom. 8.26, 27), and who reveals these things—even God himself—in Holy Scripture (2 Tim. 3.15-17). This divine Person was the Agent of the Incarnation of the Son of God in the womb of the virgin and the One who brought again from the dead our Lord Jesus and declared Him to be the Son of God (Rom. 1.4). He fulfills the will of God. He is the source of all spiritual graces in regeneration and the one who cultivates them as the fruit of the Spirit (Gal. 5.22-26).

Such a baptism is an extreme elevation of the human being. It is elevation by the grace of God in which the unworthy hovel of the spirit of this world has become the glorious temple of the Holy Spirit (Eph. 2.2; 1 Cor. 6.19, 20).

The significance of this experience is also shown by the meaning of the outpouring of the Holy Spirit on the Day of Pentecost. This is a corporate and personal significance.

For the early church and for the church in all ages, the gift of the Holy Spirit is the highest continuing proof of the resurrection of Christ. In his Pentecost day proclamation, Peter made a passing reference to the fact that there were present witnesses who had seen the resurrected Lord (Acts 2.32). So far as this occasion was concerned, these witnesses could not show anyone the risen Lord. He was not to be seen on the day of Pentecost.

Peter's main argument for the resurrection and ascension of Christ is the outpouring of the Holy Spirit: 'This same Jesus God raised up, of which we all are witnesses; therefore, since He has been lifted up to the right hand of God and has received the promise of the Holy Spirit from the Father, He has poured out this which you both see and hear' (Acts 2.32, 33). His argument and conclusions are as follows: Christ has been raised from the dead; He has been exalted to the Father's right hand. At the Father's right hand, He has received the gift of the Father, which is the Holy Spirit. The resurrected and ascended Lord has poured out this gift.

Peter could have shown them an empty tomb, but an empty tomb does not prove the resurrection of the former occupant of that tomb. He could call eyewitnesses that had seen the resurrected Jesus, but he could not on this day show them Jesus in the flesh. The primary proof, then, of Christ's presence with the Father is the outpouring of that Spirit whom the Father had promised.

So we return to the conclusions drawn from Jn 20.19-23. The bestowal of the Holy Spirit is the ministry of the risen Lord. It is His high priestly work to receive the gift of the Father and in turn to give that gift to believers (Eph. 4.7-16).

If these things are true for the body of Christ corporately, they are true for the individual members of His body. A personal Pentecost is our highest evidence of Christ's resurrection. This evidence rises above the evidences of sight and apologetical argumentation. It is well and good to be able to point to the empty tomb to show the physical evidences of resurrection, and to list all of the polemic arguments for resurrection; but the only saving evidence of the resurrection of Christ is the testimony of the Holy Spirit (cf. Rom. 1.4).

The Old Testament relationship between Passover and Sinai prepares us for understanding the relationship of the Cross to the Day of Pentecost. Sinai (and the giving of the Law) gave meaning to Passover and distinction to the Old Testament church. Sinai interpreted Passover as God's saving act. Sinai also interpreted beforehand life as it was to be lived in the land of Canaan. It was the law of the new and redeemed life. By Sinai, Israel was set apart from all other religions and nations. Her distinctive was redemptive, ethical, and covenantal.

The outpouring of the Holy Spirit on the Day of Pentecost sets this event in fulfillment of the typological prophecy of Sinai. As the Cross fulfilled Passover, Pentecost fulfilled Sinai (the giving of the Law). The New Testament experience fulfilled what was anticipated in the Old Testament experience.

Pentecost is the interpretation of Calvary. Pentecost, in the personal ministry of the Holy Spirit, instructs in the way of life to be followed subsequent to Calvary. Pentecost fulfills the redemptive and ethical significance of Sinai. Pentecost sets the Church apart in its redemptive experience and ethical role.

The gift of the Holy Spirit identifies God's people as Sinai identified the church in the wilderness (Exod. 19.5, 6). Sinai set Israel apart from her old life and from all her neighbor nations. In the same way, the gift of the Holy Spirit set the New Testament Church apart. They were no longer precisely identifiable with the Jews' religion. This is a distinction that would grow until it finally produced a rupture. The Church was not identifiable with any other religious, social, or ethical system. This gift identified this congregation as God's 'chosen family, a royal priesthood, a holy nation, (and) possessed people' (1 Pet. 2.9).

As the corporate body is identified and set apart by the gift of the Holy Spirit, so is the individual. The individual who is baptized with the Holy Spirit is identified by Spirit's personal presence and indwelling. The Spirit is the Father's authenticating and identifying seal upon the Church as well as upon the individual.

From the standpoint of the individual's relationship to the Holy Spirit, there is far reaching significance. This is an interpersonal relationship between the divine person (the Holy Spirit) and the human person (the believer). This significance is related to the Spirit's sovereignty and holiness.

As sovereign, the Holy Spirit enters as Lord, absolute Master, and as ruling Spirit. Spiritually, the entire inner nature is committed to the search, purification, and domination of the Holy Spirit. Mentally the believer is committed in thought to the Spirit's search, purification, and dominion. Bodily, the believer is committed as the temple of the Holy Spirit, to all purity, to all manifestations of the Holy Spirit and to all ministries of the Spirit.

From the standpoint of His holiness, it is the nature of the Holy Spirit to form in the believer those graces that manifest the nature of Jesus Christ. These are the fruit of the Spirit (Gal. 5.22, 23). He forbids those traits of character that are offensive to the nature of Christ and the holiness of His Spirit (Gal. 5.24-26). The application of this truth is that holiness of life is the primary manifestation of the Holy Spirit filled life.

9

THE CONDITIONS OF BAPTISM WITH THE HOLY SPIRIT

The conditions, which we look at here are conditions that relate to the initial experience of baptism with the Holy Spirit and the manner of life that proceeds from this experience. We are not dealing with a once-for-all experience, we are dealing with a continuing spiritual condition which may be defined as being filled with the Spirit.

An important clarification needs to be made. We are not using the term 'conditions' in the sense of merit; we do not imagine that one can do good deeds and gain the Holy Spirit baptism. We use this term as a descriptive term. We are attempting to describe relationships that are important to spirituality and the blessing of the Holy Spirit.

Clarifications: The conditions that we may legitimately set forth must be in harmony with the personal nature of the Holy Spirit and must be based on Scripture. We lay this foundation in order to avoid certain pitfalls. Brief attention to four of these pitfalls will be helpful.

The first pitfall is one that ties the seeking and the experience itself to certain emotional conditioning and experience. The tendency here is to create a traditional manner of receiving the Holy Spirit; certain kinds of emotional phenomena are prescribed as necessary to the baptism with the Holy Spirit. This may run to all extremes depending on the social, religious, and psychological appreciations of the individual or the group. Some insist that one can receive the Holy Spirit only if he/she becomes emotionally frenzied; others insist that a pensiveness scarcely discernible from transcendental meditation is the correct condition for receiving the Holy Spirit.

These positions are in error for two reasons. The first and most important is that they do not represent scriptural judgments. The second is that they equate baptism with the Holy Spirit with a pre-scribed emotional condition.

The second pitfall is that of prescribing certain practices of worship, which are not established in Scripture as conditions of receiving this blessing. This error appears under all conditions of worship. It is the assumption that the creature can devise practices of worship and then claim divine blessings for having fulfilled his own conditions. God alone is the object of worship; His Word alone prescribes the patterns and practices of worship. Worship practices that are not authorized in Scripture cannot prepare the believer for baptism with the Holy Spirit. We have no right to introduce these practices into worship and no authority for encouraging believers to seek baptism with the Holy Spirit through them.

The third pitfall is to create special practices and restrictions of life as conditions for baptism with the Holy Spirit without scriptural authority. The establishment of ordinances 'after the command-ments and doctrines of men' (Col. 2.20-23) cannot be set forth as proper methods of seeking for the infilling of the Holy Spirit. This may take the form of requiring certain actions or practices in what is thought to be obedience to God. It may take the form of placing unbiblical limitations on one's liberties in Christ.

The fourth pitfall is the attempt to produce the phenomena (such as speaking in tongues, prophesying, and ecstasy) of the Holy Spirit baptism by behavioral manipulation and imitation. This pat-tern removes such things as speaking in tongues from the activity of the Holy Spirit. They become humanly provoked and not divinely inspired. This practice also removes the distinction between the true baptism with the Holy Spirit and merely imitated experience.

The fundamental error of all these devices is that they are un-scriptural. We have no authority to create worship devices of our own and then use them to claim God's blessings. We have no right to create 'practices of holiness' and then call them the essence of godly living and the conditions of divine blessing and approval. Such attempts deny the authority of the Word of God.

The second basic error here is that these devices mistake psycho-logical manipulation (sometimes self—manipulation) for the mov-ing of the Holy Spirit. The attempt to equate the blessing of the Holy Spirit with a pre-established emotional experience (whether that experience is bold and external or quiet and covert) is a work of the flesh. The attempt to 'learn' how to manifest the work of the Holy Spirit denies His sovereignty in manifestation. These devices have a wrong center; their center is humankind and not God.

The Nature of the Holy Spirit in Relation to Baptism with the Holy Spirit

The nature of the Holy Spirit is determinative of the conditions of baptism with the Holy Spirit. He is personal, so an interpersonal relationship with the Holy Spirit is essential to baptism with the Holy Spirit. The manifestations of the Holy Spirit are human personal responses to this divine Person, and they are governed by Him. It is the personal condition of rapport in which the worshiper is responsive to the moving of the sovereign Spirit.

The Holy Spirit is sovereign God. He is Lord. Submission to Him is essential in us if we are to enjoy His ministries and if we are to manifest His will.

The Holy Spirit is the Spirit of Christ. He manifests Himself upon, in, and through those who belong to Christ. He manifests Himself for the glory and witness of Christ; He ministers through and in those who are themselves committed to the glory and witness of Christ.

As the title Holy Spirit indicates, He is holy. Those who would be baptized with the Holy Spirit must themselves be holy and be committed to the fulfillment of that purity of life.

In the light of these broad relationships, there are some specific applications that must be made. These are essential conditions of baptism with the Holy Spirit. It is also important that we take the order of experience seriously. These are conditions of baptism with the Holy Spirit and not products of the baptism of the Holy Spirit.

Baptism with the Holy Spirit is promised to believers in Christ. This fact distinguishes the baptism with the Holy Spirit from conversion experiences. Justification is promised to the ungodly (Rom. 4.5). Repentance is commanded of the impenitent, and is promised to those who 'oppose themselves' (2 Tim. 2.25). Regeneration is promised to those who are dead in trespasses and sins (Eph. 2.1-5). Adoption is promised to those who are not by nature the children of God (Eph. 2.3; Rom. 8.14, 15). The Holy Spirit is promised to those who already know Him because they know and believe in

Christ; He is not promised to the world because the people of the world do not know Him and cannot receive Him (Jn 14.16, 17).

The point of this review is to show that by the nature of the experience conversion is distinct from baptism with the Holy Spirit. God calls for no preconditioning of the sinner for the mercy whereby He saves him. The coming of the Holy Spirit is not promised to the sinner, the ungodly, or the impenitent. This blessing is promised to those who have already entered a covenant relationship with Christ.

This reasoning is further supported by specific Scripture statements. Our Lord makes this clear in His promises in John 14-16. He promised to pray for the gift of the Holy Spirit for His disciples (14.16). He specifically notes that the world cannot receive the Holy Spirit because the world does not know Him (14.17). In contrast, the disciples of Christ do know Him because He abides in them (14.17). Discipleship is presupposed when Christ repeats the promise in Jn 14.25, 26.

More specifically, the Holy Spirit is promised to obedient believers: 'And we are witnesses of these words, and so is the Holy Spirit, which God has given to those who are obeying Him' (Acts 5.32). Obedience to God's will is an important relationship for the receiving of the Holy Spirit.

The Holy Spirit is promised to believers who have already shown evidence of discipleship by bearing fruit: 'In this has my Father been glorified in order that you bear much fruit and you shall be my disciples' (Jn 15.8). He is the Spirit of testimony; He is promised to those who have been witnesses of Christ. It is for this purpose that the Holy Spirit is sent. The Holy Spirit will witness of Christ (Jn 15.26). The receiver of the Holy Spirit is also to bear witness (Jn 15.27).

The witness of Christ is essential in the Holy Spirit's eschatological function. The disciples had been witnesses of Christ in their proclamation of the kingdom of God. They could proclaim, 'The kingdom of God is at hand'. They could point out the physical presence of Jesus for the authority to preach and for evidence of their announcement of the presence of the Kingdom. Upon Christ's physical departure, they needed 'another Paraklete' who could and would confirm their authority in the announcement of the kingdom of God. This other Paraklete is the Spirit of Christ and of God whose Kingdom is being announced.

The Holy Spirit is promised to those who despise this world's attitude toward sin, righteousness, and judgment. The Spirit, by the nature of His holiness and by His being the Spirit of Christ, stands in condemnation of the world: 'And when that one has come, He will prove the guilt of the world in relation to sin, in relation to righteousness, and in relation to judgment' (Jn 16.8). Each of the convictions deals with the world's attitude toward Christ. The world is convicted of sin because it has not believed on Christ (Jn 16.9). The Holy Spirit judges the world concerning righteousness because Christ has gone to the Father. Christ has been declared the Son of God and justified before God. The Holy Spirit is the agent of that declaration (Rom. 1.4; 1 Tim. 3.16). His presence is the conviction of that sin which rejects the righteousness of Christ (Jn 16.10). The Spirit convicts the world in relation to judgment because Christ has judged the prince of this world order (Jn 16.11); Christ's resurrection and ascension are His triumph over all principalities and powers (Eph. 1.19-23). Those who refuse to acknowledge this lordship are convicted by the Holy Spirit.

It follows from these statements that the Holy Spirit will be poured out only upon those who have come to this same spiritual attitude toward the world, its value system, its standard of success, and its measure of happiness.

In a direct sequence of these conditions of promise, our Lord prayed for His disciples (John 17). He prayed that they might be made one in Him and with the Father (vv. 8-10, 21, 22). He prayed that they be kept from the evil in the world—separate from the world as Christ himself is (vv. 11, 12, 15). The instrument of this keeping is the name of God (vv. 11, 12). This name designates their nature and their distinction from the world. It is also the power of God by which believers are kept from the world. He prayed that they might be filled with joy (v. 13). He prayed that they might be sanctified (vv. 17-19).

The sequence of these chapters in John indicates the pattern of experience, which the disciples (and we) could expect of the promise of the Holy Spirit and the preparation for His coming. We may safely reach the following conclusion: there can be no expectation of baptism with the Holy Spirit where these conditions do not prevail. There is no point in seeking the experience if we are not committed to these standards.

If these conditions of the promise are valid as conditions for baptism with the Holy Spirit, they are also the conditions of the free operation of the Spirit in our life subsequently. The vows and spiritual steps that were necessary (that is, biblically prescribed) in seeking baptism with the Holy Spirit are also necessary if we are to walk in the Spirit and to be continually filled with the Spirit.

10

The Outward Manifestations of Baptism with the Holy Spirit

The Circumstances of the Baptism with the Holy Spirit

The circumstances under which the Holy Spirit fell on believers in the Book of Acts will be instructive for us. We should also notice the effects of this experience in the persons receiving it. The following passages must be reviewed: Acts 2.1-13; 4.31, 32; 8.14-17; 9.17; 10.44-48; 19.1-7. Our purpose in this review is to determine what is normative to baptism with the Holy Spirit.

On the Day of Pentecost (Acts 2.1-13) the believers were continually engaged in the worship of God—blessing and praising Him (Lk. 24.52, 53). They continued from the day of the ascension of Christ 'with one accord in prayer and supplication' (Acts 1.14). On the Day of Pentecost, they were in spiritual unity—'with one accord in one place' (Acts 2.1).

When the Holy Spirit fell, He manifested His presence by the sound of a rushing wind and by the divided tongues like fire. The recipients of this outpouring began to speak with other tongues because the Holy Spirit was giving them that power—the power to speak as the oracle of God (Acts 2.4). Peter preached the gospel of Christ boldly with the same prophetic authority.

On another occasion when the rulers of Israel attempted to stop Peter and John from preaching Christ (Acts 4.1-22), these two apostles sought respite among the saints (Acts 4.23). Here the company of believers 'lifted up their voice to God with one accord' (v. 24). Their prayer follows. They praised God as the Creator of all things—heavenly and earthly (v. 24). They praised Him because He was master and owner of heaven and earth. He is governor and God over all—the rebellious and the obedient (vv. 25, 26). They glorified God and praised Him for His rulership over such enemies as Herod and Pontius Pilate, the Greeks and the Jews (v. 27). They knew that these enemies had done with God's Son only that which God's hand and counsel had established (v. 28).

Then the disciples prayed that God would intervene. They prayed for boldness to speak God's Word (v. 29). They asked God to extend His hand in healings and signs and wonders (v. 30).

After they had prayed, God poured out His Spirit anew and they were all filled with the Holy Spirit (v. 31). They spoke the Word with boldness (v. 31) and came together with one heart and one mind (v. 32).

In the Samaritan renewal (Acts 8.5-17), Philip proclaimed the gospel. Scripture had earlier testified that he was full of the Holy Spirit and wisdom (Acts 6.3-5). In Samaria many believed but they had not received the baptism with the Holy Spirit (Acts 8.15, 16). Peter and John, sent out by the apostles (v. 14), prayed for the Samaritan believers that they might receive the Holy Spirit (v. 15). After they had prayed for the disciples, Peter and John laid hands on them. Then they received the Holy Spirit (v. 17). Whatever happened here was outwardly observable as is shown by Simon Magus' response (vv. 18, 19). He wanted power to create the same response that he had seen when Peter and John laid hands on the disciples.

In Acts 9.17, 18 Luke records Saul's encounter with Ananias. Saul's spiritual condition as a believer in Jesus Christ already is amply established (Acts 9.6, 11, 15). The purpose of Ananias' visit was for Saul to receive his sight and be filled with the Holy Spirit (v. 17). Ananias ministered these blessings to Saul by laying his hands on him (v. 17). Nothing is said here of outward signs except that Saul was healed of his blindness and that he was baptized (v. 18).

In Acts 10 we are provided with the details of the encounter of Cornelius with Peter and the spiritual experience of Cornelius and those of his house. Cornelius was a devout man (vv. 1-4) and a 'God-fearer'. He had been fasting and praying (v. 30). God responded to his prayers by giving him a vision (vv. 3, 4), by ministering to him through an angel (v. 30), and by sending Peter to him (vv. 19-21). Cornelius was obedient to the message of God (vv. 31-33). Peter was convinced of Cornelius' sincerity and communion with God (vv. 34, 35).

Peter began to preach Christ to them (vv. 36, 37); but this was not a strange message to Cornelius. Peter affirms that they knew the word of peace, which God had proclaimed through Christ. He also indicated that they knew of the preaching and baptism of John (v. 37). They had not clearly heard the full message of the gospel, but they knew and believed the promises of God.

The action of God is dramatically described in v. 44: 'While Peter was still saying these words [i.e., that which is recorded in vv. 34-43], the Holy Spirit fell upon all those who were hearing the Word'. God's action is also described in v. 46: 'For they [i.e., the brethren who had come with Peter] were hearing them speaking with tongues and magnifying God'.

The believers at Ephesus are designated as 'disciples' (Acts 19.1). Paul asked them, 'Did you receive the Holy Spirit after you had believed?' (v. 2). They responded that they had not you heard whether the Spirit had been given (v. 3). When these believers indicated that they had been baptized in John's baptism, Paul explained the relation of John's baptism and message to Christ (v. 4). The Ephesians believed this message and they were baptized in Christ's name (v. 5). Critical in this incident is v. 6: 'When Paul laid hands on them, the Holy Spirit came upon them, and they were speaking with tongues and they were prophesying'.

The Pattern of Experience in Baptism with the Holy Spirit

These examples are instructive. They establish a pattern of religious experience. This pattern establishes that which is normative in baptism with the Holy Spirit as it is recorded in the Book of Acts.

The first principle that these incidents establish is that baptism with the Holy Spirit is distinct from regeneration or the initial experience of believing on Christ. On the Day of Pentecost, the Holy Spirit fell on those who had seen the resurrected Lord and who were awaiting His fulfillment of promise. In Acts 4, the Holy Spirit filled those who were being persecuted for Christ's sake. At Samaria the people had already believed on Christ and had been baptized before they received the Holy Spirit. Paul had already believed on Christ when Ananias came to him in order for him to receive his sight and to be filled with the Holy Spirit. Cornelius and those of his house were devout and 'God-fearers' when Peter preached to them. The Ephesians were believers on Christ and were baptized before they received the Holy Spirit.

The second normative is that the Holy Spirit came in situations of divine worship. The believers on the Day of Pentecost were continually worshiping God. The believers in Acts 4 were engaged in common prayer when the Holy Spirit fell on them. At Samaria the apostles laid hands on the believers; this act of laying hands on individuals is consistently used in worship (Acts 6.6; 8.17; 9.12, 17; 13.3; 19.6; 28.8). Ananias ministered to Saul of Tarsus at the instruction of the Lord by laying his hands on Saul 'in order that you might receive your sight and be filled with the Holy Spirit' (Acts 9.17). Those who were in Cornelius' house were hearing the gospel proclaimed when the Holy Spirit fell on them (Acts 10.44; 11.15). At Ephesus the believers had been baptized in the name of Christ; Paul laid his hands on them and the Holy Spirit came upon them (Acts 19.6).

The third normative is that baptism with the Holy Spirit is outwardly manifested by the recipients' speaking in tongues.

A careful study of the language of Acts 2.4 shows a causative relationship between being filled with the Spirit and speaking in tongues: 'And they were all filled with the Holy Spirit, and they began to speak with other tongues because (καθὼς: because) the Spirit was giving them inspiration to speak'. When they were filled with the Spirit, the Spirit became the agent and origin of their speech. They were not empowered to speak before the Holy Spirit filled them. This is the force of Luke's language; they began to speak and kept on speaking because the Holy Spirit continued to give them the speech. The origin of this speech is also reflected in the sublimity of their speech; their utterances were oracular or inspired in their nature. The Holy Spirit's presence is signaled by His speech.

The same causal relationship is reflected in the language of Acts 10.44-46. 'And the believers out of the circumcision who accompanied Peter were amazed that even upon the Gentiles the gift of the Holy Spirit had been poured out; for they were hearing them while they were speaking with tongues and magnifying God' (vv. 45, 46). The source of their amazement was that Cornelius and those of his house had received the Holy Spirit' Clearly they were not prepared to believe that this would happen. The evidence that was to strip them of doubt was that the recipients received the Holy Spirit and spoke with tongues. Peter in response to this awareness ordered that they should be baptized in water and confirmed that the Gentiles had 'received the Holy Spirit in the same manner as we' (v. 47). His words show that he sees the same correlation between being filled with the Spirit and speaking in tongues that was observed in Acts 2.4.

Peter continued this line of reasoning when he reviewed and defended his actions before the Jerusalem leadership: 'And as I began to speak the Holy Spirit fell upon them just as also upon us in the beginning' (Acts 11.15). He repeated this reasoning also in v. 17. These arguments satisfied the believers in Jerusalem (v. 18).

The coming of the Holy Spirit upon the Ephesian believers was accompanied by their speaking in tongues and prophesying; 'And when Paul had laid his hands on them, the Holy Spirit came upon them and they began to speak with tongues and to prophesy' (Acts 19.6). The correspondence between the coming of the Holy Spirit and speaking in tongues is direct. The coming of the Holy Spirit produced the manifestation of tongues and prophecy.

At the beginning of this section we set as our goal to determine that which is normative in the experience of the baptism with the Holy Spirit. In the course of our study we have observed many manifestations of the Holy Spirit's presence. We have not emphasized all of them because they do not appear with such regularity that they can be designated as normative. Among these non-normative manifestations are the rushing wind and tongues of fire (Acts 2.2, 3), the shaking of the place where the believers were assembled (Acts 4.31), the restoration of sight (Acts 9.18), and prophesying (Acts 19.6). These are repeated experiences, but they do not become the basis of argument for the baptism with the Holy Spirit. Speaking in tongues is so used.

In summary, we may list the following aspects of this spiritual experience, which we may expect as it continues to be claimed and experienced in the church. The experience is the gift of God; it is bestowed by God. It is bestowed by God under circumstances of divine worship. It is given to believers in a special act of faith on their part, so, baptism with the Holy Spirit is distinct from the new birth. Its initial externally observable manifestation is speaking in tongues by the inspiration of the Holy Spirit.

Speaking in Tongues

Much has been said about speaking in tongues. We should be clear that what we say about it and the experience that we claim harmonize with what the Scriptures say. Every instance studied earlier shows that speaking in tongues originates in the movement of the Holy Spirit and not in the will or action of believers. This is the whole significance of the phrase 'as the Spirit gave the utterance' (Acts 2.4). The immediate provocation of speech was the Holy Spirit. The language shows that the believers spoke because and as the Spirit gave them the oracle to speak.

On the other hand, we do not wish to imply that the believer is passive in this experience. This experience represents a profound rapport between two persons: the divine Person, the Holy Spirit, and the human person, the believer. These two persons meet together through kinship and affection in such intimacy that the believer becomes fully responsive to the Holy Spirit. As He acts, wills, and communicates, the responding believer speaks and acts. This act of submission and responsiveness is essential to other acts of submission and responsiveness to the Holy Spirit.

Speaking in tongues as the Spirit gives utterance is not a learned response. It is not a practiced response. It is not a humanly initiated action. If the Holy Spirit is moving upon the individual, these are unnecessary. In fact, these human efforts destroy the aspect of faith in receiving baptism with the Holy Spirit. They substitute the human will for the divine will. They impose human gibberish and nonsense syllables for the oracle of God. Our efforts to imitate the work of God interfere with the work of the Holy Spirit and reject His sovereignty.

The circumstances reviewed above suggest specific applications. We can expect the coming of the Holy Spirit when the body of Christ meets in one mind and one accord. We can expect the outpouring of the Holy Spirit where believers join together in praising and blessing God. We can expect the Holy Spirit to baptize believers when they all join in prayer—in both intercession and supplication. We can expect the gift of the Spirit to be bestowed while the Word is being preached. We can expect baptism with the Holy Spirit to be given when hands are laid on fellow believers in obedience and faith. These are important observations because in each one the central act is the worship of God, not the singular seeking of a gift or an experience. God is not a reluctant giver of His gift, He delights to give His Spirit to those who ask Him (Lk. 11.9-13). In all of our seeking we must place greater affection on the Giver of the experience than upon the experience.

In the course of this chapter we have placed great emphasis upon those events where speaking in tongues has been specifically mentioned. It would be irresponsible to dismiss as irrelevant those passages where speaking in tongues is not mentioned. So we turn now to those passages. Our purpose in this segment of study is to determine if these passages are as near silent as is often assumed and if so is the silence determinative in this doctrinal consideration.

There are three instances in which the Scriptures do not mention specifically this sign for baptism with the Holy Spirit. The first is Acts 4.30, 31. In this instance the group who was filled at this time had already been baptized with the Spirit on the Day of Pentecost. This is a renewal experience and not an initial experience. So the question of speaking in tongues as the initial outward evidence of baptism with the Holy Spirit is irrelevant in this passage. Speaking in tongues may have—probably did—occur, but the mentioning of that phenomenon is not important to the record in this context. The silence of the record on this issue in not a determinative silence.

The Samaritans' experience in receiving the Holy Spirit is recorded in Acts 8.14-17. No mention is made of their speaking in tongues. However, the passage is not as silent on this issue as it is sometimes supposed. Luke describes the coming of the Holy Spirit with the same terminology that he uses in other places (Acts 10.44, 46; 11.15; 19.6). He intends to show that the experience of the Samaritans was parallel with the other experiences in the Book of Acts. This would include the outward manifestations of the gift. This is further implied by the reaction of Simon the sorcerer when he observed the experience (vv. 18, 19). The language indicates that there were outward and observable evidences of the baptism of the Holy Spirit.[53] It was this aspect of the experience that caught the attention of Simon and excited his covetousness. The inward spiritual evidences (which always accompany the baptism with the Holy

---

[53] See also Anthony A. Hoekma, *What About Tongue Speaking?* (Grand Rapids: Eerdmans, 1966), p. 70.

Spirit) were not immediately observable. The most reasonable conclusion for this incident is that speaking in tongues was the sign of baptism with the Holy Spirit; it was such power as that which Simon coveted.

At the time that Ananias visited Saul of Tarsus, he laid hands on him in order that he might receive his sight and be filled with the Holy Spirit (Acts 9.17, 18). Saul's immediate personal response is not here mentioned. The Scriptures record that his blindness was lifted, Saul arose and was baptized. The silence of the Scripture on the experience of speaking in tongues is not indicative here. The record passes over Saul's personal experience without comment.

By our emphasis on speaking in tongues, we must not imply that this is the only effect of baptism with the Holy Spirit upon the believer. There are other effects, which are essentially inward transformations. They are not immediately observable. They are more clearly seen as the life of the believer is transformed by the rulership of the Holy Spirit. These effects are the subject of our next study.

11

THE INWARD EFFECTS OF BAPTISM WITH THE HOLY SPIRIT

It is not possible or desirable to separate the inward from the outward in religious experience. In a form of hypocrisy, the outward may be imitated with no concern for the inward reality. In another form of insincerity, one may claim an inward experience that is never externally acted upon. This is a strange asceticism that sublimates all external duty to inward commitment and fulfillment. So it is essential that we consider both the external manifestations of the Holy Spirit-filled life and the internal effects of the Holy Spirit-filled life.

In the previous chapter, we discussed the outward manifestations of Spirit baptism with particular attention to speaking in tongues. As we observed there, this experience is not external alone. It is an external manifestation of what the Holy Spirit has done and is doing in the spiritual nature of the believer. There is an immediate external responsiveness to inward divine work. This is true in conversion as well. Conversion involves both inward faith (to believe in the heart that God has raised Christ from the dead) and confession with the mouth unto salvation (Rom. 10.9, 10). This text highlights both aspects of conversion, and the unity of both of these with the other. Certainly when one believes in the heart on the Lord Jesus, he/she is saved; but it is a natural and spontaneous response for the new believer to confess the Lord Jesus to others.

There is a similar unity between baptism with the Holy Spirit and the response of speaking in tongues. It is not that one must speak in tongues to prove Spirit baptism, but that there is a deep spiritual union between the inward experience and the oral manifestation of the experience. It is most natural and congruent that the Spirit of witness would manifest His presence by witness. The witness that is most consistently and normatively displayed in Scripture is speaking in tongues as the Spirit gives utterance.

The Holy Spirit and Truth

The Scriptures, however, extend the results of baptism with the Holy Spirit to other evidences in the life of the church and individual believers. The immediate subsequent history of the early church reveals the following evidences of the baptism with the Holy Spirit. They continued in the teachings of the apostles. They continued in fellowship and in divine worship (Acts 2.42-47). In addition to these effects, we need also to observe the effects of the Spirit's presence which reflect the person and work of the Holy Spirit. These are the subjects of our consideration at this time.

The Holy Spirit-filled church was characterized by its commitment to truth ('the teachings of the apostles'), to fellowship, and to worship (Acts 2.42). The strength of this statement may be reflected in the following paraphrase: 'They were in constant perseverance and commitment to the teaching of the apostles'. The Holy Spirit is the agent of this perseverance and commitment. The three commitments here are important to our life in the Holy Spirit.

The Holy Spirit-filled person is committed to the truth. Here the truth is represented by the instruction that the apostles gave the early believers. That instruction is demonstrated in the messages that are recorded in the Book of Acts. These speeches (or sermons) constitute the teaching of the apostles. Though there are individual variations of speeches, there are certain elements in all these speeches that consistently appear.

The broadest categorization that we may give of the content of these messages is that they were the proclamation of Christ. This is demonstrated in Peter's sermon on the Day of Pentecost (Acts 2.14-36). Briefly he defends the disciples against the charge of drunkenness (vv. 14, 15); then he shows that this outpouring of the Holy Spirit is an eschatological fulfillment of prophecy (vv. 16-21; cf. Joel 2.28-32). The rest of this sermon deals with Christ.

In other speeches in the Book of Acts, the outpouring of the Holy Spirit is not the primary subject of the proclamation, yet in those contexts there is a strong emphasis on Spirit baptism as well. In Acts 8.14-17, Peter and John went to Samaria in order that they might pray for the Samaritans and lay hands on them to receive the Holy Spirit. Here again the subject of proclamation is Christ, but the mission of the two apostles is also that the Samaritan believers receive the Holy Spirit (Acts 8.14, 15). In Acts 10.44-48 (cf. Acts 11.15-18) the Holy Spirit fell upon the believers as they heard the proclamation of Christ. In Acts 19.1-6, the Holy Spirit is the subject of Paul's inquiry concerning the Ephesian believers' experience. He was not satisfied with his ministry to this group until he had baptized them in water in Christ's name, and had laid hands on them that they might be filled with the Spirit.

This subjection of the witness of the Holy Spirit to the preaching of Christ is as it should be in 'Pentecostal preaching'. The Holy Spirit is operative in all these instances as witness to Christ and as empowerment to preach Christ. Christ had so designated the work of the Holy Spirit. His reproof of the world is centered in His witness to Christ (Jn 16.8-11). He shall not speak of Himself, but of Christ (Jn 16.13); He shall glorify Christ and speak to believers that which He has heard of Christ (Jn 16.14). Christ promised that the Holy Spirit's coming would empower the believers to witness of Christ until the consummation of this age (Acts 1.8).

The preaching of Christ in the Book of Acts is fulfilled by consistently recurring themes. These themes are as follows. Jesus is the promised Messiah—both human and Son of God. This Jesus was crucified for our sins. God raised Jesus from the dead, thus announcing that He was (but not making Him to be) the Son of God. God exalted Jesus to His right hand and to the throne of His father David. This same Jesus will return to judge the living and the dead. This is the teaching of the apostles reduced to its basic core. This is the saving message, and its proclamation is an act of worship by the preacher and by the hearer. This message takes place under the power and witness of the Holy Spirit.

Adherence to this message is essential to harmony with the person and will of the Spirit. Separation from it in any form of compromise is an offense to the person of the Holy Spirit.

This review of the message of the New Testament requires that we understand these truths as propositional. Propositional (or dogmatic) accuracy in these basic points is a requirement of preaching that is to be witnessed to by the Holy Spirit. The accuracy of these teachings is attested by conformity with the teachings of the apostles, not by religious experience. For the first generation of Christians, this accuracy was attested by the apostles themselves. In subsequent generations, this accuracy must be attested by Scripture.

The attempt to use religious experience (whether prophecy, tongues and interpretation, ecstatic responses, or any other form of religious experience) to confirm doctrinal accuracy places the church in authority over Scripture. This conclusion cannot be dodged by shifting this confirmation to the Holy Spirit, because it attributes to the Holy Spirit a function which He does not claim for Himself. In this error, we would be attributing to His ministries (tongues, interpretation, prophecy, and discernment) functions that are not attributed to them in biblical (and also apostolic) descriptions.

This error of confirmation of doctrine by means of religious experience cannot support the unity of the body of Christ. Experiences do not unify; their subjective nature promotes such diversity of interpretation that no common teaching can develop from them. There is no consistency of the content of proclamation; proclamation becomes a humanistic function.

What then is the function of the Holy Spirit in the teaching of the apostles' doctrine? Is this doctrine simply a 'dead orthodoxy'? Can the teachings of the apostles be truly conducted in the absence of the Holy Spirit's ministry? There is a single answer to these last questions: No!

The first functions of the Holy Spirit we have mentioned are as witness to Christ and as empowerment of proclamation. The Spirit also lifts the apostles' doctrine from the theoretical and the simple historical (without denying either) to living experience. The Spirit as teacher lifts events out of history to make them present in experience and realization. Truth is no longer merely mental consent; it is personal experience. The Word is translated from tablet to heart. The death of Christ becomes our crucifixion. The resurrection of Christ becomes imminent in our expectation and is translated into holy living.

The Holy Spirit and Fellowship

The next evidence of the baptism with the Holy Spirit in the early church is their continuance in fellowship one with another. The word for fellowship may be used strictly in a social sense of sharing. It cannot be so used in Acts 2.42. Within this context (the apostles' teaching, breaking bread, and the praise of God), the term refers to spiritual experience.

The point of this fellowship is that the author of it is the Holy Spirit. It is the immediate result of the Holy Spirit's presence in the congregation and infilling in the individuals in the congregation of God. Here the meaning of the word is demonstrated. They ate together.[54] They worshiped with each other as they met. They shared material goods with each other. Their meetings (whether social or specifically religious) were marked by joy (exultation) and simplicity. They praised God in their meetings together. Under these circumstances the social meeting becomes virtually indistinguishable from the worship meeting.

It is appropriate that, those who are baptized with the Spirit by whom the love of God is shed abroad in the heart (Rom. 5.5) should enjoy the fellowship of one another. It is a fellowship centered in Christ, experienced in the believers' union in Christ, and experienced by the moving of Christ's Spirit among and within them. This marked the newly baptized congregation.

Divisions, suspicions, jealousy, and distrust are the marks of a worldly society. They are not to be the marks of a community of saints baptized with the Holy Spirit.

The Holy Spirit and Worship

We have already anticipated the manifestation of the Spirit in worship, but more needs to be said. The circumstances of the Spirit's outpouring were circumstances of worship. The Spirit perpetuates these conditions of communion with God when He baptizes a congregation or an individual. Of the early church newly baptized with

---

[54] Some scholars think the expression 'breaking of bread' to be a term to describe the celebration of the Lord's Supper. This rite may have been involved, but the term before us must also be taken as the sharing of meals with each other. Jesus broke bread when the disciples asked Him to tarry with them at Emmaus (Lk. 24.30). He broke bread in the miraculous provision for the five thousand; He broke bread when He instituted the Lord's Supper (Mt. 26.26; Mk 14.22; Lk. 22. 19). In Acts 20.7, the expression 'to break bread' was one of the functions of the first day of the week. This is most likely a reference to the Lord's Supper. In Acts 2.46, the breaking of bread seems to be associated with a shared meal and not simply a sacramental meal.

the Holy Spirit the Scriptures declare: they were continually in prayer (Acts 2.42); wonders and signs occurred among them (v. 43); they shared their goods (vv. 44, 45); they were daily in the Temple (v. 46); they praised God in their meetings (v. 47), and they were winning others to the faith of Christ (v. 47). These are all aspects of worship. They mark the Holy Spirit-filled congregation.

All of these acts and products of worship are appropriate evidences of baptism with the Holy Spirit. The Holy Spirit inspires us to cry 'Abba, Father' (Rom. 8.15). It is by the Spirit that we confess Christ (1 Cor. 12.3). It is by the Holy Spirit that the ministries of the church are extended (1 Cor. 12.4). The Holy Spirit is the Spirit of intercession and prayer (Rom. 8.26, 27). We may both pray and sing with the Spirit (1 Cor. 14.14, 15).

The connection between being filled with the Spirit and worship is clearly shown in Eph. 5.18-20. Paul's exhortation is that we should keep on being full of the Spirit (v. 18). The grammatical connection with vv. 19 and 20 shows that those experiences listed are the expression and manifestation of being filled with the Spirit.

The first manifestation of the Spirit-filled life given here is communion in singing. Corporate singing (singing to and with one another) in this context is a product of being filled with the Spirit. This singing may be in the singing of psalms; the Book of Psalms is our inspired hymnal. The Spirit-filled congregation shares in the singing of hymns—the praise of God in song. The glory of God is also manifested in singing spiritual songs, that is, songs in the Holy Spirit (cf. 1 Cor. 14.15).[55]

These manifestations of the Spirit's presence are appropriate to His person and work. He is the Spirit of love, communion, and fellowship. He joins believers in love, communion, and fellowship in Jesus Christ. He is the Spirit of prayer and praise. He must manifest His presence in the prayers and praise of the saints. The intercessory Spirit must intercede for us with groanings which cannot be uttered (Rom. 8.26). He comes to us in response to these activities of worship. His presence is cultivated by our continuing in worship.

---

[55] The expression 'spiritual songs' is designed to show the origin and character of the songs. They were songs given by the Holy Spirit and sung in the Spirit. Paul illustrates this meaning in 1 Cor. 14.15.

12

THE MORAL AND SPIRITUAL EVIDENCES OF BAPTISM WITH THE HOLY SPIRIT

In addition to the evidences of the Holy Spirit's presence that we have already noted, there are the evidences which relate directly to the nature of the Holy Spirit as divine person. Many of these points we have anticipated already. Here, however, we wish to relate them to the pursuit of holiness and to specify the pursuit of holiness as integral to a Holy Spirit-filled life and as necessary to salvation: 'Keep on pursuing peace with all, and holiness, apart from which no one shall see the Lord' (Heb. 12.14). To interpret Acts 1.8 as empowerment for witnessing without also emphasizing empowerment for godly living is to reduce the experience to insignificance.

Names and Functions of the Holy Spirit

The names and functions, which are ascribed to the Spirit of God emphasize His loftiness of character. He strives against the rebellion of humankind (Gen. 6.3) and convicts of sin (Jn 16.8-11). In the Old Testament He gave a new heart to Saul (1 Sam. 10.6-10) and indwells the new heart (Ezek. 36.26,27). In Jesus' discourse with Nicodemus, He is the agent of the new birth (John 11-13). The Holy Spirit rebukes sin (2 Chron. 24.20; Neh. 9.20; Jn 16.8-11). He teaches the will of God and leads believers in its fulfillment (Ps. 143.10; Lk. 12.11, 12; Jn 14.26; 1 Jn 2.27). He makes the Word of God known (Prov. 1.23; Ezek. 36.26, 27), and is the Revealer of the deep things of God (1 Cor. 2.9-12). He is the Agent of cleansing (Isa. 4.4; Tit. 3.5; Gal. 5.16-23).

We recognize the nature of the Spirit by the designations that are used of Him. Some of these names indicate His divine nature and His relationship to the Father and the Son: Spirit of God, Spirit of

Yahweh, Spirit of My Father, Spirit of Christ, and others. Other of His names emphasize His attributes and works: Spirit of wisdom, understanding, counsel, might, knowledge, the good Spirit, free Spirit, Holy Spirit, et al.

The sum of these considerations is that the Spirit by name and nature is the Spirit of God, who by nature is infinitely Holy. God is infinitely holy. His Spirit is infinitely holy. By nature and function, the Holy Spirit is the agent by whom the Word of God is given. The Word is the out-breathing of the Holy Spirit. What the law of God requires, it requires because it is expressive of the very nature of God. What the promise of God offers is also expressive of the very nature of God. The Holy Spirit as personal agent by whom this Word is given is also of the same nature in holiness and grace.

In application, these principles mean that the Holy Spirit accomplishes in those to whom He ministers the graces of His own nature. In terms of law, He accomplishes that which is required, which is the holiness of His own nature: 'That the righteousness of the law might be fulfilled in us, who walk not after the flesh, but after the Spirit' (Rom. 8.4). In terms of promise, He accomplishes the graces of love and mercy therein promised, which is the formation of His nature in us.

The Proclamation of the Kingdom and the Holy Spirit

These graces have a direct connection with the preaching of the kingdom of God by the authority of the Holy Spirit. In Jesus' ministry, He and His disciples proclaimed the kingdom of God. Authority for the proclamation was Jesus' presence and His commission. Jesus reigns in His proclamation. Since Jesus' ascension this proclamation occurs by the action of the Holy Spirit in the church. The authority for proclamation is the endowment with power by the Holy Spirit (Acts 1.8). Jesus reigns also in this proclamation by the agency and power of the Holy Spirit. The proclamation and its results are the manifestation of the kingdom.

The preaching of the kingdom makes certain ethical demands. In preparation for the coming of the King and the manifestation of the kingdom, paths must be cleared and straightened. This was enforced by the ethical demands made by John the Baptist in his proclamation. What he required in his preaching was inseparable from the kingdom, which he announced. The fundamental ethical demand of John's preaching was repentance. This message was extended in application to require evidence of repentance in terms of restitution, changed lives, and a repudiation of the old life. This message was proclaimed on the basis that One was coming who would baptize with the Holy Spirit.

The ministry of Jesus combined even more specifically the spiritual and ethical demands of the kingdom, which He proclaimed. We need no greater evidence for this claim than the Sermon on the Mount (Mt. 5-7). This message is the very fabric of the kingdom and its proclamation.

The Holy Spirit, as the gift of God for the last days, enforces the same union of spiritual and moral duty with the formation of the kingdom. If the Holy Spirit—the eschatological gift to the kingdom of God—is also present, we ought therefore to live in spiritual crisis: to live as those who stand in the presence of the coming glorious and holy King.

We conclude, then, that the preaching of the kingdom of God makes certain ethical demands. The presence of the Holy Spirit as the Agent of that proclamation and of the formation of the kingdom makes the same demands. It is impossible to claim participation in the kingdom, which is formed by the presence and ministry of the Holy Spirit without also accepting the dictation of His holiness, truth, and love.

The Conflict Between Flesh and Spirit

The graces that are expanded in Paul's listing of the fruit of the Spirit (Gal. 5.16-26) are the product of the presence of the Holy Spirit. It is the Spirit's work to implant these spiritual qualities in the experience of the new birth. It is His work to free us from the law of sin and death (Rom. 8.2) in sanctification, thus relieving the fruit of the Spirit from the hindrances of the Adamic nature. Baptism with the Holy Spirit gives added growth and fruitfulness to the fruit of the Spirit. These are the graces that show one's likeness to Christ by the infilling of the Holy Spirit: that show 'Christ in [us], the hope of glory' (Col. 1.27).

The exhortations that are contained in Gal. 5.16-26 will guide us in our examination of the moral and spiritual evidences of being filled with the Spirit.

Paul's first exhortation is 'be thou walking in the Spirit and the lusts of the flesh you will not fulfill' (Gal. 5.16). The phrase 'in the Spirit' refers to the person of the Holy Spirit. Its meaning is to walk in the character of the Spirit; that is, in harmony with His nature and by His graces and power. It is an essential and inevitable conclusion that such a walk forbids the fulfilling of the lusts of the flesh. There are two antagonists here: carnality and Spirit.[56] The antagonists are not the bodily character of the human and the Spirit of God or the material nature of the human and his/her immaterial (or spiritual) nature. The antagonists are the desires of carnality and the desires of the Holy Spirit. They lie opposite each other as enemies in battle.

The reason for this antagonism is that both flesh and Spirit are agents or principles of life. It is the life that is sought by each that is at enmity with the other. They are by nature enemies. One is of this world order and the other is of the order of the kingdom of God. The consequence is that there is a tension between the Spirit and the flesh in which each reacts to the other. It is not God's will that the believer should live in this tension. To be filled with the Spirit is to be delivered from the tension—to be made free from the law of sin and death (Rom. 8.1, 2).

As long as there is a governing element of the flesh there is conflict with the Holy Spirit. The flesh corrupts the desires and needs of the physical body. Carnality becomes the governing principle of life. So, it is carnality that wars against the Spirit not the physical body. The Spirit is a restraint to the works of the flesh, and the flesh is a hindrance to the works of the Spirit. These conditions hinder the believer so that she/he cannot do the things that she/he wishes to do. It is the clash which the Apostle describes in Rom. 7.23, 'But I see another law in my members, warring against the law of my mind, and bringing me into captivity to the law of sin which

---

[56] 'Flesh' as used here is not simply the body. The works that are listed in vv. 19-21 show that 'flesh' in this context is an evil thing. It is not simply bodily nature and desire. It is contrary to Scripture to say that being in a body bans one from spiritual living or is inimical to spirituality.

is in my members'. It is not God's will that the believer remain in this conflict.

To be led by the Holy Spirit is to deny carnality its way of life and satisfaction. Obedience to the Holy Spirit and denial of the flesh are achieved without being bound by the law: 'If you are being led by the Spirit you are not under law' (Gal. 5.18). The law does indeed describe the kind of life one should live, but to attempt to live that life in our own strength is a work of the flesh; it is carnal. The Spirit, on the other hand, leads us into that kind of life without a sense of bondage and condemnation.

The Works of the Flesh

In vv. 19-21, Paul describes the works of the flesh. The first group of sins (v. 19) are sins of the bodily appetites satisfied outside the law of God: fornication, moral (sexual) filth, and indecency (of language, bodily movements, and bodily contact).

The second grouping of sins of the flesh are perversions of worship: idolatry and witchcraft (v. 20). The latter word is related to the use of drugs to produce hallucinations, which were interpreted in terms of religious experience.

The last grouping of sins is the largest. These are those sins of excesses and perversions of the emotions of human nature: hatred, variance (i.e., contention, strife, wrangling), emulations (rivalry, jealousy, quarreling), wrath (rage, fury, boiling anger), strife (putting one's self forward, courting favor), seditions (division into parties on the basis of individualistic opinion), envy (covetousness), drunkenness, and revelry (carousing, orgy).

Paul concludes his listing with the phrase 'and such things'. He has not given (or attempted to give) a complete catalog of the sins of the flesh. He has given a representative list by which the character of 'flesh' may be recognized. If this list is understood, the flesh cannot be successful in its various disguises.

Paul's conclusion about these matters was well known in Galatia; he reminds them that he is repeating what he had said to them earlier: 'I am saying that which I have said that the ones who practice these things shall not inherit the kingdom of God' (v. 21). Paul warns that even though some had made a claim of inheriting the kingdom, their claim is invalid if they do these things.

In many Pentecostal and Charismatic circles we have come to the point that we overlook carnality (and in some cases immorality) because we sense an anointing on the person. We seem to think that this so-called anointing can override the compromises of character. The Scripture makes no such allowance. The Holy Spirit's character and presence will not tolerate such an adulteration of His holiness. The person that makes such excuses does so at the risk of damnation. The church that does so runs the risk of the removal of its candlestick by the Head of the church: 'He that hath an ear, let him hear what the Spirit saith unto the churches' (Rev. 2.7).

The Fruit of the Spirit

From his warning against the works of the flesh, the apostle moves on to list the fruit of the Spirit. Paul's choice of the word 'fruit' (rather than 'works') is significant. He wishes to say two things. First, it is fruit; these graces are born out of a seed—the seed of the new nature. He thus emphasizes that this fruit is the expected product of being born of the Spirit. Second, he wishes to say that this is the fruit of the Spirit and not the fruit of human efforts—not even the fruit of the renewed person. What fruit is born is born out of the indwelling of the person of the Holy Spirit.

Although, it may seem strange that Paul uses the singular 'fruit of the Spirit' and then proceeds to give a list of nine spiritual graces, his aim is oneness of the origin of this fruit; it is the Holy Spirit. The manifestation of the Holy Spirit's presence is one, though multifaceted. This fruit presents one image—Christ: It shows one root—the Holy Spirit.

The graces which are listed here deal with all of our relationships: to God, to society, and to ourselves. I do not choose to try to separate in outline form the graces into specific categories, because they all interconnect. All of these graces contribute to the wholeness of the redeemed persons in all their relationships.

Now we look at each of these graces and examine ourselves. The first grace is love. It is the epitome of the spiritual graces in 1 Cor. 13.13. It is the grace which unites believers, reconciling and knitting believers to one another (Col. 2.2). It is the capstone grace finishing off the perfect picture of all those graces listed in Col. 3.12-14. It is the grace which reaches around all the others binding them into perfect union (Col. 3.14). The character of love is defined by God's giving of Himself to us in the ultimate gift, His Son. It is God's will that this grace abound in believers. It is the work of the Holy Spirit to see that it does.

The grace of joy is consistently used in Scripture to relate to our joy in God and in the fact that we are united to Him. It is a sense of acceptance by God and of rejoicing in His favor. This also relates to the believer's relationship to others, manifesting itself in joyousness of life and receptivity to others and graciousness toward them. This is one of the petitions of our Lord in His prayer for our sanctification: 'And now I come to thee; and these things I speak in the world, that they might have my joy fulfilled in themselves' (Jn 17.13).

Peace is also a fundamentally God-related grace. It is especially the product of our forgiveness and justification. It is life in reconciliation. The ground of our enmity against God has been removed, and there is peace. This peace is radiated from the life of the Spirit-filled believer. It is then the ground of peace with others.

Long-suffering presupposes that there are provocations to anger. This grace triumphs over these provocations to bear them patiently, whether they are afflictions, abuses, tribulations, or persecutions. God's long-suffering with us in our disobedience, obstinacy, and disbelief is definitive of this grace and an example of it. The Holy Spirit wills that it should be implanted and flourish in us. God's patience with us lays on us the demand of our patience with our fellowman, especially with our brothers and sisters.

Gentleness is reflected toward us by God in leading us from impenitence and rebellion to repentance. It is the attitude of a gracious benefactor, even if there have been provocations by the beneficiary.

The term 'goodness' is related to one of the terms used to designate righteousness; hence, we take this to be a general statement of purity of morals and holiness of life. It carries with it the concept of kindness as well.

Faith is the grace by which we receive and rest upon Christ. It is also the grace by which we continue to live in Him (Rom. 1.16, 17). It is the grace by which the believer's life comes to its fulfillment; note Paul's series of questions in Gal. 3.1-5. This spiritual characteristic is linked with being full of the Holy Spirit (Stephen, Acts 6.5; Barnabas, Acts 11.23, 24). It is clear that faith is also

Barnabas, Acts 11.23, 24). It is clear that faith is also bound to obedience; hence, the expression the 'obedience of faith' (Rom. 1.5). The term, then, does have a specific ethical connotation.[57]

The basic ethical connotation is the moral obligation that all are morally obligated to believe on Jesus Christ. This ethical implication must also be applied to the obligation to obey God (cf. Jas 2.14-18).

Meekness is attributed to Christ, and it is exhorted by our Lord. It is the exemplary attitude when one sees another in a fault (Gal. 6.1) and when it is necessary to rebuke those who are in error (2 Tim. 2.25). This grace also represents an attitude toward oneself (Gal. 6.1). It represents mildness of manner and a subordinate attitude toward God. Such an attitude compels one to considerateness even when it is necessary to exercise discipline and to rebuke another (2 Cor. 10.1).

Temperance refers to the mastery of one's desires. The believer is to rule them; they are not to rule the believer. This grace refers especially to control of one's physical appetites. An important aspect of this grace is that it stands in control of that which is allowable. It is not a prohibiting standard, but a standard by which one regulates desires in the interest of obedience to God and one's own spiritual well-being. Temperance in this context is not simply the product of self discipline and moderation. It is the fruit of the Spirit. The Spirit's presence and filling are the origin and cultivation of this grace.

This list of graces is not an exhaustive list; it is exemplary and suggestive. To know these things is to be able to identify spiritual living—the fruit of the Spirit. Paul says of this fruit, 'Concerning such things as these there is no law' (v. 23). These cannot be prescribed and produced by a legal code. It would be a mistake, a radical mistake, to try to transfer this list of graces into a set of regulations by which one could achieve righteousness.

---

[57] Some scholars take this reference to faith to be referring entirely to the ethical relationship of good faith or integrity in dealing with others: 'It is clear from the subordinate place here assigned to πίστις that it does not here denote the cardinal grace of faith in God, but rather good faith in dealings with men, and due regard for their just claims' (F. Rendall, "The Epistle of Paul to the Galatians", in *The Expositor's Greek Testament*, III, p. 188). This seems to be a weak basis of exegesis in the light or the basic meaning and application of the word πίστις. This view is further weakened by the fact that moral integrity is conveyed in other graces listed here.

On the other hand, the one who is cultivating and practicing these things by the indwelling presence of the Holy Spirit is not under the law. This person is not subject to the condemnation of the law and yet he/she is in harmony with the holiness and purposes of the law.

In vv. 24-26, Paul gives fundamental relationships of the Holy Spirit-filled life. The first of these relationships is our relationship to the flesh. Those that are Christ's have crucified the flesh with its passions and lusts (v. 24). It is a fact of our commitment to Christ that we have also committed our carnality (not this physical body as such, but the sinful control of it) to Christ's cross. It is His work and the Holy Spirit's to accomplish the redemptive act of crucifixion and cleansing.

The second relationship is with the Holy Spirit—to be walking in Him: 'If [as it is true, according to Paul's presupposition] we are living in the Spirit, let us also be walking in the Spirit' (v. 25). To walk in the Spirit is to live in harmony with the nature of His righteousness and holiness. The words 'to walk' that are used here mean to walk in a row or to walk in the steps of another: hence, the application: 'Let us walk in the nature and in the steps of the Spirit'.

The third relationship is with one another: 'Let us not become vainglorious, challenging one another and envying one another' (v. 26). The ambition for glory is the key to this exhortation. Vainglory creates that sort of contention for praise that provokes imitation in the body of Christ. In such a climate the coming of glory to one member provokes covetousness of that glory in others. Envy is inseparable from vainglory. A Holy Spirit-filled body is the only answer to this problem.

Since He is the Spirit of Christ, the Holy Spirit's will and work is to produce Christ's nature in us. As our Lord explained the graces of holy living—the graces of His own godliness—it became more and more evident that the Holy Spirit's ministry was essential to the church's existence and victory. The Pharisees had shown what happens when people attempt to achieve spiritual excellence without the Spirit of God.

This Holy Spirit is the Spirit of grace and the Implanter of grace in believers. He is the Spirit of all the graces, which belong to the nature of Christ. Their presence is witness of His presence. The prime evidence of a Holy Spirit-filled life is the visibility of Christ in the believer. It is the work of baptism with the Holy Spirit to cultivate these evidences.

13

The Unity of the Body of Christ and Life in the Spirit

The heart of our consideration of this subject is 1 Corinthians 12. Three observations are appropriate. First, too much theological jargon and too many so-called technical terms have been developed out of this chapter. The words of the Apostle Paul in this letter were easily understood by the people at Corinth. We should not attempt to make technical terms of this language unless usage can demonstrate that this is the intention of the author.

Second, we should not take contemporary jargon and read it back into the original and call that exegesis. The problem is that we often make our own definitions of our language/vocabulary and impose that on the first century text.

Third, and most important, it is the aim of the Holy Spirit to produce unity in the body of Christ—the fellowship of believers. This unity is achieved by living in the Holy Spirit. This is true for individual members of the body; that is, they must have a sense of union with other members of the body and of submission one to another in the body of Christ. Paul lists three manifestations of being filled with the Spirit in Eph. 5.18-21: (1) communing with one another in psalms, hymns and songs in the Spirit, (2) thanksgiving and (3) submission one to another. An attribute of humility toward our brothers and sisters in Christ is a quality of life in the Spirit.

All of these are community relationships. They are spiritual qualities; that is, they are out of and like the Holy Spirit. They are social qualities; that is, they are in the pattern of the sociality in the Holy Trinity which is the biblical pattern of all of redemptive society. By the Holy Spirit and by union in the body of Christ the church is to fulfill a social order patterned after the Trinitarian community.

The unity which is manifested in individuals is also a mark of the body of Christ corporately. So we are not just talking about an individual's life in the Spirit. We are urging that life in the corporate body of Christ must be life in the Spirit. This is the message of 1 Corinthians 12. Paul shows this by two major themes in this chapter: (1) the unity of the baptizing and ministering Spirit and (2) the unity of the body into which we have been baptized.

The Unity of the Baptizing and Ministering Spirit

The first witness of the Holy Spirit to the unity of the body is that He bears but one testimony. Paul represents this witness in a confessional form which makes a negative and positive declaration. Negatively, no one who speaks in or by the Holy Spirit can speak of Christ as accursed (v. 3).[58] The Holy Spirit can, in this connection, witness but one thing, and that is that Jesus Christ is blessed of God and not cursed. Any witness to the contrary is not from the Spirit of God.

Positively, the confession, 'Jesus is Lord' is the witness of the Holy Spirit. No one can make this confession as a saving confession unless he/she is so moved by the Holy Spirit (v. 3). This confession is probably the citation of an ancient Christian confession, perhaps the oldest creedal confession of record in the Christian church (cf. Rom. 10.9; Phil. 2.11). To make this confession is to speak by the power of the Holy Spirit, and it is to be in the body of Christ.

This testimony is unique for two reasons. First, it is unique because it is out of the Holy Spirit. This is His unique function in the world (Jn 15.26, 27; 16.7-15). Second, it is unique to the church. Only those who speak by the Holy Spirit can give this witness. Our Lord assured the Apostle Peter that his 'Great Confession' had been given to him by divine revelation (Mt. 16.13-20).

---

[58] It may seem difficult to comprehend why Paul would even suggest that any would presume to say that Jesus is accursed. However, there were (and are) religious systems which go under the name of Christian that do just that. Any confession that denies the bodily resurrection of Jesus Christ our Lord says that He is accursed. Such is a claim that Jesus died under the judgment of God for sin and that He is still under that curse. Sometimes these systems attempt to distinguish between the body of the crucifixion and the body of the resurrection. Other of these theological positions teaches that the body of the crucifixion was physical and the body of the resurrection was spirit. These systems of doctrine call Jesus accursed.

The ministries of the Holy Spirit contribute to and are essential to the unity of Christ's body. These ministries are described here by Paul by varying terms. The Apostle uses three terms: gifts (χα-´ρισμα, v. 4), administrations (ministries, helps, διακονία, v. 5) and operations (workings, ἐνέργημα, v. 6). There are several points which are common to all of these. First, they are diverse: the ministries of the Holy Spirit are many. Second, these ministries are from the same Source: referred to under the divine designations God, Lord and Spirit. This emphasis on oneness (and unity) runs throughout vv. 4-7. The recurring theme is 'the same Spirit', 'the same Lord' and 'the same God'. By these designations Paul shows the unity of the Holy Trinity in the diversity and distribution of spiritual gifts. Third, they are designated as manifestations of the Spirit (v. 7). These things make the person and presence of the Holy Spirit evident. Fourth, these ministries are gifts given by the sovereign and divine Holy Spirit.

The essential character of a gift is that it is distributed by the authority of the giver; so gifts are always unearned and undeserved. To create a scale of piety for receiving a spiritual gift destroys its quality as a gift. To create a series of steps for the achievement of a gift also destroys its quality as a gift.

The fourth point is especially the claim of v. 7. The manifestations of the Spirit is bestowed on believers and manifested in their lives by the Person and presence of the Spirit of God. Believers do not by works of virtue earn or have a right to these ministries. Neither do they dictate to the Giver the manner in which His gifts are distributed. The Spirit does place these gifts in the ministries of individuals in the body of Christ for ministry to and for the entire spiritual body. The words 'profit withal' show that the aim of the Holy Spirit is to provide for the well being of the body of Christ.

Though fulfilled in individual ministries, the manifestations (ministries) of the Holy Spirit are in, through and unto the body of Christ. To serve this end the ministries must be varied—as varied as the needs of the church and all humankind. The ministries are individually designated.[59] They are listed in vv. 8, 9.

---

[59] The word χαρίσματα (viz., charismatic gifts) is used in this list (vv. 8, 9) only of the gifts of healing. We should not make this word a technical term as if it by nature referred to the ministries of the Holy Spirit. The nature of this term should be understood. It is related to the Greek word χάρις which carries the

The different kinds of ministries of the Spirit are illustrated by the list which Paul gives in vv. 8-10. Two are special enablements of the mind: the word of knowledge and the word of wisdom (v. 8).

---

ideas of pleasantness, beauty, goodwill, favor and favor upon one who does not deserve favor; hence the New Testament uses the term in the sense of grace or undeserved favor. Paul argues consistently that the idea of grace excludes any appeal to works or merit (Rom. 11.5, 6). The word χάρις is much richer than this, but our purpose is to show that it is the basis of our word charisma (χαρίσ-ματα).

Charisma may be translated as 'gift'. It is translated in that way in the KJV in the following places, and with the accompanying uses. Paul wished to impart some 'spiritual gift' (χάρισμα...πνευματικὸν) to the Roman believers (Rom. 1.11). This word is equated with the gift of salvation throughout Paul's explication of salvation by grace in Rom. 5.15, 16; 6.23. It is used of the 'gifts (χαρίσ-ματα) and callings of God' which are irrevocable (Rom. 11.29). It is used of the diverse ministries in the body of Christ in Rom. 12.6. Here these ministries are specifically designated as the 'gifts which are according to the grace given you'. This designation is followed by a list of ministries which are properly 'gifts according to grace': prophecy, ministering (διακονία), teaching, exhortation, giving, rulership and showing mercy. Those who function in these roles are all treated as members of the body of Christ (Rom. 12.4-8). In several points this list parallels Paul's discussion in 1 Corinthians 12-14. Paul wishes that the Corinthians not be deficient in any gift as they wait for 'the revelation of our Lord Jesus Christ' (1 Cor. 1.7). Paul uses the tem 'gift of God' (χάρισμα ἐκ θεοῦ) in relation to the ability to perform ministry under varying personal circumstances (1 Cor. 7.7). Paul used the term 'gift' as a bestowal upon him 'by many persons' apparently referring to a monetary gift given him by the churches for his ongoing ministry. The Apostle uses the term as a designation of the ministry placed upon Timothy 'through prophecy by the laying on of the hands of the presbytery' (1 Tim. 4.14). Timothy was also urged 'to rekindle the gift of God (τὸ χάρισμα τοῦ θεοῦ) which is in you through the laying on of my hands' (2 Tim. 1.6). This word is used of the gift by which each one ministers to others in the body of Christ (1 Pet. 4.10).

The above information may be summarized in the following points: (1) The heart of the idea of the gifts of God (whether the ministries of the Holy Spirit or any other gifts) is the doctrine of grace. The bestowal of gifts is a benefit from God which none deserves. (2) The term 'gifts' is appropriately used of the ministries of the Holy Spirit in the body of Christ. (3) It is used of specific gifts from one individual to another. (4) It is used in parallel with the covenant calling of God.

This awareness helps us in the use of the term χάρισμα in 1 Cor. 12.9, 23, 30, 31. In vv. 9, 28 and 30 Paul uses the term in relation to healing—gifts of healing. In v. 31 he uses more general language and seems to question whether the Corinthians are seeking the 'best gifts'. He does not use this term in 1 Corinthians 13 and 14. However, by comparing 1 Corinthians 14 with Rom. 12.4-8 we learn that the ministries (prophecy, exhortation etc.) may indeed be called 'gifts'. This kind of generalization shows us that the word χάρις (χαρίσματα) is not a formal (or technical) word for the ministries of the Spirit. It shows us that these ministries of the Holy Spirit are bestowed out of the grace of God and they are given by His authority.

There is no clear indication that these enablements imply miraculously revealed facts. Knowledge and wisdom are treated as spiritual graces and endowments by God. Some ministers are especially privileged to be ministers of knowledge and wisdom in the body of Christ. Paul explains in 1 Cor. 14.6 that he may speak to them 'either in a revelation, or in knowledge, or in prophecy, or in teaching'. The phrase 'in knowledge' perhaps interprets for us the meaning of 'the word of knowledge'. It is a ministry of the Spirit to communicate knowledge to the church. We may then say the same for the 'word of wisdom'. These two ministries impart to the body of Christ wisdom and knowledge not immediately available by research or study. Our Lord predicted at least one example of the manner in which such a gift would operate. He promised that, in times of persecution and accusation before the synagogues and magistrates, 'the Holy Spirit will teach you in that same hour what you ought to say' (Lk. 12.11, 12). This example is instructive for us concerning the manner in which the word of knowledge and the word of wisdom can be used of the Holy Spirit.

The third ministry here is faith. This ministry is not elaborated on in other parts of Scripture, at least not using this terminology. The use of the term 'faith' and the benefits of faith aid us in the understanding of this text. Faith is the instrument of grace by which all the benefits of Christ are offered. These benefits include the gift of salvation, the walk in Christ and the claim of special benefits such as healing, deliverance and the supply of needs. We may judge, then, that the ministry of faith is a special ministration of this powerful grace in and for the church. Some believers seem to be especially gifted to believe when other members of the body find it most difficult. They are the Holy Spirit's ministers to those who are in a struggle to believe.

The next two ministries which are listed relate to special manifestations of power in the physical world: the gifts (χαρίσματα) of healings and the working of miracles (vv. 9, 10, 28). The plural in the phrase 'gifts of healings' (vv. 3, 28) is interesting. It is probably used here because of the plurality of the manifestations of this benefit of grace. It is clear that this benefit is intended to minister to people who are physically infirm; this is not unusual in the New Testament, and God does not intend that it be unusual in the church in any age, including our own. James clearly gives instruction on one way in which physical healing is ministered in the New Testament (Jas 5.14-16). God has provided for physical healing by direct divine intervention.[60]

The working of miracles is also a special ministry of the Holy Spirit in physical and natural matters.[61] This ministry may involve physical healings, but it includes much more. In Jesus' ministry physical things were affected by His power (wind, sea, water, fig trees, etc.). The Holy Spirit still ministers in these areas by His gifts. This ministry is appropriately designated as the 'working of miracles'. One of the recurring phrases in the book of Acts is the phrase 'signs and miracles'.[62] Peter noted that the ministry of Jesus was marked by miracles and wonders (δυνάμεσι καὶ τέρασι καὶ σημείοις: Acts 2.22). Wonders and signs (τέρατα καὶ σημεῖα)

---

[60] Some expositors attempt to turn the ministry of healing to emotional and spiritual healing and even psychosomatic healing. They avoid the expectation that God provides physical healing in the atonement. The attempt to read this text as referring to spiritual healing alone makes a mockery of the language of the text. Christ's ministry of healing included physical healing. In Mt. 8.17 Matthew cites Isa. 53.4 as fulfilled in physical healings in the ministry of our Lord. The LXX had translated this text in such a way as to mean the healing of spiritual infirmity, but Matthew cites the original text; his translation is based on the original Hebrew text and not on the LXX. As Matthew cites the text he clearly shows that the healings predicted by Isaiah and fulfilled by Jesus were deliverances from physical infirmity.

It is not true to the language of Scripture to separate healings into two categories: one spiritual and the other physical. Christ's ministry involved healing in its wholeness which delivered the afflicted from all sorts of infirmities (Ps. 103.3; Jas 5.13-16). His ministry is the paradigm for the ministry of the church in the power of the Holy Spirit. On the theological issue whether healing is provided in the atonement, we note that Isaiah 53 is an atonement chapter; so v. 4 clearly placed healing in the atonement. To take healing out of the atonement theologically destroys much of the meaning of the chapter. What other source for the benefits of grace is there other than the atonement? It is a choice between grace and merit. Atonement places healing under grace.

[61] The word δύναμις is variously translated: power, ability, virtue (viz. Mk 5.30; Lk. 6.19), strength, might, mighty deeds, miracles (Mt. 7.22; 11.20, 21, 23; 13.54, 58; 14.2; Mk 6.2, 5; 9.39; Lk. 10.13; 19.37; Acts 2.22; 8.13; 19.11; 1 Cor. 12.10, 28, 29; 2 Cor. 12.12; Gal. 3.5; Heb. 2.4). The contexts in these cases shows that the predominant use of this word is to describe extraordinary divine actions in the physical realm. This seems to be the meaning in this passage as well. So 'miracles' is an appropriate translation of the Greek word. It certainly does also apply to miracles of healing.

[62] This phrase appears in the earliest records of the Old Testament in describing divine intervention for Israel. So the New Testament community was prepared to understand the meaning of this kind of language to explain God's mighty acts in the physical world.

marked the ministry of the Apostles (Acts 2.43). The body of believers with whom Peter and John prayed following the threats of
the Jewish court prayed that God would stretch forth His Hand (an
Old Testament metaphor referring to the Holy Spirit) 'to heal and
that signs and wonders (σημεῖα καὶ τέρατα) may be done in the
name of thy holy Child Jesus' (Acts 4.23-30). Acts 5.12 notes that
many signs and wonders (σημεῖα καὶ τέρατα) were accomplished
in the ministry of the Apostles. The same evidences (τέρατα καὶ
σημεῖα) accompanied the ministry of Stephen, showing that these
miracles were not limited to the ministry of the Apostles (Acts 6.8).
Stephen recalled that Moses 'showed wonders and signs (τέρατα
καὶ σημεῖα) in the land of Egypt' (Acts 7.36). The Lord granted
grace that signs and wonders (σημεῖα καὶ τέρατα) were done in
the ministry of Paul and Barnabas (Acts 14.3; 15.12). In Joel's Pentecost prophecy he uses the single word σημεῖα (sign) to mark the
outpouring of the Holy Spirit (Acts 2.19). This word is used of the
healing of the paralytic at the temple (Acts 4.16, 22), and it is used
of the miracles in the ministry of Philip at Samaria (Acts 8.6).

The remaining four ministries in this list are 'word ministries' of
the Holy Spirit; that is they are ministries of speech or communication: prophecy, discernments of spirits (διακρίσεις the ability to
discriminate), 'different kinds of tongues', and the interpretation of
tongues (v. 10). These ministries and their interaction with each
other are more extensively dealt with in 1 Corinthians 14. We will
look at them in the next chapter of this study.

Paul concludes the listing of these ministries of the Holy Spirit
with another statement of their unity. These are all the works of 'the
one and self-same Spirit (v. 11). The Holy Spirit is also the Sovereign over the distribution of these ministries in the body. He 'di-
vides to each one as He wishes' (v. 11). These are gifts of grace
from the Holy Spirit. Distribution is according to His will, not the
will of the seeker, or the church, or any special group in the church.

It is also clear from this verse (v. 11) that these ministries rest
upon and are exercised by individuals in the body of Christ. This
does not deny that these ministries are given to the church. They
are given to the church by their being placed upon individuals who
are ministers in and of the body: i.e., the church. The distribution
which the Holy Spirit makes is wise and proportionate. The Apostle
explains the proportioning in terms of the members of the body

(vv. 12-25; Rom. 12.3-8). This distribution shows that diversity is not a violation of unity, but is vital to it. Diversity and unity in the body are mutually supportive. The Holy Spirit fulfills this unity in His witness and ministries.

The Unity of the Body into Which We are Baptized

Verse 12 introduces the subject of the body of Christ. This is Paul's application of vv. 1-11 to the ministry that is to take place in the church. Christ is the Center and Pattern of the unity that is to be seen in the body. It is essentially a spiritual unity—a unity which exists in the body because of its union with the Head, Christ. This unity is accomplished by a baptism which is administered by the Person of the Holy Spirit (v. 13). A series of statements emphasizes this unity. This baptism is by one Spirit. We are baptized into one body. We are made to drink of one Spirit. Life in the Spirit begins with this baptism.[63]

This common experience of baptism provides for and enforces the unity of the body of Christ. This is the spiritual experience of entering into the body of Christ so that what has happened to Him as Redeemer happens to the believer as redeemed. Paul's explanation of this experience is in Rom. 6.1-10. It is baptism into the

---

[63] This baptism should be distinguished from baptism with the Holy Spirit. The baptism that is here described is into the body of Christ (cf. Rom. 6.3-5; Gal. 3.27, 28). The personal Agent who administers this baptism is the Holy Spirit. The element into which one is baptized is Christ: His death, burial and resurrection.

In baptism with the Holy Spirit the element into which we are baptized is the Holy Spirit. The personal Agent who administers this baptism is the Messiah (Mt. 3.11; Mk 1.8; Lk. 1.16; Jn 1.33).

These are distinct baptisms, both spiritual in nature. They are different in the element of baptism. They are different in Agents of baptism. These baptisms are also distinct from water baptism. John distinguished the baptism with which he baptized from the baptism with which the Messiah would baptize—baptism with the Spirit. This distinction was maintained consistently in the book of Acts. Water baptism preceded in time the outpouring of the Holy Spirit on the Samaritans (Acts 8.12-17). The Holy Spirit fell upon Cornelius and his household while Peter was preaching to them; afterward they were baptized in water (Acts 10.44-48). At Ephesus Paul baptized the believers in water (Acts 19.5). Subsequently, Paul laid his hands on them, and the Holy Spirit came upon them (Acts 19.6).

Water baptism may be distinguished from spiritual baptism. First, water baptism is administered by a human agent. Second the element of baptism is a physical, temporal element. Third, it is sacramental in nature. Finally, it is fallibly administered; that is, the act of baptism does not save.

death of Christ (Rom. 6.3). It is burial with Christ (v. 4), and it is resurrection with Him (v. 4). As the resurrection life for Christ follows His death, burial and resurrection, our newness of life follows our dying with Him, being buried with and in Him and being raised up to newness of life with and in Him (v. 4). All of this is drawn out of the fact that in Christ our 'old man' was crucified in redemptive provision (vv. 5, 6). It is in our faith that we walk in this newness of life.

In application, Paul enforces the unity of the body of Christ against all human barriers. Racial and former religious schisms are broken down. There is neither Jew nor Greek in the body of Christ (1 Cor. 12.13). Social and economic barriers are destroyed because there are no bond servants or free people in the body of Christ. Though these social, economic and racial barriers may continue to exist in society at large, they must not exist in the body of Christ. In our own day the church cannot afford such distinctions as educated and uneducated, white and black, cultured and uncultured, male and female (Gal. 3.28), better society and lower society. These are not spiritual measures and distinctions; they are carnal (1 Cor. 3.1-4).

Through this common experience of baptism, God establishes an organic union of members of the body. The unity of Christ's body is that of a living organism and not that of mechanical organization.

An organization is unified around various elements. It may be unified by its instrument of organization: its constitution or bylaws. It may be unified around its structure of government: its offices. Inspirationally, it may be unified around its officers. Its center of unity may be a common cause. None of these centers of unity affects the nature of the people who are drawn into the organization.[64]

An organism is unified by its source of life. It is cellular in nature and structure; its cells are joined to each other in the life flow of the organism. This is demonstrated in the human body. There is one life flow throughout the body; this life flow provides the necessities

---

[64] What is said here implies nothing negative about church government and denominational organization. However, it is a warning; we cannot do with church organization what God intends to do in the organism of the body of Christ. If we try, we will miss the purpose of God in the body of Christ. Our efforts will become schismatic and excluding.

of the body (nutrition, oxygen, even life itself) and gives the members the power to function.

Division and malfunction in an organism are far more damaging to the organism than division in an organization. Division in an organization creates rough running machinery, and it may retard the achievement of purpose. It may even bring about a breakdown, but that is the worst that can happen. Division in an organism creates disease and damages the health of the body. The worst that can happen here is drastic—the death of the body.

The applications of this analogy to the body of Christ are important. The single life source of the body of Christ is Christ who is Head of the body. This body lives because of and by the flow of His life from cell to cell—from member to member. In and by this common life source each member is joined to all other members. Each one draws life from the others, and each contributes life to the others. Disease in one member is corrupting to all the body and each of its members. Severance of one member is painful and traumatic to the entire body.

On the other hand, all these applications may be turned positively. In health and in the free flow of life each member contributes to the health and strength of all other members of the body. Each member of the body of Christ has a spiritual obligation to contribute to the health of the whole body.

In vv. 14-26 Paul makes some obvious simplistic statements about the human body in order to teach important lessons about the body of Christ. No member of the body can deny that it is a member of the body simply because it does not do or cannot do what another member of the body does: 'If the foot should say, because I am not the hand, I am not of the body, is it therefore not of the body?' (v. 15). How could the body function if it were only an eye (v. 17)? The same could be asked of any function. God established each member and its functions when He made the body (v. 18).

God has made the members of the body interdependent. Exactly as the eye cannot claim to be the whole body, it is dependent on other members such as ears, hands and feet (v. 21). God has added another dimension of this dependency. Members of the body which we regard as weak God has made necessary (v. 22). Those members of the body which we regard as less attractive (such as internal organs) God has given a more necessary function in the health of the body. To the more attractive members (such as the outwardly attractive members) God has given less necessity (vv. 23-25). God did this to provide for the full and balanced operations of the body.

In v. 16 Paul shows the unity of the body by the mutual sensitivity of the members of the body: 'If one member suffers, all the members suffer together; if one member is exalted, all the members rejoice together'. It is impossible to separate the well-being and pleasures of one member of the body from the entire body and of all members in particular.

These are obvious lessons from the human body. We must learn them and apply them in relation to the spiritual body. God has established different ministries in the church and He has given to each believer a membership function: 'You are the body of Christ and members individually' (v. 27). By this statement Paul applies all that he has said of the human body (vv. 14-26) to the church.

Function in the body of Christ is set by God; this is a sovereign appointment. It is also an appointment in grace. There is a representative list (though not a complete list) of these functions in v. 28: 'In the first place apostles, in the second place prophets, in the third place teachers, next miracle workers, next gifts of healings, helpers, leaders [helmsmen; governors], kinds of tongues'.

By his designations 'first...second...third...next...', the Apostle definitely established an order of placement in the body. He has also shown that these functions are distinct from each other. The clear indication is that each should fulfill its own function and be content in that ministry (cf. Rom. 12.3-8). Paul enforces this conclusion with the series of questions in vv. 29, 30. These are all rhetorical questions, and they anticipate a negative answer. The answer is, 'No'. All are not apostles; all are not prophets; all are not teachers. This answer is applicable to all the questions raised here.[65]

---

[65] One of the questions in this series is, 'do all speak in tongues?' The answer is still, 'No'. Does this contradict the Pentecostal emphasis on speaking in tongues in personal devotions and as evidence of baptism with the Holy Spirit? Many scholars feel that it does, but that answer takes the question out of context. The context of this question is asking, 'Do all speak with tongues as a ministry function in and to the rest of the body of Christ?' Clearly they do not, exactly as all are not prophets, teachers, etc. In 1 Cor. 14.5 Paul says, 'I wish that all of you spoke with tongues'. Here he clearly intends tongues to refer to personal edification. So a negative answer to this rhetorical question is not inimical to Pentecostal teaching.

It is appropriate that we relate the ministries of the Holy Spirit to the analogy of the body. Paul has laid the foundation for this in vv. 14-26. The ministries of he Holy Spirit (both the gift and the gift receivers) are dependent on each other. All members of the body of Christ must respect all other ministries that God has placed in the church. God has placed the variety of functions in the body in order to provide for the full equipment and health of the whole body, the church.

These concepts govern the attitude of the ministries to each other. There are other attitudes necessary for the body to have toward its ministries. The church must not bestow an inappropriate honor upon any gift or gift-bearer in the body. God calls individuals to specific functions, places on them appropriate gifts for their ministry and ordains them (i.e. appoints them in the body). These gifts of ministry are given by the grace of God. They do not represent merit and achievement on the part of the minister. The exercise of a gift or gifts is not a mark of superior spirituality. It is a mark of the grace of God in that He gives ministers the privilege of being instruments of His work in the church and in the world.

The church must not exalt the glamorous and dramatic gifts and despise the less glamorous. God has established greater honor on the 'uncomely parts' by way of their greater need in the body. He has established less honor on the 'comely parts' (vv. 23, 24). These so-called comely parts are gifts of the Holy Spirit that may be spectacular in operation, such as the working of miracles or the gifts of healings. There are gifts which are not so spectacular ('uncomely') such as a word of knowledge, or a word of wisdom or discernment. God has adjusted these to each other in order to provide all the needs of the body and to avoid carnal division in the body.

At the conclusion of all that he has said Paul raises a final rhetorical question: 'But are you seeking the best spiritual gifts?' (v. 31a).[66] The expected answer is, 'No'. It is clear from tenor of this

---

[66] The KJV and most other translations treat this text as an imperative and translate it, 'But covet earnestly the best gifts'. This is the translation which this author followed in the first edition of this volume. *I no longer feel that this is the correct translation.* The original Greek uses a verb form that can be an imperative verb (as in the KJV) or an indicative interrogative verb. I have chosen to translate this sentence as a rhetorical question expecting a negative answer. 'But are you seeking the best gifts? No, you are not.' This translation makes this sentence consistent with the language of vv. 29, 30. The questions in those verses are all rhetori-

166 *Living in the Spirit*

entire book and from what Paul says in chapters 13 and 14 that the Corinthians had distorted the body of Christ by their carnal attitudes toward individual ministers and particular forms of the ministry gifts of the Holy Spirit.

It is appropriate that members of the body of Christ seek to be used of God in the gifts and ministries of the Holy Spirit. Passivity in this matter is not acceptable, and it is not healthy for the body of Christ. So, this text translated as a rhetorical question expecting a negative answer also shows that it is right to seek to be used of God in spiritual ministries.

In his concluding statement 'and yet show I unto you a more excellent way' Paul offers a kind and spiritual rebuke of the Corinthian believers. This statement catches up all that he has already said about ministries, ministers and gifts. Paul is saying to them, 'There is a better way to minister, and this is what I have laid out for you'. He is also anticipating the impact of love (chapter 13) and order (chapter 14) on the proper exercise of spiritual gifts.

---

cal questions expecting a negative answer. I see this verse as the climax of a series of rhetorical questions. It shows that the Corinthian believers had misplaced their values and they were not seeking the best gifts, but were elevating the spectacular above the quiet and unostentatious manifestations of the Holy Spirit.

The following is a quotation of the final paragraph for this chapter as it appeared in the first edition of this work. 'At the conclusion of all that he has said about spiritual gifts, Paul gives the exhortation, "Be thou seeking the higher gifts" (v. 31). Two observations may be drawn from this exhortation. First, a passive attitude toward the exercise of the gifts of the Holy Spirit is not God's will. We are to seek to exercise spiritual ministries in the body of Christ. Second, we are to seek those gifts which are greater—that is, those which serve the needs of the body in the best way.'

It is the author's hope that the reader will see that the translation chosen in the current edition offers the better understanding of 1 Cor. 12.31.

14

TONGUES AND PROPHECY

Tongues, interpretation and prophecy dominate the considerations of 1 Corinthians 14. Other ministries are discussed in their relationship to the body of Christ in 1 Corinthians 12. The transitional material between these two is 1 Corinthians 13. The content and position of this chapter shows how these ministries ought to operate; love must be the dominant spiritual grace in the relationship of all ministers and ministries in the body of Christ. If the Corinthian believers had allowed love to hold sway over their operations as it is described in chapter 13, the difficulties that are discussed in 1 Corinthians 12 and 14 would not have arisen.

From the attention given to the issues of speaking in tongues and prophesying, it appears that these were the primary areas of conflict and disorder among the Corinthian believers.

Putting the Issues in Perspective

'Pursue love' (1 Cor. 14.1a) is the exhortation that places the operation of spiritual gifts in perspective with spiritual graces such as faith, hope and love. These graces show our likeness to Jesus Christ; this is fundamental to our exercise of spiritual gifts. The exhortation above precedes and supercedes the seeking of spiritual gifts.

This is an important understanding. The first perspective necessary is that spiritual gifts serve temporal needs; spiritual graces are eternal in origin, in need and in quality. The temporal nature of spiritual gifts is related to the fact that they minister to the needs of believers and the world in this world order. These gifts serve believers while they are on their way to the perfect. When the perfect has come in its full glory, the need for these spiritual gifts will have ceased (1 Cor. 13.10). The development of such graces as faith, hope and love is for eternity (1 Cor. 13.8-13).

The second perspective that is necessary here is the functions of tongues and prophecy in relation to ministry. Tongues serve for the personal edification of the believer who speaks in tongues: 'For the one who speaks in tongues, he is not speaking to men but to God' (1 Cor. 14.2).[67]

These instructions cannot reasonably be taken as a denigration of speaking in tongues. Paul is clear. Speaking in tongues is proper, and it is of the Holy Spirit. It is not uncontrolled enthusiasm, and it is not satanic in origin. However, tongues speech as it is being discussed here cannot be understood by the people who speak it and hear it without a divinely given interpretation: 'In the Spirit he is speaking mysteries' (v. 2). This is a mystical experience which is inspired by the Holy Spirit and in which God is being glorified. Such a ministry, however, cannot edify others. The one who is speaking in tongues is 'building up' (edifying) himself/herself (v. 4). His/her understanding and the understanding of the church is unfruitful (v. 14).

Prophecy stands in contrast to speaking in tongues because it is addressed to the people in the language which they understand. It ministers immediately. Prophecy and proclamation/preaching (κηρυγμα) are not the same, though their functions may overlap. We are using the term 'prophecy' here as a ministry of the Holy Spirit in the body of Christ. Paul has explained its place in the body and the place of the prophet in relation to other offices of the church in 1 Corinthians 12. Now he is explaining the exercise of this ministry in the worship of the congregation.[68]

1 Corinthians 14.3 names three specific purposes of prophecy: edification, exhortation and comfort. For clarification we may sub-

---

[67] There are those who would limit speaking in tongues to a miracle by which one speaks in an identifiable human/world language. Some of them further assert that the purpose of such a divine act is to witness to people who could not otherwise be reached because of language barriers. This is clearly not the case here. The person whom Paul is describing here is not by intention (either of the Holy Spirit or the believer) speaking to other people. In fact this language cannot communicate with other people without divine interpretation. This is not the case with all tongues speech (note Acts 2.4-11).

[68] There were ministers in the early Christian church who were identified as prophets (Acts 11.27, 28; Agabus is named among them). On occasion they gave predictions of things to come (Acts 11.28; 21.10, 11). Women were among those who ministered in prophecy (Acts 21.8, 9; 1 Cor. 11.5). Prophets ministered in calling and appointing others to the ministries of the church (Acts 13.1-3; 1 Tim. 1.18).

stitute synonyms: building up, encouragement and persuasion. These are all positive functions. There are places in Scripture where the Holy Spirit revealed secret sin and announced divine judgment (viz., Ananias and Sapphira, Acts 5.1-11). In the incident of Ananias and Sapphira, the Scripture record does not designate the spiritual gift(s) that operated in this revelation. It certainly could have been a prophetic word, or it could have been a word of revelation; the two are not mutually exclusive. Later in this chapter Paul notes that the ministry of prophecy, with the discernment of the rest of the body of Christ, brings judgment and the secrets of the heart are revealed (vv. 24, 25).[69]

These observations do not take away from the fact that Paul is concerned that the ministry of prophecy be an instrument of spiritual cultivation by edification, exhortation and comfort. This purpose is emphasized by Paul's statement, 'The one who prophesies builds up the church' (v. 4).

The third perspective that Paul establishes is the relationship between the two ministries of tongues and prophecy. First, he commends speaking in tongues: 'I wish that all of you would speak in tongues' (v. 5). It is a strange kind of 'exegesis' which sees in this statement a disparagement of this ministry or an implication that it should be discouraged or withdrawn.[70]

Second, Paul states a greater wish that he had for the people: 'But I would prefer that you prophesy' (v. 5). It is clear why he prefers prophecy; prophecy is immediate in its communication (vv. 3, 4). The one who prophesies serves the immediate needs of the congregation because he/she is directly understood.

Paul does say that the purpose of a prophetic message may be realized through the ministry of tongues on one condition: that

---

[69] The danger of rebuke that is not moderated by discernment in the rest of the body (particularly by other prophets) is that individuals (or a small group of individuals) may become self appointed monitors of the spirituality of the congregation. This is a gnostic tendency and must be carefully guarded by the church by the authority of the Word of God and the discrimination/discernment which the Holy Spirit gives to the body.

[70] It is obvious that regulation is not a prohibition; it is a legitimizing of that which is being regulated. So, when the biblical text here and in 1 Cor. 11.2-16 places regulations on the manner in which prophecy can occur in the body of Christ, it is giving approval of its operation. If the Holy Spirit is in process of withdrawing this gift from the church, why does He regulate its use instead of simply prohibiting it?

there be an interpretation of the message in tongues. If the interpretation does not come, there is no understanding as v. 2 has shown. If an interpretation is given by the Holy Spirit, the church will receive encouragement, direction or strength (v. 5).

The Function of Tongues

There were misunderstandings about the function of tongues in Corinth; likewise, there were misuses of this ministry. The instructions that are given here do not presuppose or imply that speaking in tongues is improper or that it was not of the Holy Spirit. In fact, just the opposite is indicated.

The establishment of regulations on the exercise of speaking in tongues shows that it is a proper ministry in the body of Christ. God does not regulate that which He prohibits. Instead, He indicates the circumstances in which the ministry is to operate. This is implicit approval of this function in the body. So we conclude that it is the will of the Holy Spirit that believers continue to speak in tongues in the continuing ministry of the church.

One of the problems at Corinth was that many spoke in tongues in the church and did not interpret. They seemed to think that the church would be benefited simply by the experience of hearing someone speak in tongues. This is futile as Paul shows by his incisive question, 'If I come to you speaking with tongues, how will I help you?' (v. 6). The rest of his question suggests other speaking ministries by which they would be helped rather than uninterpreted tongues: revelation, knowledge, prophecy or teaching. All of these ministries, except revelation, are mentioned in 1 Corinthians 12. They are all ministries which address the congregation of God in its own language and are immediately understood.

The reasonableness of this conclusion is illustrated by natural things. Every musical instrument must give a distinctive sound; that is, it must give a meaningful (interpretable) sound (v. 7). The battle trumpet must give a known signal or the soldier will not know when or if he should prepare for battle.

Paul extends his illustration to foreign language. Every language in the world has significance, but only to those who understand it. However, the fact that a language has meaning to those who understand it gives it no meaning to those who do not understand it. The

Apostle's conclusion is, 'Unless I know the meaning of the language, I shall be to the one speaking a foreigner and the one speaking shall be a foreigner to me' (v. 11).

Paul seems to belabor his illustration, but it was necessary. People seem to think that spiritual experience and communication do not operate on the same principles of intelligibility that are required in natural things. This is a devastating error. It allows experience to operate without the moderation of reason and without the clear understanding of the divine word in the vernacular. Such a system allows everyone to be both ruler and judge of his/her own truth. This is the pattern of Gnosticism.

Believers must seek excellence in spiritual things as they do in natural things. The aim of this excellence is the strengthening of the body of Christ (v. 12): 'For this reason, let the one who speaks in tongues pray that he may interpret' (v. 13). Paul places the obligation to interpret first on the one who speaks in tongues. This does not mean another may not interpret, but it does impress the necessity for interpretation on those who speak in tongues in corporate worship.

Prayer and praise/singing in the Holy Spirit are appropriate. Prayer and singing in tongues are proper. However, this does not enlighten the understanding—not even the understanding of the one who prays or sings in tongues (v. 14). Does this forbid praying and singing in the Spirit? No!

Note Paul's answer: 'What is it then? I will pray in the Spirit, and I will pray in the understanding; I will sing a hymn of praise in the Spirit, and I will sing a hymn of praise in the understanding' (v. 15).[71] These are valid spiritual experiences. The Apostle extols the worth of both forms of worship: praise and hymn singing (Eph. 5.18, 19).

The spiritual value of an individual's experience does not give it significance for those who do not know what is being said, even if God is being truly worshiped. Though the individual may be truly praying and giving thanks, it has no meaning for those who do not know what is being said. The one who listens but does not understand cannot affirm the worship by 'Amen'. This is important because congregational worship is reciprocal. Those who listen to a

---

[71] The Greek word here is ψαλλω: 'I will psalm [sing a psalm]'.

message (whether preaching, speaking in tongues or prophesying) participate in the message by saying, 'Amen'. By the 'Amen' both the speaker and the entire worshiping congregation are joined in giving the message and in worshiping God. If the listener does not know what is being said, he/she cannot affirm it and join in the proclamation (v. 16).

Equally damaging to corporate worship is that the congregation is not being edified when uninterpreted tongues are being spoken (v. 17).

Paul uses himself as an example in order to impress this lesson. First, he establishes the fact that he does approve of and practice speaking in tongues: 'I give thanks to God that I speak in tongues more than all of you' (v. 18).[72] This is not a boast, but it is an answer to any of his accusers in Corinth. They could not argue that Paul had no appreciation for or experience with this ministry of the Holy Spirit.

Second, Paul places the exercise of tongues in perspective with speaking in the language of the people. He speaks in extremes, but his point is well taken. Five words of instruction in a known language are better than a deluge of uninterpreted tongues (v. 19).

Third, Paul pleads with the Corinthians to grow up; 'Brethren, do not be children in understanding' (v. 20). The word here translated as 'understanding' is used only here in the New Testament, but it is used in other literature to refer to the heart. In the Septuagint it is so used in several places in the translation of the Proverbs. So Paul has in mind the believer's total spiritual perception. He has in mind total spiritual maturity. He enforces this with the exhortation that follows: 'But in understanding [again the same word as above] be perfect': i.e. mature (v. 20). The Apostle recognized that there is danger that misunderstandings over the exercise of spiritual gifts will produce disputes, even divisions; so, he exhorts, 'In malice, be children' (v. 20).

---

[72] There are those who attempt to explain this verse by understanding the word 'tongues' to refer to Paul's linguistic ability, claiming that Paul must have spoken several languages. If it is the case that Paul spoke several languages (and it may well be), no other reference in Scripture appeals to this ability. This is not responsible exegesis. Paul uses the term 'tongue(s)' in this case as he has been using it throughout this discussion. His reference here to speaking in tongues is clearly a reference to his 'speaking in tongues' in a manifestation of the Holy Spirit.

A Comparison of Tongues and Prophecy

Paul cites Isa. 28.11, 12 as a prophetic anticipation of speaking in tongues. The most immediate fulfillment of this text was that God used the Assyrians of 'stammering lips and another tongue' to convey a message of divine judgment on the people of God. Israel is once again in the position of disbelieving the revelation of God. It is necessary for God to speak to them by this principle: 'In the law[73] it is written, With men of other tongues and other lips will I speak unto this people; and yet for all that will they not hear me' (1Cor. 14.21).[74]

Paul now clarifies the function of tongues. They are not a special sign to believers of the working of God in the church; believers do not need this. Tongues are, therefore, a sign to unbelievers (v. 22). God shows His power to unbelievers by special divine intervention. In this case God intervenes by placing in the lives of believers the strange tongues uttered in the power of the Holy Spirit.

This is not to be understood as if speaking in tongues were some sort of magical sign of God's power. It is the revealing of the 'secrets of the heart' through tongues and interpretation that convinces the unbeliever that the power of God is at work. There is no magic in speaking in tongues; it can easily be imitated. This is the reason and explanation of the warning in v. 23: 'If, therefore, the whole church enters into the same place, and [if] they all speak with tongues, and [if] the ignorant or unbelieving enter, will they not say that you are out of your mind?' The form of Paul's question answers itself. Certainly unbelievers would conclude that a whole congregation that was doing nothing but speaking in unknown tongues was insane. The purposes of God are not served by such behavior.

---

[73] 'Law' is used here to refer to the totality of the law and the prophets. No technical distinction is intended between the law and the prophets.

[74] Paul speaks here of the fulfillment of prophecy by principle. He is appealing to the fact that as it was necessary for God to speak to Israel in the Old Testament by people of a foreign language, it is again necessary to speak to Israel in the New Testament by similar divine intervention. If we understand this passage in this way, it is understandable that the expressions 'other tongues' and 'other lips' are used in two different ways. 'God spoke to Israel in the strange Assyrian tongue in retribution not to confirm their faith, but to consummate their unbelief. The glossolalia may serve a similar melancholy purpose in the church.' [G.C. Findlay, "St. Paul's First Epistle to the Corinthians", in *The Expositor's Greek New Testament*, II, p. 910].

On the other hand, there is evidence of divine power and knowledge when sins thought to be hidden in the secrets of the heart are exposed.

In contrast to tongues, prophecy is a sign to believers. All that Paul has said about prophecy can also be used to the glory of God to unbelievers as well. Again, prophecy serves its purpose because it is in the language of the people and is immediately understandable by both believers and unbelievers. Though the unbeliever may approach it with a great deal of skepticism, he/she does understand what is being said in the power of the Holy Spirit.

The Apostle explains the reaction of an unbeliever to prophecy in these words, 'But if all prophesy, and any unbeliever or ignorant person enter, he will be shown his error by all [that is, by all the congregation in prophesying]; he will be judged by all' (v. 24). In this case prophecy serves a convicting purpose because it is the oracle of God (note also Jn 16.8-11). The sinner cannot avoid its convicting impact because prophecy is the oracle of God and it exposes the 'secrets of the heart' (v. 25). 'And thus are the secrets of the heart made manifest; and so falling down on his face he will worship God, and report that God is in you of a truth' (v. 25).

In the course of this chapter we have discovered two functions of prophecy. First, in relation to the church prophecy serves to edify, exhort and persuade (v. 3). Second, in relation to the unbeliever, it exposes and convicts of sin (vv. 24, 25).

In order to avoid confusion and promote unity, all the ministries of the body must be in proper order. The problem does not (and did not at Corinth) relate to tongues and prophecy alone. Paul chides the Corinthians because they come together in an atmosphere of competition for attention and dominance: 'Why, then, brethren? When you come together, everyone has a psalm, has a teaching, has a revelation, has a tongue, has an interpretation' (v. 26). Corinth was fragmented with varied ministries, and the people were apparently unwilling to yield to each other in the interest of order or humility. The basic answer for this problem is, 'Let everything be done for edification' (v. 26). A competitive spirit leads to confusion and abuse both of the body of Christ and of the gifts of the Holy Spirit. It is necessary to establish order in the exercise of the ministry of the Holy Spirit. Many people fear this requirement of order because they are afraid that they will 'quench the Spirit' (1

Thess. 5.19). This is an unfounded fear because the Spirit is never quenched or grieved when His instructions for order are being followed.

In this discussion Paul establishes the order in which tongues may be used in ministry to the church and in personal worship. If anyone speaks in tongues to the church, he/she is to expect an interpretation. In this expectancy, and in order to allow for interpretation, those who speak in tongues are to speak one at a time. Paul allows that this may be done without interpretation two or three times; by that time an interpretation should be given. This is the burden of v. 27: 'If someone speaks with a tongue, (let it be) two or three and one at a time, and let one interpret'.[75] Earlier Paul has indicated that the one who speaks in tongues should pray for an interpretation (v. 13). Here he shows that interpretation can come from someone else. Proper order is still maintained.

If an interpretation does not come when this order is followed, the one who is speaking in tongues is to be 'silent in the church' (v. 28). It is essential that we observe carefully what Paul says and what he does not say. First, he does not say that tongues which are not interpreted are spurious. He does not say that they are 'in the flesh'. He does not say that they are not from the Holy Spirit. Second, he does say that tongues uttered under these conditions are not to continue audibly to the church without an interpretation. Such is not edifying to the church because the church does not understand what is being said.

Paul assumes that tongues spoken under these circumstances are of the Holy Spirit, but they are for personal edification. So he says, 'Let him [that is, the one who is speaking in tongues] speak to himself and to God' (v. 28). This is a parallel circumstance with what Paul has said in vv. 14 and 15. God is being properly worshiped; the individual is worshiping in his/her spiritual nature; public worship proceeds undisturbed, and the Holy Spirit is not being grieved or quenched by the process.

Paul next establishes the order in which prophecy is to be given in the church. Prophets are to speak in an orderly fashion, and they are to be subject to the discernment exercised in the body of Christ and especially in the discrimination of other prophets: 'And proph-

---

[75] Paul is not here requiring a legalistic 'count down'; he is giving guidelines for what a congregation should expect in terms of order and interpretation.

ets, let one or two speak; and let the others discriminate' (v. 29). It would appear that this is one of the ways in which the ministry of the discernment of spirits (1 Cor. 12.10) is to operate in conjunction with the ministry of prophecy. A prophecy uttered is subject to the approbation of the rest of the body of Christ; that approbation is to be expressed by others to whom the message is being given or confirmed. This is an important safeguard. There is great danger when one person (or a small and select group) is made the singular and private source of messages from God. Such a person has a powerful weapon by which he/she may subjugate the entire church to his/her notions. The person becomes answerable to none. The instructions of Scripture, especially the chapters under study here, do not allow it.

Another safeguard is that those who prophesy are to do so in deference to each other: 'If it is revealed to another sitting by, let the first keep silence' (v. 30). This allows the prophetic message to be a corporate message and not a private message. This also provides for corporate confirmation of the message.

Orderliness in the expression of prophetic messages does not quench the Holy Spirit or stifle the message: 'For you are all able to prophesy one by one' (v. 31). This order is in the interest of learning and exhortation: 'In order that all may learn and in order that all may be comforted' (v. 31). Paul's simple explanation for this is, 'And the spirits of the prophets are subject to the authority of the prophets' (vv. 32). The expression 'spirits of the prophets' refers to the spiritual nature (its impulses and unction) of those who exercise the ministry of prophecy.

The sum of all that the Holy Spirit has said in this passage of Scripture is, 'God is not [a God of] disorderliness, but of peace' (v. 13). God has placed spiritual gifts in the church in order that the full and healthy functioning of the body may take place. This provides for the building up of the body. These ends are best served and most fruitfully accomplished if spiritual gifts are fully functioning and if they are functioning in accordance with the wisdom and instructions of the Holy Spirit. He is never grieved when His instructions are being followed.

15

LOVE: THE ESSENTIAL PERSONAL ATTRIBUTE

Paul's masterpiece on love (1 Corinthians 13) does not command us to love anyone, not even God.

The subject of discussion here is not loving people in general or anyone in particular. It is not even about loving God. What is being discussed is a quality of being. Love is a spiritual grace that identifies the essence of one's nature. As a personal characteristic love determines our responses and responsiveness to others under any and all circumstances.

The closing line of 1 Cor. 12.31 is the introduction of 1 Corinthians 13: 'I show you a way that is still more excellent'. Paul has just described the organic unity of the body of Christ. This way of life in the body is marvelous. This way of life crowned with love is even more excellent.

With this introduction we establish the essential unity of chapters 12 and 13. It is from chapter 12 that we know that unity is in Christ through the agency of the Holy Spirit: 'For by one Spirit we all into one body have been baptized' (12.13). In the course of this baptism 'the love of God has been shed abroad in our hearts through the Holy Spirit who has been given to us' (Rom. 5.5).

By this baptism we enter into an organism—a living body made up of living cells in which each cell draws life from other cells and transmits life to other cells. This organism has a single life source—the Lord Jesus Christ who is Head and Savior of the body. That life source is love because 'God is love' (1 Jn 4.8).

Such is the nature of the body of Christ. All of its parts (members/ministers) relate to each other and function together in love. The individual ministries (i.e. the parts of the body) fulfill their functions without envying the roles of others and without usurping the authority of others. The only way this can work is in the love of God. Love of an organization will not do this. Love of a common goal will not do it. Loving people is not sufficient.

In this chapter Paul discusses love from three perspectives: the necessity of love, the character of love and the endurance of love.

The Necessity of Love

The necessity of love is related by Paul to specific exercises: excellency of speech, exercise of spiritual gifts and the fulfillment of spiritual services.

In terms of the ability to speak, Paul imagines the possibility of reaching the height of human excellence. He raises the prospect of his becoming the most sublime of human orators. He is still not satisfied; so, he imagines that he might speak as the angels speak. He masters the graces of heavenly language.

Even if one could achieve these heights of speech, the achievement would be empty without love. In terms of sound, Paul places contradictory sounds together. It is as if he said, 'If from my mouth the beauty and harmony of angel speech flows; and if I do not have love, I have become a raucous, discordant sound'. His actual words are, 'I have become and still am a clank of brass and a clanging cymbal'.

Paul does not say here, 'and have not love for God, or man, or any specific thing'. Rather, he speaks of having love as an attribute of his personal nature. It is a quality of existence. To be a human being and not to have the quality of love is to be nothing—a silver trumpet that sounds like a tin rattle.

The writer does not say that he would become 'like a clanging cymbal'. He says that he would 'be a clanging cymbal'. It is the person who has become vain and discordant, not simply his/her words.

Love is necessary to the exercise of spiritual gifts. Paul compares love to the exercise of three spiritual gifts here: prophecy, word of knowledge and faith. The first of these, prophecy, is listed in chapter 12.10, 28, 29, and it is explained in detail in chapter 14. This is the ministry of the Holy Spirit by which revelation and the oracles of God are spoken. The exercise of this gift was a problem in Corinth.

The knowing of all 'mysteries' seems to be best understood as relating to the word of knowledge and the word of wisdom (1 Cor. 12.8). The terminology and grammar of 1 Cor. 13.2 seem to point in this direction as well. Yet this is beyond the mere knowing of a thing; it is a spiritual understanding that can come only from divinely given insight which is a spiritual gift.[76]

In this ministry Paul is not talking about special intelligence or the acquisition of massive amounts of facts or theories. He is talking about knowledge that is especially given, and a depth of comprehension that can come only from a gift of the Holy Spirit. This certainly fits the description of a 'word of knowledge'.

The next gift that Paul mentions here is the gift of faith. It even has the potential of removing mountains. Faith works the same for everyone, but there are special ministries (and ministers) of faith in the body of Christ. Such ministers believe by the gift of the Holy Spirit, and they have special ministry in the body of Christ through this gift.

The three gifts that Paul mentions in this text are representative of all the gifts of the Holy Spirit. For Paul's purpose here these three are important. One represents the speaking of the revelation of God. One relates to understanding the revelation of God. The other relates to believing the revelation of God.

---

[76] The word 'mystery' is used in a variety of ways in the New Testament. It is used to refer to the kingdom of God (Mt. 13.11), to the restoration of Israel (Rom. 11.25), to the gospel message (Rom. 16.25), to the will of God (Eph. 1.9), to the nature of the resurrection (1 Cor. 15.51), to the union of Jews and gentiles in the body of Christ (Eph. 2.3, 4, 9), to the union of Christ with His body the church (Eph. 5.32), to Christ Himself (Col. 4.3), to faith (1 Tim. 3.9), to the Incarnation ([the mystery of godliness] 1 Tim. 3.16) and to the seven churches of Asia (Rev. 1.20). These are not the only places where the word 'mystery' appears in the New Testament. The references cited above are representative of the texts that deal with God and His relationship with the world.

The thing which the references have in common is that they depend on divine revelation for knowing and understanding. These 'mysteries' are recorded in Scripture, but their presence there is by special revelation, and the understanding of them is a ministry of the Holy Spirit.

There is a vast difference in the way that the New Testament uses this term from the manner in which it is used in Gnosticism. The mysteries in Gnosticism were for the 'elite' (the highest rank in the cults). They were privately received and held, and were used as powers of control over others in the cult. They were instruments of bondage, and were to be kept from anyone in the lower ranks of the cult.

The mysteries in Christ were given to be shared with all the members of Christ's body; they were even proclaimed to the world for the salvation of the lost. They were revealed by the Holy Spirit in order to free the body and demonstrate the equality of all believers. They were not instruments of control.

By comparing love with these gifts the author has placed love over against all spiritual gifts. These gifts standing in themselves (and they cannot in fact stand apart from love) do not give worth to anyone. Only love gives worth. Paul's supposition here is hypothetical (not actual); but if a person could have all these gifts and not have love, he/she is nothing. All other elevations of character and power cannot make something of the person who is devoid of love. It is significant that Paul says, 'I am nothing', not simply, 'I have nothing'.

Next Paul compares love with personal sacrifice (v. 3). These are acts of spiritual significance: the giving away of all of our substance,[77] and the giving of our life.

To feed the needy was especially meritorious by Jewish standards. It was carried over into the Christian consciousness (Acts 6.1-7; Gal. 2.10). Here the Apostle suggests such extreme giving as to give away all that one possessed at the time.[78]

The next sacrifice that Paul suggests is giving his own body for sacrifice in order that he may have glory. Martyrdom is implied here. The idea is that of being sacrificed in religious devotion.

Both of these suggestions (giving one's substance and giving one's life) are designed to gain religious merit. If they are offered in the absence of love, they have no merit: 'I am made to profit nothing'.

It is possible for one to impoverish himself/herself in order to feed the hungry, but this has no spiritual value. It is also possible for one to place himself/herself in a position that will assure assassination for a cause that she/he believes in—even Christianity. If the motives and origin of these exclude love, there is no spiritual value in them.

In vv. 1-3 Paul has shown a specific progression. Love is essential in all relationships mentioned. It is essential in the natural ability of sublime speech, of the operation of spiritual gifts (prophecy,

---

[77] The word used here 'to feed the needy' is a tender word. It is often used to describe the feeding of an infant by placing a bit of food on the mouth of the child. Paul's comparison is not a cold, calculating and mechanical giving. Giving even in the tenderest human manner still requires the love of God.

[78] The verb here (aorist subjunctive) does not suggest that such giving calls for a life long vow of poverty. It is not a pledge to keep on giving all that one receives. It is a gift of all that one possesses at the time.

knowledge and faith) and in the exercise of the religious service of giving to the poor and the sacrificing of one's own body.

The Character of Love

After Paul shows the necessity of love, he shows the nature of this spiritual grace. He personifies love and describes it as having certain personal and spiritual qualities. In other places Paul lists these graces as fruit of the Spirit and of light (Gal. 5.22, 23; Eph. 5.9-21). This is compatible with Col. 3.14 where love is the 'bond of perfectness' holding together all other spiritual graces.

Our author attributes the graces here listed to love, not to the people who love. His praise is not for the 'perfect person' but for the perfect virtue of love. It is not the believer who achieves these graces, but love that imparts them.

These graces are not mere abstractions or 'ideals' because love is neither an abstraction nor an ideal. It is a specific identifiable quality of relationship with God and with people. Love is known when these qualities are seen in action.

The text before us identifies three fundamental relationships: with God, with other people and with one's self. These verses do not deal predominantly with defining our relationship with God. This has already been established in the testimony of Christ and baptism into the body of Christ (1 Cor. 12.3, 13). This presupposition shows itself in the manner in which the love of God relates us to others and to the understanding of ourselves.

There are three graces which stand in relationship with other people: patience, kindness and unselfishness. The first attribute of love—patience and long-suffering—is a temperate attitude in occasions of offense and injury. It is slow to anger in the light of provocation. Love is also patient in waiting for the fulfillment of a promise.

Patience by itself may be only passive; love must go beyond that. So the next grace is active; it is kindness. Love extends to others to do them good even in the face of provocation. It is also careful of the sensitivities of the other person.

Love is unselfish ('charity envieth not'); it refuses to be envious. It rejects jealousy and angry, destructive zeal that is inconsiderate of other individuals or ministries in the body of Christ.

The next graces that are mentioned relate to self—actually the relation of love to itself: 'Love is not vainglorious; it is not proud; it does not act unbecomingly; it does not seek its own things; it is not irritable; it does not imagine evil'. The humility of love creates a naturalness of display that it can be seen; love is observable. Though it is seen, it does not put on a proud display. Love does not show itself in this manner; it is not a strutter.

Displays of this nature are embarrassing to see. Love does not behave in such an unbecoming manner and in a manner that puts others ill at ease. There is a refinement in love that will not degrade itself by ostentation and crudity.[79]

Love will not seek its own things. The condescension and life of our Lord are held out as examples for this aspect of love: 'Look not every man on his own things, but every man also on the things of others' (Phil. 2.4; cf. also Rom. 15.1-3).

The problems that violate love (as in vv. 4, 5) arise because of a false and lofty self-image. To do the things that are here spoken against is to think of oneself more highly that one ought to think (Rom. 12.3). Where love is absent or flawed, ministers and ministries of the body of Christ begin to envy one another and exclude one another. Love is necessary in order to avoid this kind of division in the body of Christ. Love is the regulator for the operation of the gifts of the Holy Spirit. The ministries of the gifts are interrupted and impeded where love is absent of flawed.

The inflated self-image leads to the problems next anticipated—a quick temper and paranoia. Love is not easily irritated or exasperated. Neither is love quick to imagine evil and meditate on it. Love does not harbor hurt even when there are evil actions and intentions.

Those who imagine and harbor such do so with an inordinate sense of importance. Love corrects this sense of importance by giving a correct center of concern. The correct center of concern for love is not self, but God and then others.

---

[79] 'Doth not behave itself unseemly'. The word used here suggests vulgarity in physical exposure; however, the emphasis in this context is the sense of refinement which love has. The Scriptures are very plain-spoken about physical vulgarity in other places, but this does not seem to be the thought here. The use of such strong language does show how intensely the Apostle considered this issue.

The next relationship of love is its relationship to other spiritual graces. Negatively, love does not take any pleasure in unrighteous thoughts or deeds. It has no communion with injustice. On the other hand it rejoices together with the truth. There is union and communion between love and truth, which is well represented in the psalmist's line, 'Behold, thou desirest truth in the inward parts: and in the hidden part thou shalt make me to known wisdom' (Ps. 51.6). The connection between truth and love is essential. Paul notes this connection in Eph. 4.15 in his expression 'speaking the truth in love'.[80]

That which is spoken may be correct in factual content, but if it is not spoken in love and if it is spoken in the service of injustice, it is morally wrong. When truth is spoken outside the context of love, its character is so far violated that it is no longer truth. Truth and love must be united in order to complement and fulfill each other.

Truth is the antithesis of injustice here. A wrong deed toward another is a lie in action. That it is acted out and not spoken does not relieve it of the charge of being a falsehood. Love which rejoices together with the truth cannot at the same time rejoice in iniquity.

As injustice and truth are antithetical, love in its affections rejects the one and rejoices with the other. To rejoice together with the truth is to join it in its victory and superiority over falsehood and injustice.

In v. 7 Paul envisions two circumstances. The first is love's relationship to circumstances of life. Love bears up under all things. It is brave and strong under the most trying and threatening of circumstances. The second circumstance seen here is the relation of love to people. Love believes all things. There is a loyalty in love that seeks to believe the best of others. Love refuses to give up hope in the one who is loved. It, therefore, endures many apparent violations of love and trust in its hope for good.

In all of this text love is personified. It is described as if it were a person who is known by the qualities here discussed. This means that love is not properly known (recognized or experienced) if it is separated from these personal considerations. True affection there

---

[80] Paul used an interesting term here which may be paraphrased to say 'truthing in love'.

may be, but love as the highest of spiritual graces must incorporate all other virtues in itself.

Love, as it is defined here, is a revelation of the character of God. It is, therefore, a revelation of God's will for humankind. Every person who does not love is in moral default and is under divine judgment. The commandment of God is not that we should not hate our enemies, but that we should love them (Lk. 6.27). Everyone who does not love is incomplete in humanness.

We cannot pass off this obligation by our time worn excuses such as, 'I don't hate anyone', 'I don't hold anything against anyone', 'I would not do anyone harm' etc. We have not fulfilled God's will for us until love has become in us what it is in God—a personal attribute, an essential of our nature as men and women in the image of God. If it is this, it is self-extending and self-giving even in the presence of rebuff.

The Endurance of Love

Spiritual gifts are the provision of God's grace for our temporal life. Spiritual graces are the promises of the indwelling of God's nature in us, and they are promises for eternity. Therefore, Paul places a specific contrast between the endurance of love and the duration of the exercise of spiritual gifts.

Paul's bold statement is, 'Love absolutely never ceases'. This is not to say that some people do not cease to love. It does say that love as perfection in God and as a grace communicated to those who are in God does not ever cease. 'God is love, and the one who exists in love exists in God, and God exists in him' (1 Jn 4.16). Love is an essential attribute of divine nature and of those who abide in Him. It is, therefore, eternal.

In contrast, spiritual gifts serve temporal functions. God will bring prophesyings to an end. Tongues (i.e. speaking in tongues as the Spirit gives utterance) will cease. The word of knowledge shall be terminated as a special ministry of the Holy Spirit.[81]

---

[81] It is evident that Paul uses the term 'knowledge' in reference to a 'word of knowledge' (1 Cor. 12.8). Verse 12 of this chapter shows that knowledge as such will continue and be perfected in our glorification. So the reference here is to the special ministry of the Holy Spirit in the word of knowledge.

These spiritual ministrations have limitations. They are limited in their nature. Even with the gift of prophecy, God does not reveal the entire future. With the word of knowledge all knowing is not bestowed; God does not impart omniscience to any creature. There are also limits based on the nature of the creatures in whom these gifts are placed. They are of this temporal order and this order cannot be stretched into eternity.

So Paul says of knowledge, 'We know in part': i.e., by individual segments of knowledge. Such knowledge is incomplete because it is temporal in nature and because it serves a temporal purpose. This is not the same as saying that such knowledge is erroneous. That which is known in part is still known. We know in part; that is, we do not know the whole, but we do know.

Prophecy has similar limits. Prophecy as prediction by nature moves to a fulfillment. When the fulfillment has come, the prophecy itself has served its purpose. Not all prophecy is predictive; it may be hortatory. It is still of temporal application because the need for action is a passing situation (for example, the care for the believers in Judea: Acts 11.27-29).

The aim of these statements (v. 9) is to set spiritual gifts in perspective. The two that are mentioned here (knowledge and prophecy) are representative of all other spiritual gifts. Their functions will not be needed in the order of the eternal kingdom. These gifts are aids that the Holy Spirit has given while the fullness of the kingdom has not yet come.

That these gifts are 'in part' does not mean that they are flawed. They are flawless because they are God's gifts. They serve specific purposes in God's plan, but they are not the whole plan. When God's purpose has been fulfilled in the return of our Lord and the final fulfillment of His kingdom, God will bring spiritual gifts as we know them to an end. Paul explains this in vv. 10-12.

God's will is 'to bring all things under one purpose in Christ' (Eph. 1.10). When that has been done, the 'perfect' will have come. The clause 'that which is perfect' refers to the fulfillment of a prescribed goal. By this term Paul has in mind the end of this age and the arrival of the kingdom of God in its fullness.[82] 'The apostle is

---

[82] Various interpretations have been suggested for this passage. The interpretation above is supported by the explanation in the context and by Paul's use of the word 'perfect' in other passages.

saying nothing about the cessation of χαρίσματα in this life: prophesyings and knowledge might always be useful. All that he asserts is that these things will have no use when completeness is revealed.'[83]

All those gifts of the Spirit which God has provided for us to serve our needs in the period of waiting and serving will have fulfilled their purpose when all divine promises have been fulfilled. When the Lord of glory appears without sin unto salvation (Heb. 9.28) for all the waiting ones, living and dead, there will be no further need for spiritual gifts. They will, therefore, cease; but love will continue.

The Apostle explains this order by his analogy of growth: 'when I was a little child, it was my practice to speak as a child speaks, to think as a child thinks, and to reason as a child reasons; since I have become an adult, I have put aside the things of a child' (v. 11). In comparison to the life that is to come when Christ appears, our present level of understanding and speech is immature.

Paul explains this further. In this present age, we see only dimly. His word picture depicts our looking into a reflection made by our looking into crudely polished steel. Such a mirror provides only a dim reflection of the face. What is seen is obscure, even an enigma. This important truth is twofold. First, we see only a hazy reflection. Second we see a true reflection, though lacking in detail. That which we see is real and not imaginary. It is true and it is divine promise. That which we see is only a dim reflection of the excellent glory which is to appear.

When the Lord of glory appears, the perfect will have come. We shall see Him face to face. To see the face of the Lord is to enter

---

Among other interpretations we note and reject are the following. The 'perfect' is the end of the apostolic age. It is the completion of the canon of Scripture. The difficulty with these views is that they are foreign to the text. They are concepts which the Corinthians would have had no way of understanding. Even in the apostolic age signs and wonder were not limited to the ministry of the Apostles. What guidelines would tell the early Christian believers when the gifts were to cease? If we push this to the point of absurdity, were believers to stop speaking in tongues, prophesying and receiving a word of knowledge upon the expiration of the last surviving Apostle? Does the term 'apostle' refer to the twelve only or to Barnabas who is also called an Apostle (Acts 14.4)? To say the least this statement would have been meaningless in the first Christian century.

[83] Archibald Robertson and Alfred Plummer, *A Critical and Exegetical Commentary on the First Epistle of Paul to the Corinthians* (2nd ed.; T & T Clark, Edinburgh, 1917), p. 297.

into His presence; it is to see Him and to know Him as He is and to be transformed into His likeness (Phil. 3.20, 21).

In application, Paul says we now know in part. That which is known is truth, but we do not know fully. Then, when He appears, we shall know thoroughly. Paul intensifies his language here: 'Even as also we are known'. Paul does not say that we will come to know God as fully as God knows us, for that would require omniscience. Paul speaks here of the manner of our knowing and the purity of our knowing. As we are known fully and clearly, we shall know fully and clearly.

The eternal nature of all spiritual graces is affirmed in v. 13. The phrase 'and now' has the effect of saying, 'And now, having said all of this, faith, hope and love remain'. This places these graces in contrast and superior to all spiritual gifts.

Faith reflects our reliance on God and His mercy for our salvation. This grace remains because we are in eternal need of Christ's intercession (Heb. 7.25).

Hope is related to our expectations of God. These also continue into the kingdom age. We will not possess the totality of our existence in a single moment of eternity. So, we will continue to look to God with expectancy. Eternal life is a life of expectancy and excitement.

Love completes the 'trinity' of spiritual graces. The aim of all that Paul has said earlier is to define love.

In his words 'these three' Paul places great emphasis on these virtues. He also shows their unity. Love is the very character of God; faith and hope give us entrance into His presence and provide our union with Him.

Out of all these graces love stands as the greatest. It is so much identifiable with the nature of God that John declares, 'God is love' (1 Jn 4.16).

Our eternal purpose is not to prophesy, to speak in tongues or to heal the sick. Our eternal purpose is to become like God, and God is love.

The Relationship of 1 Corinthians 12 and 14 to 13

This chapter (13) is an essential transition from chapter 12 to chapter 14. It is from chapter 12 that we know that this love is in Christ.

We are baptized by one Spirit into one body. It is in this baptism that love is shed abroad in our hearts by the Holy Spirit (Rom. 5.5), and in which we enter an organism whose life source is love. This is the body of Christ. All its ministries (parts) relate to each other and function together in love. The individual parts of the body fulfill their individual functions and do not usurp the functions of others because they are joined in love (not because they must do so for efficiency).

This quality of love is essential if there is to be no schism (12.25), and if members are to rejoice and suffer with each other (12.26).

Chapter 13 describes this attribute of personalness that accounts for these relationships in the body of Christ.

It is in chapter 14 that we see specific examples of how this love functions in ministry. Love for the body of Christ and for individuals and specific ministries in the body of Christ produces and maintains order. One prophet waits on another (14.29) because of love. Interpretation of tongues is expected and waited for because of love (14.27, 28). One does not impose on the whole body his/her own personal edification with continuous uninterpreted tongues (14.13-19). One does not shatter the decorum of the church by a cacophony of tongues, prophecies, revelations and psalms (14.26). The reason for these restrictions is love. Love is the operating principle by which these regulations are fulfilled harmoniously.

There are those who attempt to apply the instructions of 1 Corinthians 12-14 in a mechanical, impersonal and authoritarian manner. To do this is to miss the point of Paul's instructions.

Two things stand out in this context and the manner in which Paul arranged this material by the guidance of the Holy Spirit. The first of these is the nature of the body. The second is the chapter on love (chapter 13).

As to the first (the nature of the body) the regulations are to be applied because the members of the body choose to work in the unity of a healthy organism. Failure to do so will bring disease (disease) in the body. A healthy body seeks and promotes the well being of all its members and of the whole body.

As to the second of these (love) regulation carried out in love is always a caring function. Those who exercise authority are a part of the community of love. Those who are being directed are in a relationship of love for all the body and for those who are in authority. This is the reason that the material in chapter 13 stands between the material in chapters 12 and 14.